The Guerilla Guide to Teaching

Related titles

Getting the Buggers to Behave – Sue Cowley
Getting the Buggers to Write – Sue Cowley
Starting Teaching – Sue Cowley
Protecting Children – Janet Kay
Readings for Reflective Teaching – Andrew Pollard
Reflective Teaching – Andrew Pollard

The Guerilla Guide to Teaching

Sue Cowley

continuum
LONDON • NEW YORK

Continuum
The Tower Building
11 York Road
London SE1 7NX

370 Lexington Avenue
New York
NY 10017-6503

First published 2003

British Library Cataloguing-in-Publication Data
A catalogue record for this book is available from the British Library.

ISBN: 0-8264-5836-X (hardback), 0-8264-5837-8 (paperback)

Typeset by BookEns Ltd, Royston, Herts
Printed and bound in Great Britain by MPG Book Ltd, Bodmin, Cornwall

Contents

Dedications   ix
Acknowledgements   x
Introduction   xi

Section 1: Anatomy of Teaching

1   Teaching as a career   3

The upsides   3
The downsides   4
The facts   5
Tips for long-term survival as a teacher   6
Voices of experience   7

2   Teacher training   20

Routes into teaching   20
What's in the degree?   23
Applying for teacher training   23
Financial incentives   23
QTS   24
First steps   24
Useful books for student teachers   38

3   Surviving and succeeding on teaching practice   40

Preparing for teaching practice   40
The first day   42
Observing the class   43
Observing the teacher   45
Potential problems   48
Planning   49
Teaching   52
Getting your class to behave   53
Useful books on behaviour management   55

4 Finding a job 57

Job hunting 57
The independent sector 59
Types of state school 60
Applying for jobs 61
Job interviews 63
After the interview 71

5 Your first year 72

What's it really like? 72
The first week 74
Survival tactics 76
The induction process 80
Starting out 89

6 Anatomy of a school 101

Typical school management structures 101
Head teacher 102
Deputy head teacher 106
Assistant head teacher 109
Head of department or faculty 112
Subject coordinator 115
Head of year 115
Advanced skills teacher 118
Form tutor 119
Classroom teacher 124
Teaching assistant 125
Special educational needs coordinator (SENCO) 129
Educational psychologist 129
Educational welfare officer (EWO) 130
School librarian 130
Office staff 134
Bursar 135
Caretaker 135
School governor 135
Inspector 136

7 Preparing to teach 140

Lesson planning 140
The National Curriculum 142
Special educational needs 143

Contents

Schemes of work 146
Resources and equipment 146
Setting up your room 151

8 Classroom teaching 156

Classroom management 156
Behaviour management 157
Differentiation 170
Marking 171
Assessment 173
Self-evaluation 176

9 Beyond the classroom 179

Admin 179
Recording and reporting 181
Examinations 183
Pastoral work 184
The parents' evening 187
Extracurricular activities 188

10 Pay, promotion and career development 190

Teachers' pay 190
Working conditions 190
Promotion 191
INSET 193
Teaching and other careers 194
Educational shows 195
Private tutoring 195
Teaching overseas 195

11 Other issues 202

Supply teaching 202
OFSTED 208
Pensions 211
Support systems 212
The teaching unions 213
General teaching councils 217
Disciplinary procedures 223

Section 2: Case Studies

12 Planning in the primary school **227**

13 Planning in the secondary school **241**

Section 3: Teachers' Toolkit

14 Sample documents **259**

Job hunting 259
Teaching 269

15 Terminology **279**

16 Checklists **281**

Section 4: ICT

17 ICT and the teacher **295**

Using ICT 295
Managing ICT use 297
The internet in teaching 299

18 Software **302**

Some general tips 302
Word processing 303
Spreadsheets 307

Section 5: Directory **313**

Index **334**

This book is dedicated to Tilak, to BB,

to my Mum, and to all the girls at the

October Club.

Acknowledgements

It never ceases to amaze me how generous those in the teaching profession are with their time and expertise, especially considering the huge workload that comes with the job. This book would not have been possible without the generous help of a large number of teachers, student teachers, and others working in education. To everyone who contributed their thoughts and experiences, whether or not these are featured in the book, a very big 'thank you' for your time! Many thanks also go to the excellent ETeach website.

Special thanks must go to Carl Smith and Tracey Nightingale, working teachers who went out of their way to help me, and who were happy to answer a seemingly endless stream of questions without a murmur of complaint. A special mention, too, for Nichola Beech, Steph Leach and Lisa Simpson, whose regular emails kept me updated, informed and amused. Thanks to Alexandra Webster and Anthony Haynes at Continuum, and to Tilak for lending me his spreadsheet expertise.

Introduction

Teaching really is one of the most wonderful jobs in the world. Of course, it has its difficulties, and if you're going to do your job properly you've got to be really dedicated and hard-working. But for every downside and for every difficult day in the profession, there are a million reasons for teachers to love their work. What other job allows you to spend time with your favourite subject, day in, day out, as secondary specialists can? What other profession gives you so many rewards: the chance to see a student learn something new, the look of joy on a child's face when you praise them for a good piece of work, the opportunity to be your own boss in your own classroom? And what other job gives you the opportunity to inspire future generations, to hear those priceless words: *'you made a difference to my life'*?

This book will help you negotiate the minefield that is the teaching profession. It's realistic, practical, and stuffed with valuable information. It will prove useful to student teachers, and those already working in the job. It will also be helpful to those interested in taking up other posts within a school, for instance as a teaching assistant or school librarian. A crucial part of the book is the interviews that I conducted with all different types of people working in the education sector. I spoke to student teachers and to teachers who've spent their lives in the profession. I talked with newly qualified teachers, and with those right at the top of the management and advisory structure. I also interviewed the unions who support us in our working lives, and organizations such as the General Teaching Council. So, if you have a question about teaching that you want answered, then you should be able to find what you need here.

As a profession, teaching gets a lot of press attention, sadly much of it negative. All parents have to educate their children, and consequently it's a subject close to most people's hearts. We all went to school, of course, and we can remember the good and bad bits of our own time in the world of education. For some of us, though, our school days were a long time ago, and there have been huge changes in the years since we last walked out of the school gates. This book will help you understand the world of education as it is today. It gives you information on the most important aspects of the profession, and an insight into what working as a teacher is really like. Above all, if your quest is to become a teacher, this book will help you fulfil your goal.

Teaching is a profession in a constant state of change. Every five minutes, it seems, a fresh initiative is launched, an extra set of tests is brought in or a new curriculum idea tried out. For many of my interviewees, this constant flux, and all the administration and paperwork that goes with it, was one of the biggest difficulties of their working lives. Teaching also seems to lurch from one crisis to another: schools 'failing' their students; not enough teachers to go around; not enough money to attract 'good' graduates to the profession; the low status of teachers in society. There are plenty of people out there who will try to put you off the idea of becoming a teacher (some of them teachers themselves).

Although this book doesn't try to hide the less wholesome facts about the job, its overall message is that it really is worthwhile entering the profession if you've got the requisite dedication and energy.

Above all, I'd like to wish you luck in your quest to work as a teacher, or in the field of education. As I said at the start of this introduction, it really is one of the best jobs in the world. If you're willing to give it your best, and to dedicate your life to helping children succeed, you really couldn't make a better choice of career.

Sue Cowley
www.suecowley.co.uk

Please note:
Acronyms are rife in teaching, but confusing for the newcomer. For explanations of all abbreviated terms, see Chapter 15 'Terminology'.

Both government policies and website addresses are subject to seemingly constant change. Although every effort has been made to include up to date information, please accept that some of the details mentioned in this book may have changed since the time of writing.

Section 1

Anatomy of Teaching

1 Teaching as a career

So, you're looking at a career in teaching. You might be just turning the idea over in your mind, unsure about whether it's the right choice for you. If you've mentioned your prospective career to others, you've probably had reactions ranging from 'you're completely insane' to 'you'll have to be a total saint'. Maybe you're at the stage of applying for a PGCE or a degree with QTS. Perhaps you've already embarked on your training, or are in the first few years of your job, and questioning whether you've made the right decision. This chapter gives you information and advice about teaching as a career choice. It explores the upsides and the downsides of a teaching job, and looks at the facts about teacher retention in the profession. It also gives you the chance to hear from some 'voices of experience' – those teachers who have stuck it out in the job for a substantial part of their working lives.

The upsides

Why go into teaching, then, or why stay in teaching for the long term? Below is a list of just some of the upsides of the job. If you're already working as a teacher, and wondering whether it's still the right career for you, why not read through these upsides to make yourself feel more positive?

- Above all, a job in teaching is rewarding and worthwhile. If you like children, and are willing to work hard to help them succeed, then there is nothing like teaching for a sense of satisfaction.
- Teaching is both a profession and a vocation. Although it's not respected as much as it once was, it is still a good career choice for graduates.
- Teaching will stretch you in a number of ways – intellectually, physically, emotionally, psychologically. If you want to challenge yourself on a daily basis, teaching is a great option.
- Teaching gives you a good range of transferable skills. Times are changing, and the tendency is more and more towards moving between different jobs during your working life. As a teacher, you will learn skills that other employers are keen to utilize.
- The job offers good security in the long term. There will always be a need for teachers, and once you are qualified it is unlikely that you will ever be out of work for long.
- Teaching is a 'mobile' profession – you can work pretty much anywhere in the country, or even in the world. Teachers who speak English are in great demand in international and language schools as well as in the UK.

- The job is reasonably well paid, and there is a defined and rising salary scale as you gain more experience or take promotion.
- The teachers' pension offers an excellent deal, especially if you stay within the profession long term.
- You will be working with other, like-minded people, who are educated to the same level as you, and who share your sense of vocation.
- On the whole, teaching does get easier the longer you do it and the more experienced you become, a point that is well worth remembering if you're finding your NQT year hard!
- In a secondary school, or in higher education, you get the chance to work with the subject you love, day in and day out.
- In your own classroom, despite all the dictates from above, to a large extent you are still your own boss.
- Although it might be tiring and stressful, the job is almost never boring. You might be learning about a new topic, or going out on a trip with your students, but every single day will offer you a different challenge.
- Potentially, the job combines well with bringing up children.
- You really do have the opportunity to make a difference to the lives of other people. Some teachers have a genuine, long-term impact on the students with whom they work.
- The holidays are great!

The downsides

For every 'upside' in teaching, there is of course a drawback. The decision you have to make, when considering a career in teaching, or when deciding whether to stay in the profession long-term, is whether the upsides still outweigh the downsides for you. As far as I'm concerned, with teaching, there is no middle ground. The job is far too important to do half-heartedly, or to spend your time moaning about what's wrong. Here are some of the downsides for you to consider.

- Although it's not true for every school, there is some seriously bad behaviour out there. There are some students (and parents) who will abuse you both verbally and physically.
- There is a lot of stuff in teaching that has little to do with being a teacher. Paperwork and meetings often get in the way of the important bits of the job, such as preparing good lessons and helping the children to learn.
- The job can be very stressful, whether this is to do with excessive workload or poor behaviour. It can also 'take over' your life if you let it. See Anne Cowan's wonderful advice (page 8) about keeping the professional separate from the personal.
- The job is very tiring. Some teachers suffer from work related illnesses such as stress, breakdowns or simply exhaustion.

- If you want promotion, you must be willing to take all the additional paperwork, pressure and politics that come with a management post.
- To earn a really decent salary, you will need to leave the classroom (perhaps the reason you entered the job in the first place!) and move into senior management.
- The pay will never be all that great. Even right at the 'top of the tree', there is still a huge gap between a head teacher's pay and that for an equivalent position in the business world.
- You'll never be given a company car, health insurance scheme, gym membership, bonus, or any of the other perks of a job in the commercial sector.
- Many teachers work very long hours in order to do the job as well as they can, or even simply to get the job done at all.
- Teaching is often used as a 'political football', and there is a lot of interference from governments of whatever persuasion. You are likely to find yourself battling to keep up with new initiatives and seemingly endless changes to the curriculum.
- There is less and less freedom for teachers to move outside the statutory curriculum areas, and to be creative in their approaches to the job. Time is especially tight in the primary school.
- The nature of the job has the potential to lead to cynicism and a negative attitude. Some teachers do have a tendency to moan.
- There are a few teachers in the job who are not up to it, or who have been worn out by it. You will find yourself covering for these people, both in dealing with the issues that arise in their classrooms, and literally covering for them, when you have to take their classes because they're not in school.
- You may find yourself spending much of those lovely long holidays dealing with all the work you couldn't fit in during term time.
- There is no flexibility in when you take your holidays, and you will be taking them at the time when they are most expensive.

The facts

Information about the numbers of people leaving the profession is surprisingly difficult to pin down. Surveys and reports have been undertaken, but official statistics are hard to come by. Some of the reported figures and other details are listed here, although the numbers given do vary considerably. Be warned: these figures make worrying reading.

The information given is taken from the *Guardian* education website (www.education.guardian.co.uk) and from a report by Alan Smithers and Pamela Robinson of Liverpool University for the National Union of Teachers (www.teachers.org.uk). Reasons given for leaving the profession included workload, pupil behaviour, government initiatives, salary levels and stress.

- Two out of five teachers leave the profession within five years.
- Up to 40% of teachers leave within the first three years.
- 58% leave teaching within the first three years (this figure includes those leaving during and after teacher training).
- Out of 100 final year student teachers, 40 don't go into the classroom, and another 18 leave within the first three years.

Primary school teachers who do not expect to be teaching:

- 31% in five years
- 56% in 10 years
- 77% in 15 years

Secondary school teachers who do not expect to be teaching:

- 26% in five years
- 51% in 10 years
- 71% in 15 years

Tips for long-term survival as a teacher

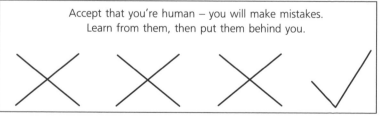

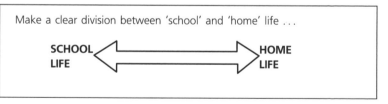

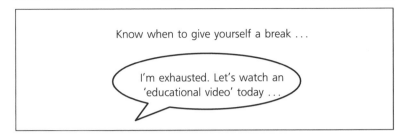

And of course, never forget,
at the end of the day, it's all about the kids ...

Voices of experience

The three interviews that follow give you a good idea about what it's like to spend a large part of your working life as a teacher. My interviewees don't pull their punches, but from each of them comes a sense of the joy of teaching, as well as an honest appraisal of some of the more difficult aspects of the job.

> Primary school teacher – retired, 33 years' experience
>
> Now a freelance journalist
>
> Anne Cowan

Q. Could you tell me a bit about what made you go into teaching in the first place?

Anne – On the rebound from a Bob Cratchit like year as an insurance clerkess, I decided to be a teacher because I had loved my own primary school days.

Q. And what teaching qualification did you take?

Anne – I took the three-year course for primary teachers at Moray House College of Education, Edinburgh, qualifying in 1962.

Q. What about your 33 years as a teacher? Where did you work and in what type of schools?

Anne – After two difficult years in a Glasgow housing scheme, I gave up and worked my way to San Francisco. On my return to Scotland there followed three years in the inner city, 16 in a former mining community and 12 years in the small town school I went to myself. Each time I changed job, teaching got easier and more enjoyable.

Q. And what do you think makes some people stay in the profession, while others leave after only a few years?

Anne – If there's one thing which keeps the unpromoted teacher's nose to the chalkface it's pay, followed a close second by pension prospects. Many of us who qualified in the sixties are from the first generation of our families to have stayed on at school beyond the age of 14. We've seen what long hours in menial jobs for low pay are like and do not want to be old and cold. Lots of teachers who have children expensively educated at university spring from a respectable working class which abhorred debt. If that's where you're coming from, you stick in at school. I didn't give up teaching for writing, but by a stroke of luck got early retirement at 55. Much as I had enjoyed my job I had been at it too long and was exhausted.

Q. What advice would you give young teachers who hope to stay in the profession for a long time? How did you stick it for so long?

Anne – How did I survive at the chalkface for 33 years? The ability to switch off, to forget all about work once you're off the premises, was crucial. There is life beyond the school gates, so don't be scared to get out there, relax and enjoy it. Anybody needs to get out and meet people, to do something different after work, all the more so teachers, whose work involves controlling and educating conscripts.

Q. And on a day-to-day basis in the classroom? How did you survive in the tougher schools?

Anne – Surviving teaching reminds me of aircraft safety demonstrations. Adults, fix your own oxygen mask first or you won't be able to help the children. Teacher, save yourself. At tougher schools we showed more TV programmes than was strictly necessary. It settled difficult classes and gave the teacher a breather to catch up with correction. If uproar is about to break out, play a quiet game for five minutes. I must confess to being a closet whole class teacher when juggling groups was driving me to despair. The old fashioned arrangement, rows of seats facing the front, concentrates juvenile minds wonderfully, if you can get away with it. One thing I would have appreciated is the book, *Getting the Buggers to Behave*.

Q. Have you got any advice for new teachers?

Anne – Unfortunately many young teachers feel pressurized and fall victim to the creeping cult of presenteeism. Where competitive parking is the norm, they put themselves into self-imposed detention under the illusion that a car on show is an indicator of commitment to the job. Also when new schemes are introduced, there's the temptation to think that this is the right way to go about things. Teaching is not an exact science. There is not one right way.

Q. Could you tell me a little about what you feel makes primary school teaching such a great job?

Anne – One of the best things about primary teaching comes when the class feels like a family. Everyone gets to know each other, they gel and when something absurd happens, you roll your eyes and they all laugh with you, not at you. There's something very nice about gathering them all round to tell a story, go off at a tangent and have a blether. The sad thing is that so much of the spontaneity has been knocked out of the primary school. With strict guidelines and having to keep written pupil assessments of everything except how they blow their noses, teachers are stressed out. Another innovation I would have found disconcerting and inhibiting is having other adults in the class most of the time.

Q. And what sort of teacher would you say you were?

Anne – You'd have to ask my former pupils what kind of teacher I was! I'd say that I was never a perfectionist, that I liked a firm but informal approach, and that I loved teaching creative writing and art and doing projects which involved both of them with getting out of school.

Q. Could you describe some of the best memories that you have of your teaching career?

Anne – One of my favourite things was sussing out the Edinburgh Festival Fringe and taking a new class of a couple of days up to town 23 miles away. We'd go with parent helpers to one of the children's events at the Edinburgh International Book Festival in Charlotte Square in the morning, eat lunch sitting watching the jugglers and fire-eaters at the foot of the Mound, then walk up to the Old Town to see free exhibitions, street theatre and performances up closes and in back yards. Then back at school next day we'd plunge into the creative explosion of words and colour and enthusiasm. I always thought that the epitaph to my teaching would read 'she muddled through' and was genuinely astonished at the nice things people kindly said when at the age of 55 I finally tottered out the school.

Another surprise was the joy of continuity. I ended up teaching with people who had taught me and who had been at school with me. There were pupils from families of which I knew/had known four generations. That was really interesting and they do say that a sense of belonging is one of the most important things in life. It came as an unexpected bonus and I'm glad I was part of East Lothian small town life again. I loved teaching at my old school.

I used to joke that the two great educational advances were women teachers being allowed to wear trousers and the October break. Seriously though, parents' nights make the world of difference. So much good can result and misery be avoided now that teachers get the chance to speak to the people who know the child best. Parents' nights help everybody.

Q. You stayed in the classroom. Was that a deliberate decision? What do you think about going for promotion within the profession?

Anne – What do I think of promotion? I hardly give it a thought. As one of nature's employees and not officer material, I've never been interested in it. In Scotland the post of senior teacher was supposed to reward the best teachers while keeping them in the classroom. Instead it became part of the career structure and a stepping stone to greater things. This post is being phased out and a new superteacher grade, chartered teacher, introduced. This also looks set to become a rung on the promotion ladder. One thing is certain, the head teacher sets the tone and a good head is vital to the morale of other staff. Having smashing colleagues who become friends makes all the difference in the world.

Q. You moved into another career after you left the classroom. Could you tell me a bit about how and why you started writing?

Anne – A recurring theme in every staffroom, a constant topic of conversation is how to get out of this job. What can a teacher do to exit the classroom for the last time? There was a time when each morning as I wrote the date on the board, it seemed as if this heralded another long day of my life to be spent between four classroom walls. It was freelance journalism that saved my sanity and opened many doors. For a while, after school on a Thursday, I'd go up to *The Scotsman* office in Edinburgh, go through the press releases, find a fashion theme and write it up. Work for *The Herald* and *Times Educational Supplement Scotland* followed, the latter mostly about the wackier side of teaching. But my escape might just as well have been into hillwalking, salsa dancing or advanced patchwork quilting, though journalism paid better.

Q. What about teaching as a profession? How do you view the current perceptions of the job?

Anne – Teachers don't get a great press. Their job is perceived in many quarters to be a doddle, thanks largely to the long holidays. However many teachers feel that if they work nine months of the year the remuneration reflects this. They are paid the equivalent of three quarters of a salary. Perhaps the image of the profession lacks lustre because of the working environment. When I started I was told that the only non-residents who go into deprived areas are teachers, police officers, doctors and nurses. Teaching is not glamorous though higher salaries would undoubtedly make it more attractive. Having said all that, I was really lucky to have had great teachers myself.

Q. And how do you think things have changed since you left teaching? Are the changes for the better or not?

Anne – In the five years I've been a freelance journalist I've been hearing of the ever-changing new regimes and pressures being inflicted on primary schools. At times it seems as if the relaxed atmosphere and much of the fun are but fond and distant memories.

Q. Finally, what do you feel could be done to make teaching a more attractive profession?

Anne – Teachers' pensions, like those of the forces and police, should not be based on 40 years' service. It keeps too many tired, burnt out people, for reasons I stated, at the chalkface. It is doing pupils no favours and more early retirement or the adoption of a 30 year career structure would breathe fresh life into the schools. On the other hand, the plain speaking of the old staffroom cynic is the perfect antidote to all the jargonese and daft innovations to which teachers are subjected.

> Surviving teaching reminds me of aircraft safety demonstrations. Adults, fix your own oxygen mask first or you won't be able to help the children. Teacher, save yourself.

Secondary school teacher – 25 years' experience

Head of Faculty – Design & Technology

Name withheld

Q. Why did you decide to go into teaching?

A. I came into teaching when I was 25 after working in industry, mostly in chemical and aerospace companies. Reasons? Well I felt I'd enjoy it having had spells as an instructor to engineering apprentices; it would be a challenge and seemed at that time to provide a good career structure. Money was not an issue. To be honest I also liked the holidays as it fitted in with my climbing passion and allowed me to go abroad on expeditions.

Q. What route did you take into teaching?

A. I left school at 16 with six 'O' levels. Then I did five years in further education to HNC standard in Product Design. My PGCE course was at Manchester University. After that I did some teaching in further education then moved into secondary teaching.

Q. Do you think it's better for teachers to gain work experience like you did, before going back to a career in the education system?

A. Certainly it was (for me) better to enter teaching with experience at 26 than it would have been to have followed a more conventional sixth form route and entered earlier.

Q. How long have you been teaching, and what's your current job?

A. 25 years this September. I work at an 11 to 16 comprehensive. I'm the Head of Faculty for Design and Technology. I teach all years with a high percentage of GCSE in Electronics.

Q. What has been your best moment in teaching?

A. There are too many to recall. The best times seem to revolve around personalities, relationships and situations. I've enjoyed foreign visits with students, outdoor challenges, absorbing project work and the satisfaction of getting results. It's also nice to have ex-students come back years later and say you made a difference; something that is not always evident at the time.

Q. And what about the worst moments?

A. Again, many. Aside from personal tragedies that have affected colleagues and students it has to be the depressing grind of trying to be an effective teacher when paperwork, lack of funds, lack of time, poor facilities gets in the way. It was good until the mid-eighties but has got worse year on year since then. It is depressing to see once good teachers crack under the strain.

Q. What are the best and worst things about teaching your particular subject and age group?

A. I enjoy my subject because it allows me to be creative and still challenges me.

The worst thing is the lack of resources. Never enough time to prepare lessons as I'd wish. Masses of admin and chasing faculty problems. Behaviour has declined markedly over the past five years. It's hard to get any time for decent INSET.

Q. Tell me about being promoted. What's it really like? Is it worth the extra hassle?

A. I've been promoted several times to my current position. I turned it down initially . . . not worth the money, I'd rather have a life. Only my own self-esteem keeps me going. I thought I would have a chance to really develop a faculty and weld a team, instead you are given no management time (time to have a vision, think, plan etc.). I have moved a faculty on and am proud that it's one of the best in the area and has excellent results, but it has been at a cost.

Q. Has being promoted taken you away from classroom teaching?

A. I wish it had! One of the great myths. Just about all middle managers retain their full teaching load and run a faculty . . . an impossible task. I teach 34 lessons out of 40; 50 per cent is GCSE work and I lose more doing cover each week. Only at SMT level does the teaching load drop away.

Q. And what about the future? Would you like to be promoted further?

A. I'd like to move out of teaching. Certainly no higher in a school.

Q. What support have you experienced during your teaching career?

A. I've had support from many sources. My wife (excellent), my colleagues (very good), the unions (OK), senior staff (varied . . . some good, some not so good escapees from the classroom), the LEA (has fallen away over the years).

Q. Would you recommend a teaching career to others?

A. Absolutely not! This is not the profession it was. The workload is horrendous, the support is often poor, politicians will lay every ill of society at your door, you will work in poor conditions with limited resources. Morale is very low and I can't see where the next generation of teachers will come from. It is rare indeed to find a student who says they wish to become a teacher . . . and many will try to dissuade them. Only if you are teaching full time in the current climate and have been for a while will you understand.

Q. What could be done to make teaching a 'better' career, then?

A. Time, resources and some appreciation. Time to prepare/plan. A year out every seven years. A better career structure.

Q. What was it like when you first started teaching? Has education changed? Are the changes for the better or not?

A. I enjoyed teaching when I started. It seemed more relaxed. People had time for you and vice versa. You got to know students better. Class sizes were smaller (considerably). I had a good induction year. NQTs now seem to be thrown in the deep end so it's little wonder many quit within a year or two. I have seen change upon change for over ten years with much of that soon ditched and no one held accountable for the lost energy, time and money thrown at it. We were recently (as a staff) forced to watch a DfEE video as an INSET activity that told us that the new thinking was that lessons should have a beginning, middle and end (which would be called a plenary) and should be structured to be effective . . . to think we'd missed that over the years.

Q. What about the future? What are your plans?

A. Not too sure. Maybe to change schools and have a fresh challenge with a new set of faces; that could be revitalizing. Failing that to expand a business venture I've been involved in for several years and see how far that goes. I have two children to put through university and the expense of that is now starting to weigh so a decent income remains a priority.

Secondary school teacher – 11 years' experience

Second in Science Department/Form Tutor

Turves Green Girls' School and Technology College, Birmingham

Carl Smith

Note: You can read more about Carl and his work in Chapter 13, 'Planning in the secondary school'.

Q. Why did you decide to go into teaching?

Carl – I had gained a degree in Chemistry at the age of 26. Six years on and the company that had sponsored me through college had no idea what to do with me. I was working as a foreman on the shop floor and going nowhere. I had always thought that I could be a teacher since I first left school and spent four years working in a teacher training college as a lab tech.

Q. Tell me about your training.

Carl – My degree was with the Royal Society of Chemistry (GRSC Parts I and II). At 32 I gained a place on the PGCE course at the University of Birmingham.

Q. What was the PGCE course like?

Carl – It had a good structure and was well presented by the Science lecturers. Teaching practice was three weeks in the first term and 12 weeks after Christmas. On the downside was the EPS (education and professional studies) lectures. These were on the whole extremely boring, delivered by a bunch of out of touch academics who it seemed had not been inside a school for years. In many cases they just seemed to want to deliver their brand of political dogma, which, to me, bore no resemblance to the real world (the 21 and 22 year olds on the course lapped it up).

Q. Any tips for students on PGCE courses right now?

Carl – The best training is to watch, assist and follow on from experienced teachers in real classrooms. Talk to them in the staffroom and listen to what they have to say. This also applies to the first years in the job, and still applies for me today. Sadly we still sometimes get training videos where actors/ teachers perform in front of 'Stepford Wives' type classes where the teacher raises an eyebrow and a pupil is immediately subjugated, good for a laugh at least!

Q. How long have you been teaching now, and what's your present job?

Carl – 11 years. I'm at Turves Green Girls' School and Technology College, Birmingham, teaching Science at Key Stages Three and Four. I'm just completing my sixth year there.

Q. And will you be looking to move on soon?

Carl – No. I'm completely happy where I am thanks.

Q. Tell me about your job as a form tutor. How do you see that role?

Carl – In my present school I have a Year Nine group of 31 girls. I acquired them at the start of Year Eight and will hand them on at the end of this term. There are a lot of good things about the job of form tutor: day-to-day interaction with the group, acting as an 'uncle' to quite a few when trying to help with the many problems that modern pupils bring into school. I think of the role as being a mentor for the form and on occasions being their advocate. Obviously there are times when you need to be firm and 'heavy' but thankfully with my current form

15

these have been few (apparently the current Year Seven form that I will pick up in September contains a fair few 'darlings' who have already made their presence felt!).

Q. Are there any drawbacks to being a form tutor?

Carl – The main drawback of the job is the admin. Many schools fail to give adequate time to the job. It can be difficult as some weeks the job merely entails calling the register but there are some weeks when you would need an hour each morning to go through the notices, room changes, letter and reply slips, absence notes, etc. Chasing absence is probably the least enjoyable part. You end up moaning at the pupils about the lack of notes whereas of course it is the parents who are responsible. Occasionally you end up putting a pupil in detention because a note hasn't arrived despite phone calls home and letters (the letter I use only requires a sentence and a signature but many parents can't be bothered). Usually a small number of pupils account for the majority of the absences. In some cases these absences are condoned by the parents. The school seems powerless to bring these parents back into line, educational social workers, home visits, constant phone calls seem to have no effect.

Q. What else do you have to do with your form during the year?

Carl – The school has recently instigated a 'target setting' process that entails the form tutor interviewing each of the form for fifteen minutes to discuss their progress and set some targets. The first interview takes place around October and the parents are invited into school (about 30 per cent come in). The second meeting takes place around April when targets can be reviewed and reset. Targets apart (which I think can be a bit naff!) the chance to sit down with each pupil in a quiet spot on comfy chairs with soft music playing and to discuss how they are finding school and to praise and encourage them is worthwhile. Frequently pupils will talk about or raise issues that they would not raise in the normal run of the school day. These interviews take a whole day (you usually get to see about 24 pupils in a day; those with SEN are usually seen by the SENCO and the 'Naughties' by a year head or SMT).

Q. What about those special moments as a teacher? Can you describe one for me?

Carl – At my previous school (a boys' Comp) there was a pupil who had been in my tutor group for Years 10 and 11 and who had had a very chequered career. He came back to see me two years after he'd left to tell me how he'd got a job as a motor mechanic (using a reference I had given him) and was now at college on day release, had been promoted and was really doing well. In Year 10 he had been very close to total exclusion and even prison.

Q. And how about the downside?

Carl – I can't really think of one really bad moment although there have been one or two close calls. Walking into a room in my first weeks at my first school and finding two Year 10 boys fighting, being urged on by the rest of the class. Instinctively I grabbed both boys by the hair and pulled them apart (fortunately I am six feet tall and at the time played rugby) and held them until they stopped swinging. I remember sitting down in a quiet corner afterwards and I couldn't keep a limb still.

Q. What's the best thing about teaching Science?

Carl – When a pupil says that he or she would love a career in science, or when a pupil stays behind to ask about possible careers in science. Then I feel that I have enthused them.

Q. And the worst thing about teaching at secondary level?

Carl – The extreme bad manners of some pupils and the fact that in many cases they don't even realize that their behaviour is unacceptable.

Q. How about promotion?

Carl – When I first started teaching 11 years ago I was really keen. I took on several unpaid responsibilities at my first school with the intention that the experience would stand me in good stead when I sought paid promotions. My only 'promotion' at my first school was as a temporary year head covering a term's medical leave. It was a Year Seven first term (September to Christmas) and included an OFSTED inspection!

Q. And at your present school?

Carl – When I moved here it was to take up the post of Second in Science. I've been unsuccessful three times in trying to become a year head when vacancies arose (one temporary and two permanent) but each time the post went elsewhere. I have since taken on responsibility for Health and Safety (one point) and this keeps me plenty busy! Now I am older and wiser, I have plenty to keep me busy in school and at home and the extra hassle isn't worth the increase in salary.

Q. How about support for you as a teacher? Where has that come from?

Carl – At my first school the department had a core of experienced teachers who had worked together for many years, and the department seemed to run telepathically. New teachers quickly got used to this and the support that these teachers gave was tremendous.

Q. Any resources that you find particularly useful?

Carl – The website Just for Teachers is good. I try to avoid books on teaching; I read the staffroom copy of the *TES*. Four years ago we introduced 'Science Now' at Key Stage Three. It revolutionized how we deliver science. Now we're looking for a replacement to cover the new syllabus.

Q. Would you recommend teaching as a career?

Carl – I think that for certain people I would encourage them to become teachers but I think that they should come to it after spending some time working in the 'real' world.

Q. What could be done to make teaching a better career?

Carl – Smaller classes, more classroom support, less prescription, a suitable curriculum for the lower ability pupils.

Q. And thinking back to when you were an NQT, what was it like?

Carl – It was called 'probation' then. Birmingham arranged five INSET days, some of which were useful.

Q. How did you find that first job?

Carl – The school phoned my university to ask if they had any students who might consider a mixed Maths and Science timetable. They had advertised but had no takers. I went along to look at the school, got on well with the heads of Science and Maths and so applied.

Q. You sound remarkably uncynical for a teacher with eleven years in the job. Any tips for NQTs on staying positive?

Carl – Only the usual ones. Don't try and run before you can walk. This is especially relevant now I think. As more staff leave or opt for quality of life over promotion the temptation is to load more responsibility onto younger (keener?) staff. To an NQT starting on the bottom of the scale I can see that an extra £1K or so can be very tempting. Develop a healthy cynicism, don't trust any politicians whatever the party. Always think of the good pupils you have taught that day. Remember that some of them are a lot cleverer than you are and will go a lot further, thanks to you. Remember that almost every child that you have taught today has made some progress, acquired some extra knowledge or skill that they didn't have yesterday. There will always be pupils who drive you nuts, but let it go, don't allow that five per cent to dominate your thought or conversations (this is really difficult). Keep a sense of humour at all times and never take anything too seriously. After all, even in your worst lesson nobody died!

Keep a sense of humour at all times and never take anything too seriously. After all, even in your worst lesson nobody died!

2 Teacher training

This chapter covers the 'nuts and bolts' of becoming a teacher. It gives you information about the different routes that you can take into the profession, and looks at the decisions you need to make before entering teacher training. It will also give you an idea of what these different routes involve, and how to go about applying for them. In addition, you can hear from some people taking their 'first steps' towards a teaching career – student trainees who have made the decision to move into the profession.

Routes into teaching

England and Wales

The two most common routes into teaching are via an undergraduate or postgraduate university course. However, a third possibility has recently been added – the 'employment based' route. Whilst this might seem like an attractive option, there are a limited number of places available, and some prospective teachers report limited success in finding placements. You'll find details about this and the 'traditional' routes below.

STEP ONE
You must have:
GCSE in English and Maths
(Grade 'C' or higher)

STEP TWO
'A' Levels or Access Course

STEP THREE
Degree/Postgraduate Certificate
CHOICE OF 3 'ROUTES'

ROUTE ONE

Undergraduate route
'Teaching degree', with subject specialism

- BEd/BA/BSc with QTS
- Usually primary level
- Full or part time
- Three or four years (five-year part-time courses available)

If you are one year into a non-teaching degree, you can apply for a two-year course. This is especially suitable for mature entrants.

OR ...

ROUTE TWO

Postgraduate route
'Subject specific degree', then teaching qualification

First degree:

- For primary preferably related to the National Curriculum
- For secondary the subject or subjects you want to teach

Postgraduate qualification – PGCE:

- One year (some two years)
- Full, part time, flexible learning
- Flexible learning = distance learning, evenings, weekends

OR ...

ROUTE THREE

Employment based route
Training for QTS while employed by a school

- Working as an unqualified teacher while gaining QTS
- Following an individual programme of training while you work
- School pays you a salary while you train
- You must be over 24 years old
- You must find a school willing to train you on GTP/GTRP
- Highly competitive: just over 3,000 places available in the academic year 2001–2
- Places tend to go to those offering a secondary shortage subject

Note: The different routes into teaching are subject to constant change, and you can find out a great deal more information about getting into the profession from the Teacher Training Agency (www.canteach.gov.uk).

Scotland and Northern Ireland

There are six universities in Scotland that offer teacher training, and you can find details of these on the Scottish Executive website (see the Directory for details). As in England and Wales, you can choose between a PGCE for primary or secondary, or an undergraduate course (in a limited range of subjects). There are no distance learning or part time options available in Scotland.

Universities in Northern Ireland offer both primary and secondary PGCE courses. As these universities do not take part in the GTTR scheme, applicants should apply directly to the university at which they are interested in studying. There are high levels of competition for teaching posts in Northern Ireland. You can find out more information at www.qub.ac.uk/co/students/teachni.htm.

Decisions, decisions!

Before deciding which of the three routes to take into teaching, there are various things that you'll need to consider.

- *Which 'route' is best for me?* For instance, if you are completely certain that you wish to teach at secondary school level, the normal approach would be to take a subject specific degree and then follow this with a PGCE. When making the choice between a 'straight' teaching degree, or a first degree/PGCE, think carefully about the benefits and drawbacks of each route:
  - *The teaching degree* – gives you more time to practise and develop your teaching skills, but has less flexibility should you decide to leave (or not enter) the profession.
  - *A first degree/PGCE* – gives you a much more condensed opportunity to learn while on teaching practice, but is a more flexible route for those unsure about teaching, and (in England) attracts a financial incentive (see below).
- *Which degree subject is best for me?* If you wish to teach at primary level, and decide to take the degree/PGCE route, you should ensure that your subject choice is related to the National Curriculum. If you're planning to teach at secondary level, be aware that some subjects are far more popular than others. As a consequence there is more competition when trying to secure a teaching post within that subject area. If you train to teach a 'secondary shortage subject', you are likely to find it far easier to get a job, and to gain quick promotions.
- *What age group do I want to teach?* You can train to teach in the whole of the primary or secondary sector, or a specific age group, such as 3–8 or 14–19.

- *How am I going to finance my training?* At present, some teacher training courses attract additional funding from the government. See 'Financial incentives' below for more information.

What's in the degree?

Primary school teachers are trained to teach English, Maths, Science, plus one or more specialist subjects. The undergraduate route involves a substantial amount of time spent in school, currently 24 weeks for a three-year course and 32 weeks for a four-year course. These teaching practices (TPs) are staggered over the years of the course, so that they build up gradually in length and intensity. For the PGCE course, you can expect to spend 18 weeks in school (primary) and 24 weeks in school (secondary). You can find lots more information about teaching practice in the next chapter.

Applying for teacher training

If you wish to take a PGCE, you will need to apply via the Graduate Teacher Training Registry (GTTR – www.gttr.ac.uk). For undergraduate teaching courses, the normal university applications system (via UCAS – www.ucas.ac.uk) applies. You can find full contact details for the GTTR and UCAS in the Directory at the back of this book. In Northern Ireland, students apply directly to the training institution. For 'Fast Track' teaching, you should apply via the website – www.fasttrackteaching.gov.uk.

Financial incentives

Financial incentives are currently only available for students doing a PGCE in England. In Northern Ireland and Scotland, competition for teaching posts means that it is unnecessary for the governments to encourage additional graduates into teaching in this way. Decisions about financial incentives in Wales are currently being made. Students taking an undergraduate teaching degree are not eligible for any incentives – a sore point with many undergraduate student teachers!

PGCE students receive a £6,000 'training bursary'. In addition to this, £4,000 is available two years into your career if you are teaching Maths, Science, English, MFL, Design and Technology or ICT. There are also some 'secondary shortage subjects' which attract (means tested) payments for students in addition to the PGCE training salary. These are Maths, Science, MFL, Design and Technology, ICT, Geography, Music and RE.

QTS

The QTS standards

You can find a downloadable document that explains the QTS standards in full from the Teacher Training Agency website (www.canteach.gov.uk). Briefly, the QTS standards deal with the areas of your work explained below.

- *Professional values and practice:* This covers areas such as having high expectations of your students, treating the children with respect and consistency, and improving your own teaching.
- *Knowledge and understanding:* In this section are attributes such as good subject knowledge, understanding the National Curriculum, using ICT effectively, and knowing a range of strategies to promote effective learning and good behaviour.
- *Teaching:* This section looks at three different areas. The first is planning, expectation and targets, for example setting challenging objectives and selecting and using resources. The second is monitoring and assessment, for example assessing and recording student progress, and reporting on it to parents and others. The third is teaching and class management, which covers areas such as having high expectations and organizing and managing the learning environment.

The QTS skills tests

Students training in England also have to pass the QTS 'skills tests'. These are in literacy, numeracy and information and communications technology. At present, skills tests are not required for teachers training in Wales. You can find lots of information about these tests on the TTA website (www.canteach.gov.uk). You'll also find some comments about the skills tests in the student interviews below.

First steps

The interviews that follow give you an insight into the lives of some student teachers: why they chose to move into the profession, their experiences of teacher training, and their initial impressions of working in a classroom on teaching practice. The trainees that I spoke to were working throughout the UK, at both primary and secondary levels, on BEd and PGCE courses, and as both full-time and part-time (distance learning) students.

> Student teacher
>
> Primary BEd (Drama) 3–11 years
>
> Manchester Metropolitan University
>
> Nichola Beech

Q. Why did you decide to go into teaching?

Nichola – Teaching is a career I've always been interested in, since I was young. It's the only career I've ever really considered. I've always enjoyed working with young children – when I was younger I used to help at a youth club, and I've always thought that teaching was something I wanted to do.

Q. What route are you taking into teaching?

Nichola – My course is a four-year BEd (Hons) Primary with QTS. I'm training at the Institute of Education (Didsbury), which is part of MMU. My specialist subject is Drama, but I cover all subjects because I'm training to teach in the primary sector.

Q. When you were considering the training route you would take, what was it about the BEd that made you choose it over BA/PGCE?

Nichola – I thought that my knowledge was of a more general nature and that I didn't want to specialize in as much detail as I would have done if I'd done a BA and then a PGCE. I also thought that a BEd would help me to develop as a teacher, rather than a short course of about nine months for a PGCE.

Q. What's the best thing about the course you're doing?

Nichola – The amount of time spent in a wide range of schools in different social and ethnic areas. Also the chance to work in a special needs school (where I'm about to start a week's placement).

Q. What placements do you do in each year of the course?

Nichola – In the first year we did four one-day visits to observe specific aspects of teaching, then a five-week block practice in the first half of the summer term. In the second year I did a week in a nursery in the autumn term and a five-week block during the first half of the spring term, with a focus on my main subject. We also did a one-week practice teaching only Foundation subjects. In the third

25

year we had a six-week block practice, this time teaching 'solo', whereas all the other practices had been with a student partner. Then I've got one week in a special school. Next year, I think it's going to be an eight-week block practice, but this isn't finalized yet.

Q. What about the QTS skills tests? Have you taken those yet? Any problems?

Nichola – I took and passed all my QTS skills tests back in October. I decided that the best way to practise them was to do them and I passed! The ICT test was really easy and the English was OK. I found the mental maths part of the Maths test hard, as I've never really done any mental maths except the small amount I've done in school with the kids! I booked them all online, though I had a few problems with registration, and I know a few other people at my uni did.

Q. Could you tell me about the different types of schools that you've taught in? Was there one school that really stands out as a good experience?

Nichola – I've been in Catholic schools, Church of England schools, Community schools, schools where the majority of students are middle/upper class and ones with a real multicultural mix. My third year block placement was a fantastic experience, as I was welcomed as a member of staff, not just as a student. The children responded well to me and I enjoyed teaching in that school. All the staff were kind and helpful, especially my class teacher, who helped me in any way she could.

Q. Have you been thrown in 'at the deep end' on your teaching practices?

Nichola – We always had preparation visits for our teaching blocks, so we could observe the class and teacher, and help the class teacher.

Q. What support have your university tutors given you while you're on TP?

Nichola – We always have a designated tutor to observe and help us. They usually come in once a week, and offer their telephone numbers in case we need more assistance. It's always interesting to get feedback from the tutors, although as they're not always there I find information from the class teacher and other teachers in the school more informative.

Q. What sort of planning have you had to do for your TPs?

Nichola – We have a booklet for each teaching block, which prescribes the kind of planning we have to complete. It's quite detailed and forms the basis of our assessment. We also have to do lots of analysis of our teaching, which is always read and assessed.

Q. Has there been a lot of written work on the course?

Nichola – We have at least two assignments per year. In the first year we had assignments for English, Maths and Science and also main subject and GPS (general professional studies). Our topics for assignments have included Assessment, Talking with Parents, and a study of a Foundation subject, to name just a few.

Q. What's the best thing about doing TP?

Nichola – Seeing children achieve targets that you set for them, especially those that were extremely challenging targets. Also when children enjoy my teaching and I can see them enjoying learning.

Q. How do you make your teaching enjoyable?

Nichola – I provide a lot of 'hands-on' teaching, where the children are part of the lesson, not merely observing. I like to get children out of their seats where appropriate and take an active rather than a passive role in their learning. I also try and teach topics that interest them.

Q. What's the best thing about teaching your subject and age group?

Nichola – I really enjoy seeing children becoming a part of the learning experience rather than just observing. I also love seeing children 'coming out of their shell' through drama work. Also, teaching young children, I enjoy seeing their thirst for knowledge and seeing them come on in great steps in the basics of learning.

Q. Do you ever use drama methods to teach other areas of the curriculum?

Nichola – I often use drama techniques to teach other subjects, as often during block placements this is the only way I can introduce drama because of curriculum constraints. I've taught about the Great Fire of London through drama, where the children became people in London at the time of the fire, and they wrote diaries (like those of Samuel Pepys) and letters to their friends and families. We also wrote newspaper reports based on this drama work.

Q. What forms of support have you experienced during your teacher training?

Nichola – I've had support from my tutors and from teachers that I've worked with, but I've found my mother to be the most useful form of support. As a teacher she's been able to help me in all sorts of situations, such as when you get stuck on that idea for how to present a certain area of the curriculum, or reading an essay.

Q. Did your mum advise you to go into teaching, or did she ever tell you about the downsides of the job?

Nichola – My mum has shown me both sides of the job, both good and bad, and as many of her friends are also teachers I have been surrounded by teachers for most of my life, so I've seen the good and bad things that happen. Mum has never discouraged me from being a teacher. She knows that it is what I want to do. My mum wishes that the government 'would stop "shifting the goalposts" and allow us to get on with what we were trained to do – teach'.

Q. Would you recommend a teaching career to other people?

Nichola – I would recommend teaching to anyone, if I thought they would enjoy it. It's not a career you go into because of the money, it's something you have to want to do – some may say they 'have a calling' for it. It's an immensely rewarding profession, although I do not deny that it's time consuming!

Q. What could be done to make teaching a more popular career?

Nichola – I feel that the government should make funding available to undergraduate trainees, as well as to PGCE students. I know that like myself, other people on my course feel that we are being undervalued as teachers, and in some way are not as worthy as those who do a PGCE. I also think that the press need to stop giving teaching such a bad name, and praise the positive rather than focus on the negative. Giving teachers a less restrictive curriculum to work from would be a good idea, as Foundation subjects (particularly Music and Drama) are being ousted in favour of literacy and numeracy, when I feel they have equal importance within the primary curriculum.

> Student teacher
>
> Primary PGCE (Art & Design) 7-11 years
>
> Stephanie Leach
>
> University of London, Institute of Education

Q. Why did you decide to go into teaching?

Steph – Because I'd been looking for a job that was challenging and constantly changing. I'd worked in various places (mostly offices) and found the work boring, uninspiring and uncreative. I hated shuffling paper all day. I had been thinking about going into teaching, and had spoken to a few family friends that are teachers and they all thought I had the potential to become a good teacher. The fact that the government was ploughing a lot of money into teaching and teacher training made my decision a little easier, and the concept of training for a year wasn't too scary, but I think I may have done it anyway.

Q. And did you have any experience of teaching before you started training?

Steph – When I started the application process I got a job in a local primary school for a couple of hours a day delivering the ALS (additional literacy support) scheme to seven to nine year olds. I knew after a couple of days that I was going to love school, and after a couple of months I was convinced that I had made the right decision by applying to do my PGCE. I had found the place where I belonged.

Q. What route are you taking into teaching?

Steph – I did a BA (Hons) in History of Art, Design and Film with Arts and Media Management. I'm now doing a General Primary PGCE at the Institute of Education. Although the course covers the whole of the primary syllabus, I'm specializing in later years (age seven to eleven) and in Art and Design.

Q. Why did you choose this particular course?

Steph – With my degree, I couldn't have gone into secondary teaching, and I wouldn't have wanted to either. I couldn't imagine standing in front of a class of 16-year-old boys and expecting their attention. I chose seven to eleven year olds because they are at that age when they are able to go the toilet on their own (mostly), are interested in learning, but are not too cocky like adolescents. I did

29

consider training whilst working in a school that sponsored me, but that only applies to over 24s and I'm only 22.

Q. How has the course been so far?

Steph – It's been great, but there is one word that describes it perfectly – intense. The course is definitely a full-on affair, but it is enjoyable. I know people warned me of this at the start, but it is true that you don't get a break. School holidays are spent writing essays and reflecting on everything you do and all your spare time is spent reading and completing that ever-moving sequence of teaching, assessing and planning. I feel the university element of the course has really prepared me for the school experience side, but only practice will make this feel truly my own. In conclusion, I'm tired but happy, and I still love to teach.

Q. What's been particularly good about the course?

Steph – One of the best things is the support we have received from our tutors at university. As we are clustered according to where we live we can share experiences with other group members and also know where to go if we need a chat with our tutor.

Q. And what difficulties have you experienced?

Steph – One of the most difficult things for me has been the travelling as I live quite far away from the schools I am in at the moment (but this is self-inflicted I suppose).

Q. How have you got on in your teaching practices?

Steph – My teaching practices have been fine, but exhausting. My biggest target is, as always, behaviour management. I've enjoyed both practices, but sitting in lectures making notes is far easier than doing the teaching.

Q. What advice would you give prospective student teachers about surviving a PGCE?

Steph – Stay organized, try not to miss a day as you will *never* catch up and don't worry, you don't have to read *all* the books on the reading lists. Take each day as it comes, but plan in advance. If you make yourself believe you will not have a day off for the whole year, you may actually enjoy yourself on Christmas Day or maybe your birthday (as long as it doesn't fall on a weekday, weekend or during half term). Kids are terribly behaved with every student and supply teacher, and we all have behaviour management worries.

Q. And how about the QTS skills tests? Have you got those out of the way yet? How difficult did you find them?

Steph – I've done the QTS tests and passed them all first time. I didn't think they were too difficult but it may be because I downloaded the practice tests from the internet and tried those a couple of times each. The format of the tests is fairly simple, but does take some getting used to as they are obviously not allowed to use Microsoft programmes that we are all used to using.

Q. What plans have you made for your NQT year? Have you started job hunting yet?

Steph – I've started looking for jobs in Hertfordshire as they should be easier for me to travel to. I keep taking down details of jobs I'd like, but I'm not going to worry about it too much at the moment as there will be a lot more jobs around in the summer term.

Q. Can you recommend any resources that have been a help to you?

Steph – I highly recommend www.eteach.co.uk. It's an excellent website for teachers and those in the education sector. There's also an excellent new section for students and NQTs, who are usually largely ignored. I have to recommend the *TES* and the *TES* website www.tes.co.uk is OK, but you still have to buy the publication. I don't see why there can't be an electronic version that would help save a few trees. The BBC Learning Zone is good for general resources (www.bbc.co.uk/learningzone). The DfES website is good too (www.dfes.gov.uk).

Q. Would you recommend a teaching career to others?

Steph – I think teaching is one of those professions that you either love or hate. They say it takes a special kind of person to become a teacher, and I think that's a good general assumption. If you can handle a job that is difficult, frustrating, exhausting, badly paid and under-funded, but on the other hand is rewarding, invigorating and inspiring, then teaching is for you. If you want a job where you are undervalued, underpaid and never appreciated but makes you feel like you have made a difference in the lives of the little people of this world, then teaching is for you. If you want an easy life, take a desk job or don't work at all. Teaching is not for the faint-hearted, which is why I love it.

Q. What could be done to make teaching a better career?

Steph – The most obvious answer to that is to pay us more. I don't think the starting wage is too bad at £14,000 for a graduate, but I know my student debts will amount to a lot more than that. After four years unpaid training, you would have thought you could get a better wage than this, and also to be able to advance up the scales in a shorter time than is possible.

I think OFSTED is putting a lot of people off teaching, and making many existing teachers retire early. If school inspections were a more frequent, less formal affair, I think the stress levels in schools would drop dramatically. Teaching would also be a much more popular profession if all the existing teachers stopped moaning so much! Everywhere you look there are teachers moaning about something or other. I know they deserve to be heard and most of them are making valid points, but they don't make teaching very appealing to those on the outside. No wonder there is a shortage of teachers.

Student teacher (Scotland) – qualified

BA (Hons) Craft & Design

Secondary PGCE (Art & Design)

Lisa Simpson

Q. Could you tell me why you decided to go into teaching?

Lisa – It wasn't until my second year in art school that I realized that I wanted to teach. In class, I was always looked upon as a substitute tutor by my classmates. I looked to my old secondary school for guidance. I taught there for a couple of weeks (just one morning a week) and loved it so I looked into it further. I realized that teaching came naturally to me and it gave me great personal satisfaction.

Q. And why did you decide to go into secondary rather than primary teaching?

Lisa – Because I wanted to concentrate on one specific subject. I felt that I would be more suited to teaching teens as I saw that as the most educational stage when it came to art.

Q. What was the best thing about the PGCE course that you did?

Lisa – Definitely the school placements. Although you were still studying to teach you were given full responsibility for the classes.

Q. And what about the most difficult thing?

Lisa – That was all the reading! Lots of theory and government guidelines to take in and it became quite difficult to remember it all.

Q. Could you tell me about the teaching practices you did on your course?

Lisa – We had three teaching placements which totalled 18 weeks. The first placement was a two-week induction to the school (observing and learning the ropes) and we then had four weeks teaching (in November/December). In February there was a six-week placement in a different school, with more time spent on solo teaching. Then in April there was another six-week placement. This was normally in the same school as your second placement but in some cases, due to staffing in schools and timetables, it was a different school. We were assessed six times in total by our tutors, although the head of the department was also likely to do their own assessment too.

Q. And what good and bad moments did you have on your placements?

Lisa – The best moments were during my last placement. One of them was when 12 pupils that I had taught briefly had been accepted into art school, lots of hugs and tears that day. Another was when a senior pupil had asked to see some of my own work (some of which involved staining handmade paper with coffee) and a few weeks later when I returned to visit she showed me how she had used the techniques I had shown her to present her design work. On my last day of placement I took in a T-shirt for the pupils to sign and reading the comments afterwards just reduced me to tears and reassured me that teaching is what I was meant to do in life.

My worst moment was when one pupil became quite aggressive and I failed to deal with the situation, thus making a very hard class to teach. I was reduced to tears afterwards but did not let it keep me down, I have to say that this particular pupil became one of my stars by the end of the placement.

Q. What sort of planning did you do for your TPs?

Lisa – My lesson plans were one side of A4. These detailed a brief description of the task, the aims of the lesson, a list of materials and then a checklist in chronological order of the activities, discussions, etc., to be done during the lesson. I would then do a lesson review with a pupil review as well. The length of my lesson plans varied depending on whether the lesson was part of a series of themed lessons or not. I would also run through the lesson myself (for example produce the painting or drawing). In general I didn't find the written lesson plans helpful, but going through the lessons myself was.

Q. What are the upsides and downsides of teaching Art as a subject?

Lisa – It's always a great subject to teach, the pupils are usually sick of writing and reading so Art seems to be a bit of a break for them. Although we do some writing I have to add. Ha-ha. It is a chance to actually use the other side of their brain for once. The worst thing is the preparation! Always lots of mess and each lesson has to be worked through. Also the pace of the lessons is difficult, some parts of the projects are quick and easy for some but others will take three weeks to complete the work.

Q. Where do you see yourself working as a teacher?

Lisa – I hope to teach in the Glasgow area (I live in Aberdeen right now) but want to travel over to the US or Canada at some point in my career.

Q. What would you say is different about being a teacher in a Scottish school, rather than one in the rest of the UK?

Lisa – I think the main difference is all the places you can teach up here. With remote villages and towns and also the islands, you have a chance to teach in a small and intimate community rather than in the city. Patriotism is seen as a positive thing in Scotland, and children learn a lot in History lessons about Scottish battles and also Scottish crafts.

Q. And what about actually training to be a teacher in Scotland?

Lisa – With only three teacher training (for PGCE) colleges in Scotland you feel that we are never really short of teachers. We keep hearing about the shortage in England and I always get relatives, etc., saying 'But they say that they are crying out for teachers! Why can't you get a job?' Oh, and also that the colleges in England are paying their student teachers £6,000 (or around that) to do the course! Up here we couldn't believe it! It's seen as a flat out bribe that shouldn't be needed. In Scotland perhaps we are more willing to go into teaching (or perhaps with the country being so much smaller, it just seems like it). But with the national news constantly putting down teachers and teaching in England, who knows, maybe the students will come up here.

Q. What about supply teaching, how does that work in Scotland?

Lisa – In Scotland we apply to the local council of the area we want to teach in. The application is just a general one with also a section to list any preferential schools you would like to be placed in. You then get an interview and you are put on their list. They call you with details of placements, etc., if and when they occur. You can also write to schools to tell them that you are available for supply, this gets your name around a little faster and shows that you are keen to be in their school. I have applied to do supply work in Aberdeen but the council have not given me an interview yet, which is quite annoying as I applied about two months ago! I am chasing them up about it but with the new probationers starting it is maybe the worst time for me to start.

Q. I understand that you've not started teaching yet?

Lisa – No. I'm taking some time off until next year when I'll start my teaching career. At present I'm a Graphic Designer for a small handmade gift company in Aberdeen.

Q. And have you had any interviews for teaching posts?

Lisa – No interviews yet, which is kind of depressing. I've had five knock backs for interviews but there are very few jobs going which are more than one day a week.

Q. So are there real problems with finding a job as a teacher in Scotland?

Lisa – Well, there's now a new government bill which guarantees *all* NQTs from this year on *one full year employment*! So they just graduate and they go straight into a job! Nice, huh? The forgotten year (i.e. me and the rest of the 2001 graduates) are left to fend for themselves, even though the bill was accepted in parliament only months into our course.

Q. Will it mean problems with your induction, if you don't find a job soon?

Lisa – Well, one good thing is that the General Teaching Council for Scotland has changed our length of probation from two years (school years) to only 270 days. This is an improvement but it means that if we have not completed our 270 days before the NQTs finish their one year employment, we will probably lose out on all the jobs because they will have one year's experience already. It's a mess really and I can see that there will be tough times ahead. So I think that councils at the moment are doing a very bad job.

Q. Finally, would you recommend a career in teaching to other people?

Lisa – I certainly would recommend teaching to others, it is such a satisfying and challenging career and you really see the effects you have on the kids, either negative or positive. The holidays are great too!

> Student teacher
>
> Primary PGCE (Maths) Key Stage One
>
> Part time, distance learning
>
> Name withheld

Q. Why did you decide to go into teaching?

A. During my degree I had to do placements in each year, my first was in social work and that's when I discovered I was good at working with children. So, for the second placement, I went on to a primary school (Year One class) and that's when I decided. It was too late to change to a BEd then, although I did try.

Q. What route are you taking into teaching?

A. I'm doing a part-time distance learning PGCE (Primary) course. I'm training at Key Stage One and specializing in Maths. The course takes two years.

Q. And why did you choose that course?

A. I had a baby during my final degree year and couldn't manage full time just yet. Because it's part time I still have time for my daughter and the distance learning means I save a fortune in childcare! I also get to see my daughter a lot more than I would doing a full-time course.

Q. Did the extra money for PGCE students help influence your choice?

A. Yes. The money is a major factor for me because without it I couldn't have afforded to do it, especially with the cost of childcare and books, etc.

Q. What's the best thing about the course so far?

A. We keep in contact with our tutors by email. This is really useful as it saves time trying to get phone calls returned. Also the monthly meetings at local centres are good because you get to exchange ideas with other members of the course and help each other out a bit.

Q. And what's the hardest thing about it?

A. The time it took to get us all placements. It has meant my serial attachment is now being done in the space of two weeks rather than spread over five weeks.

This causes childcare problems for me and other members of the course with children.

Q. You must have needed a lot of support, with a young baby. Have you found that people are willing to help you out?

A. Yes. The tutors are there when you want them which is good, but friends and family have been the most supportive especially with childcare. I have a few friends that are already teachers or have just finished their BEds. They have been an invaluable source of support and ideas.

Q. What have been the best and worst things about your teaching practices?

A. The best was getting the children to finally understand where speech marks go! The support from members of staff at the school has been really nice as well. The worst was feeling a bit useless at first because I didn't know what to do or where to put myself.

Q. What's special about working with Key Stage One kids?

A. They're still reasonably scared of adults so aren't too much trouble and are easier to keep in line than other older classes. They also have a fantastic innocence which makes them a delight to teach, as does their wild imaginations.

Q. What are your plans for the future in teaching? Do you hope to gain promotion?

A. Yes, but not so I won't be in the classroom teaching anymore. I'd like to do some special needs training and take on a post relevant to that.

Q. Would you recommend a teaching career to other people?

A. Yes, the pay is good (despite allegations to the contrary – none of my graduate friends earn the same or more than the starting salary I will get) and it's never ever dull!

Q. And what would you say needs to be done to improve teaching as a profession?

A. They should increase the training salary and make it available for BEd students. They also need to reduce paperwork – a lot of it seems very unnecessary (and dull). I have a friend who would love to be a teacher. She has GCSEs and a BTEC in Art. She hasn't done a degree and she doesn't have any 'A' levels (or their equivalent) but she is so keen and in my opinion would be a great teacher. However whenever she goes to open days she is told that it would take a lot of work to become a teacher (she'd need to start from 'A' levels or an Access course) and is basically told not to bother. This needs to be addressed because the profession is losing out on a lot of good teachers this way.

Useful books for student teachers

Handbook for Newly Qualified Teachers
(Second edition)
Elizabeth Holmes
ISBN: 0-11-702616-6
Publisher: The Stationery Office Limited

A very practical guide to many of the different issues faced by NQTs, this book would also prove very helpful to student teachers, especially those just finishing their course. It covers areas such as finding a job, joining a school, and the induction year, in a down to earth and accessible way. Elizabeth Holmes also answers questions from NQTs on the website www.eteach.com.

The Teachers' Survival Guide
Angela Thody, Barbara Gray, Derek Bowden
ISBN: 0-8264-4791-0
Publisher: Continuum

This book covers important areas such as voice, time and stress management. It gives a number of useful tips, and also looks at different scenarios and how a teacher might handle them. The authors also provide evidence and statistics that may be useful for student teachers writing essays.

Essential Teaching Skills
Chris Kyriacou
ISBN: 0-7487-3514-3
Publisher: Nelson Thornes

A comprehensive and detailed book for student teachers and NQTs. Chris Kyriacou deals with a wide range of important areas such as teaching skills, planning and presenting lessons, and dealing with discipline and assessment.

> *A Guide to Teaching Practice*
> Louis Cohen, Lawrence Manion, Keith Morrison
> ISBN: 0-4151-4221-0
> Publisher: RoutledgeFalmer

More theoretical than my other suggestions, this book is a set text on many teacher training courses. Useful for students writing essays about classroom practice, although probably not a text that you will refer to once you're actually working as a teacher.

> *Starting Teaching: How to Succeed and Survive*
> Sue Cowley
> ISBN: 0-8264-5108-X
> Publisher: Continuum

I must confess to a personal interest here (I wrote this book). Suffice to say, it is written from a totally practical perspective, and covers all the things that I really needed to know about when I first went into teaching. The sections on how to teach and control your classes should prove especially useful for student teachers.

3 Surviving and succeeding on teaching practice

For many student teachers, teaching practice (TP) is the most exciting (and scariest!) part of the teacher training course. It is during your TPs that you get the chance to put all that theory and reading into practice, and that you discover how challenging and rewarding the job can really be. In this chapter you'll find lots of information, tips and ideas about surviving and succeeding on TP. The advice that I give will help you cope with the practical issues you might face on TP, and also to feel better prepared for any problems that could crop up.

Preparing for teaching practice

Getting ready to go on your first teaching practice (TP) can feel like a daunting prospect for student teachers. It may be a number of years since you last set foot in a classroom, and in any case, working in a school as a teacher is very different to attending a school as a student. You may have heard worrying stories about the bad behaviour you're likely to come across. You will certainly be feeling at least a little unsure and anxious about what lies ahead. However, there are a number of things that you can do to prepare yourself for, and to survive, and succeed on TP. And with at least some advance knowledge and tips about the process, you can lessen the stress of your first TP.

Common concerns and how to address them

In the accompanying panel, you'll find some of the more common concerns and questions about TP, both ones to do with the actual classroom, and also some of the more practical aspects of TP. The answers that follow will help you feel more confident in the days and weeks leading up to your first school experience.

> Should I plan some work for the children?
> Will I be thrown in 'at the deep end'?
> Should I prepare anything at all?
> How can I find out more about my TP school?
> Do I need to bring my own refreshments with me?
> What about lunch?
> How early should I arrive?
> What should I do when I get to the school?
> I start my first TP tomorrow, and I'm feeling completely terrified
> – is this normal?

- *Should I plan some work for the children?* In short, the answer to this is 'no'. Although it is very tempting when you're a keen student teacher, it is best not to do too much lesson preparation in advance. One of the most crucial things about lesson planning is that it suits the children that you are teaching – at this point children you haven't even met!

- *Will I be thrown in 'at the deep end'?* Again, the most likely answer is 'no'. On your first teaching practice it is really highly unlikely you will be given completely 'free rein' with the class. At this point you will not have sufficient experience, and the class teacher is unlikely to want to hand over his or her students immediately. Rather, you might simply be observing what goes on, or the class teacher could ask you to work with some small groups at first. Eventually, you may be given the freedom to prepare and teach a few lessons. In fact, some class teachers will actually give you a specific lesson of their own to deliver.

- *Should I prepare anything at all?* It may help you feel better prepared if you have some brief ideas for short games, fun activities or interesting lessons that you could use if you are asked to look after the class. In any case, this type of 'mini' planning will come in handy later on.

- *How can I find out more about my TP school?* This is now a reasonably straightforward process. Look up the school's latest OFSTED reports (www.ofsted.gov.uk) and find out its 'vital statistics' on the performance tables website (www.dfes.gov.uk/performancetables). Remember, though, that these reports and statistics can only ever give you a snapshot view of a school – you may find that the reality is in fact very different.

- *Do I need to bring my own refreshments with me?* The tea and coffee situation varies from school to school. Some schools do provide their staff with mugs, tea bags, coffee, milk and hot water, but in my experience this is actually quite rare. In many schools, teachers are expected to bring in their own refreshments, and you may experience some resentment if you turn up in their staffroom expecting to 'borrow'. To save any possibility of making enemies, take in your own mug and whatever drink making equipment you might require on your first day at the school.

- *What about lunch?* Remember, too, that the school could be a fair distance from the nearest shops, and that the catering at lunchtime might not be to your taste. Better to take your own packed lunch with you, at least on the first day, until you have sussed out the situation.

- *How early should I arrive?* It really is well worth aiming to arrive extra early on your first day of TP. At this point, you will be uncertain about how long travelling to the school will take, and it's better to be safe than sorry. Nothing makes a worse impression than a teacher who arrives late – in the teaching profession it is absolutely vital that you are in school and ready to start work when your children arrive. Remember, though, that schools are very busy places first thing in the morning. It could be that you are left hanging around for a while before somebody is able to deal with you.

- *What should I do when I get to the school?* When you arrive, make sure that you report to the school reception, where you will probably be asked to sign in and perhaps be given a badge to wear identifying you as a visitor to the school. You might then be taken up to the staffroom to wait until someone can deal with you.

■ *I start my first TP tomorrow, and I'm feeling completely terrified – is this normal?* In short, yes! You may well find that you have trouble sleeping the night before your first day at school, or that you have a nervous, sick feeling in your stomach. Don't worry about this – it is perfectly normal, and indeed even some very experienced teachers still feel this way at the start of a new school year or term (I know I do).

The first day

As I said above, it really is highly unlikely that you'll be thrown in at the deep end on your first day at school, and expected to actually take over a class on your own. What is more likely is that you will be asked to observe the class or the teacher, perhaps helping out with a small group of students once they have been set a task on which to work. Here's a checklist of tips for what to do (and what not to do) on that crucial first day, followed by a more detailed run down of each piece of advice.

> **Surviving the first day**
>
> *Get your bearings*
> *Locate the facilities*
> *Find out about timings*
> *Get some information*
> *Make useful contacts*
> *Approach the staffroom with care*

■ *Get your bearings:* Start to learn about the layout of the school. If you're not automatically given a map, ask for one at school reception and take the time to study it. You might like to ask if you can spend some time during the day walking around the school buildings to familiarize yourself with them.

■ *Locate the facilities:* Find out where the most vital amenities are: especially important are the toilets, the staffroom, the assembly hall, the school office and the photocopying machine.

■ *Find out about timings:* It is important to understand the timing of the school day. Timetables vary considerably from school to school, so make sure you learn:
  ■ What time the school day starts and finishes.
  ■ How long the lessons are.
  ■ Whether time is given (in a secondary school) for students to move between lessons.

- How long the breaks are, and whether these are the same for all children (some schools run different lunch timings for different ages of student).
- Whether there is a daily or weekly assembly, and when this takes place.
- In a secondary school, whether the timetable runs over one or two weeks.
- *Get some information:* If you can, get hold of a copy of some of the more important school policies. It will prove useful to read about the school rules and the whole school behaviour policy (if there is one), especially if you are working in a 'challenging' school. That way you can study it and know what to do if a child does misbehave.
- *Make useful contacts:* Make a real effort to get to know the school secretary and the office staff. These people know a lot about the way that the school runs, and they can make your life much easier when you have a question that you need answered.
- *Approach the staffroom with care:* A word of warning: do watch where you sit in the staffroom. Teachers can be extremely territorial about their favourite chairs. Before you park yourself in a seat, do make sure to ask 'is it OK if I sit here?' This might seem petty to you at the moment, but just wait until you've got a full-time teaching job and you find a student in your own favourite seat in the staffroom!

Observing the class

At the start of a teaching practice, you'll be given a chance to observe the class or classes of the teacher with whom you're going to be working. This really is a wonderful opportunity – in fact one that would benefit many working teachers, who rarely get the chance to observe their colleagues in action. What, then, should you be watching out for and learning about as you observe your TP class or classes?

Observation Checklist

The whole class ☐
Individual children ☐
Patterns ☐
Rules and control mechanisms ☐
Expectations ☐
Behaviour ☐
Rewards and sanctions ☐
Resources and equipment ☐
Classroom environment ☐
The teacher ☐

- *The children as a whole class:* On a general level, how do the children work and behave? Are they keen to learn, concentrating well on what the teacher says and the tasks at hand. Alternatively, are they what is euphemistically known as 'challenging' children, whose behaviour must be closely regulated? Remember that you are probably watching a fairly experienced teacher, and one whom the children already know well. This will have an impact on overall levels of behaviour and work, so please do not expect exactly the same responses from them when you do get the chance to teach.

- *Individual children:* Are there any 'personalities' in the classroom, or any children who appear to have special learning needs? You might like to talk to the teacher further about these children after the lesson, to get more information about their particular difficulties. Try to avoid making judgements about your students before you get to experience them for yourself: children respond very differently to different teachers.

- *Patterns:* Does the class or day follow a specific pattern? For instance, at what point is the register taken? Do the children sit and listen to a story at the end of the day? What is the routine for going to and coming in from break and lunch? Do the children stand behind their chairs at the end of the lesson? It can prove very useful for maintaining consistency to use these patterns yourself when you do get to teach the class.

- *Rules and control mechanisms:* What classroom rules are already in place, that you can use to your benefit? Are there school rules that the children follow? Does the teacher use any control mechanisms that you can take advantage of, for instance 'hands up' for silence, or a 'silent seat'.

- *Expectations:* What level of expectations does the teacher have of the class? Does he or she expect perfect work and behaviour, or is a little more leniency applied? Remember, every teacher is an individual, and your standards or expectations may vary a great deal from those of the teacher you observe.

- *Behaviour:* If there is poor behaviour in the class, when and why does this happen? Are there particular triggers that set off bad behaviour, such as a lack of space or issues over the pacing of the lesson? Do the students sit and listen in complete silence to the teacher, or does he or she have to struggle for their attention?

- *Rewards and sanctions:* To what extent does the teacher use (or need to use) rewards and sanctions? What rewards are available for you to use? (Remember, these include verbal and written praise, as well as more tangible rewards such as merits and stickers.) When sanctions are used, when and how are they applied? Is there an 'ultimate' sanction for extreme behaviour? If detentions are set, how and when are these served?

- *Resources and equipment:* Are the children responsible for bringing in their own resources and equipment? When do they get their pencil cases and books out, and what happens if they have forgotten them? If the school provides equipment, where is this kept and how do the children access it?

- *Classroom environment:* What type of environment is provided for the students, and does this contribute to the way that they behave and work?

What are the displays like, and how do the children respond to and interact with these? Are there issues about excessive heat or cold, or lack of space?

- *The teacher:* What sort of teaching style does the teacher have? Does he or she take a strict or relaxed approach with the children, or somewhere in between? What use does the teacher make of verbal and non-verbal signals with the class? How well does he or she control the children and the learning?

Remember, too, that an observation does not have to be a static event. For instance, the teacher might set an individual or group activity, then start to move around the classroom helping individuals. This would be the perfect opportunity for you to join in – you might go to the assistance of a child with his or her hand up, or you might simply sit with one group to talk about the work. Show a bit of willing and initiative – every teacher is grateful for help. You may find that the children ask about your presence in the classroom, perhaps saying 'are you going to be our new teacher?' If they do ask, you might choose to answer them directly by saying 'in a little while', or you could give a non-committal answer such as 'only if you're really, really lucky'!

Observing the teacher

In addition to more general observations of the class, watching an experienced teacher at work also gives you a great chance to see which teaching techniques work (and which ones don't). There is no guarantee that you will be watching or working with an exceptionally good teacher, but in any case it is of course possible to learn a great deal from observing a teacher who is not particularly effective. The truth is that most of us teachers fall somewhere in between the two extremes, especially on days when we are tired, stressed, or simply in a bad mood. Again, try to avoid making snap judgements until you've actually had a chance to experience these children and this school for yourself. You may well find out that teaching the class is not as straightforward as it appears! As you observe the teacher, think about some of the aspects listed here of the way that the class is run.

Classroom control

The way that a teacher controls his or her class can have a huge impact on learning and behaviour. Think about the following:

- How does the lesson start and finish? Is there a particular pattern to the opening and ending of class time?
- What does the teacher do if it looks like a student is going to misbehave?
- How does the teacher deal with poor behaviour when it does occur?

- How does the teacher move the children from one activity to the next?
- Are there specific ways that the teacher organizes any group work?
- What techniques does the teacher use to put the curriculum across?

Verbal and non-verbal signals

Teachers constantly give out signals to their classes, whether they realize this or not. The more aware you can be of the signals that you and other teachers give, the more effective you will be as a teacher. Consider the following:

- When the teacher wants the class's attention, what verbal and non-verbal signals does he or she use?
- How does the teacher use her voice?
- Does she ever seem tense or out of control vocally?
- Does she feel the need to shout? When does this happen?
- How does the teacher use his or her face and body?
- How often does the teacher smile or frown at the class?
- What other facial expressions does the teacher use?
- How static or active is he within the room?
- Does the teacher use different height levels, e.g. crouching down to talk to a child?
- Does the teacher go to the children when they need help, or ask them to come to him?

Behaviour management

A teacher's management of behaviour is vital in ensuring that learning can take place. Here are some points for you to consider:

- Does the teacher's 'mood' have an influence on behaviour?
- Does he or she approach the class in a negative or positive way?
- What part do rewards and sanctions play in behaviour management?
- How are small incidents of misbehaviour dealt with?
- How does the teacher handle any more serious incidents?
- At what stage in an incident does the teacher intervene?
- Does the teacher ignore low level or attention seeking misbehaviour?
- Which of the teacher's strategies could you use yourself?
- What is the connection between the teacher's expectations and the way that the students behave?

TOP TIP

At some point in your observation, try to see the teacher and the teaching from the children's perspective. How would you view him or her if you were still this age? How engaged and focused on the work would you feel? Would you be inclined to behave yourself or not?

Getting on with the classroom teacher

Developing a good relationship with the class teacher is essential for a successful teaching practice. Do remember that the teacher you are working with will also have been on TP and will be aware of the worries that you might be feeling. He or she will, 99.9 per cent of the time, be keen to help and support you. Here are some tips about how you might build a positive relationship with your TP class teacher.

- *Be sensitive about the space:* Teachers can feel surprisingly territorial about their rooms. This is especially so in the primary school where a teacher has a classroom of his or her own. (Some secondary school teachers also have their 'own' rooms, but this is not always the case.) Be aware that this is the teacher's space – don't just dump down your stuff wherever you want without asking first. Try to avoid giving the sense that you are taking over. After all, you'll have a classroom of your own shortly, and you'll want it treated with respect!
- *Be sensitive about the children:* Some teachers are also possessive about their classes, perhaps a secondary school teacher with a top set GCSE group, where there is a lot of pressure to achieve good results. Do be aware that the teacher might have some insecurities about handing over the children to you (although most teachers will just be grateful to have your help).
- *See the teacher as an 'expert':* You really can learn a huge amount from the experienced teacher – make sure that you ask the teacher questions and learn as much as you can from him or her. Treat your classroom teacher as an expert on the subject of teaching and pick his or her brains whenever you get the chance.
- *Don't be judgemental:* Don't be too quick to judge the teacher with whom you find yourself working. We all have different teaching styles, and you may have a very different opinion of what constitutes 'good' teaching. Remember, too, that what you view as a class where the teacher cannot control the children, could in fact be a group of very difficult students.
- *Learn to keep your mouth shut:* Carrying on from the point above, learn to keep your opinions to yourself. Do not, on any account, gossip about 'your' teacher in the staffroom.

- *Let your teacher have a rest:* Accept that your teacher needs to take breaks – don't spend the whole of lunch break grilling him or her.
- *Make yourself useful:* If you are not kept busy with teaching at first, do offer to help put up displays, sort resources, anything that will alleviate some of the load on the teacher.
- *Find a chance to chat:* If possible, don't rush off the minute the bell goes at the end of the day. Take time to help to clear up any work and tidy the classroom. Perhaps sit down with your teacher and chat about the day over a cup of tea or coffee. This may be the only time that you get a chance to relax together, so make the most of the opportunity.

Potential problems

Of course, there will be situations on TP where you encounter problems, and it's important to know what to do to solve these. Here are some thoughts about the type of problems you might possibly encounter, and the course of action you could take.

- *'The school treats me as an unpaid supply teacher':* Occasionally, and it is rare (although certainly not unheard of), some schools do view student teachers as useful, free of charge, supply teachers. If you do find yourself pretty much abandoned to take care of a class or classes, without any decent support, your first response should be to talk to your university tutor about the situation. Bear in mind that the school has a responsibility to take your learning (and non-contact time) seriously. Until the situation is remedied, try to view this type of 'in at the deep end' situation as a good chance to experience the reality of a working teacher's life.
- *'I don't get on with my supervisory teacher':* It's inevitable that there will be occasions when a student teacher does not get on with the teacher who is supervising him or her. This can be an awkward situation to deal with, because it is fairly unlikely that complaints from you are going to lead to any changes being made, unless there is something seriously wrong with the teacher's supervision of your practice. You might choose to have a word with your tutor, and ask for some advice. Alternatively, you are probably best to just grin and bear it: keep quiet, do your best, focus on the kids, and wait for the end of TP to come.
- *'I can't control the kids!':* Behaviour management can seem incredibly difficult when you are a student teacher (and sometimes for experienced teachers too). Although you should not be given a class that is completely out of control, you are likely to encounter at least some children who are not immediately willing to do exactly as you ask. Do bear in mind that developing your behaviour management skills is a crucial part of learning to be an effective teacher, and that you are still at the 'learning' part of the process. Look closely at the section in this chapter entitled 'Getting your class to

behave', preferably before you start your TP. Look too at Chapter 8, 'Classroom teaching', which gives lots of information on behaviour management. It's also a good idea to buy yourself a general and practical book on dealing with difficult behaviour (you'll find some ideas at the end of this chapter). If you are having really horrendous problems, talk to your university tutor, or ask your classroom teacher to come in and assist you for a while.

Planning

It may be that your university specifies the format that you must use when planning lessons on your teaching practices. Alternatively, they may give you a list of areas that must be included (see below for some likely points), then leave the actual layout to your own discretion. You will probably be asked to prepare 'Schemes of work' which detail how a whole series of lessons fit together over a longer period, to cover a topic or a particular National Curriculum area. You can find some more information about planning as a working teacher in Chapter 7, 'Preparing to teach'. As you will see from the planning 'case studies' in Chapters 12 and 13, once you become a full-time teacher it is very unlikely that you will have the time or the inclination to plan in this much detail ever again.

There are a huge number of ways that you might plan a lesson, but there really is no one correct or definitive way. When you first start out as a student teacher, you will inevitably want to include plenty of detail in your plans. Once you become a working teacher, you'll probably look back at the planning you did as a student in amazement, wondering how on earth you had time to fit it all in! However, there are a number of reasons why detailed planning is actually a good idea at this stage in your teaching career.

- To please your university tutors and pass the course!
- To demonstrate that you are fulfilling the standards for becoming a qualified teacher.
- As part of your initial experimentation in what works for you and what doesn't, when it comes to lesson planning and delivery.
- To give you a sense of security, so that you know exactly what will happen (or should happen) at every point in the lesson.
- To enable you to reflect on and remember what happened during each lesson.
- To develop some top quality lessons, resources and materials that can be reused at a later stage in your teaching career.

What will be in the lesson plans?

You may be asked to include some (or all) of the following areas in your lesson plans. As you will see from the length of the list below, planning in this much detail will take a considerable amount of time. It is very helpful to create your own format for lesson planning on the computer, so that you can use this as a basis for each individual lesson. You can find a sample 'student lesson plan' in Chapter 14 of the Toolkit. You can also see a real student lesson plan in the section below.

- *Aims:* These describe the overall purpose of the lesson, providing a 'map' to show where you are going. What do you aim to achieve during this class?
- *Objectives:* Your objectives are closely linked to the learning that you wish to take place. They are more specific than aims, and explain exactly what the children will learn during the lesson.
- *National Curriculum and QCA references:* You should be able to demonstrate which of the statutory criteria your lesson is going to fulfil.
- *Literacy and Numeracy Strategy references:* Again, if you are teaching within the NLS or NNS, you will need to show how the activities you use correspond to the learning objectives of these strategies.
- *Activities:* A list of the different activities that will take place during the lesson.
- *Organization:* Under this heading you might include details of whether work will be done individually, in pairs or in groups, and how these will be organized.
- *Timing:* You may like to give quite a detailed account of the amounts of time you will allocate to each activity, although it is likely that you will deviate from this in reality.
- *Resources:* Details of the resources that you will be using during the lesson.
- *SEN:* Details of any children in the class with special needs, and how your lesson and activities will cater for them.
- *Differentiation:* Information about tasks that will be differentiated for students of differing abilities, and how this will be organized by the teacher.
- *Evaluation:* Information about how the children or the teacher will evaluate the work that has taken place during the lesson.
- *Outcomes:* A description of the learning outcomes that you hope will be achieved during the class.

You can see an example of a numeracy lesson plan below, which was written by student teacher Steph Leach (see the 'First steps' interview in Chapter 2).

Lesson: **Numeracy – addition and subtraction**

Date: Tuesday 12 March 2002 Working with: Whole Class

Learning Objectives:
We are learning . . .
To recognize the
relationship between
addition and subtraction

Links to NC, NNS, NLS, QCA:
Calculations
Mental calculations
strategies (+ and –)
■ Add or subtract the
nearest multiple of 10
or 100, then adjust
■ Develop further the
relationship between
addition and subtraction

Resources:
'Round the Class Maths'
Cards (25)
Pre-prepared +, –, =, 20,
30, 50, 500, 250, 750, 1000,
150, 850, 899, 440, 459
Textbooks
Computer example sheets x 2
Whiteboard and pens

Key questions/vocabulary:
Is this statement true?
Is there any other way that
this statement could be
written and still be true?
How many are there
altogether?
Is there always this number?
Why?
Is there anyone who is still
unsure of what we have
been doing?

Mental/Oral Starter:
'Round the Class Maths'
Each child gets one card which reads 'I have (no.)'
and 'I need (sum)'.
One child starts by saying I need (sum) and
whichever child has the answer to this sum on
their card says 'I have. . ., I need. . .' and so on
until the game gets back around to the first child
that started.
If no child volunteers an answer, ask class if
they know the answer to the sum and then ask
if anyone has this number.

Main Activity:
Using pre-prepared number and function cards
put up sum 20 + 30 = 50.
Is this statement true?
Is there any other way that this statement could
be written and still be true?
Get child to come and move numbers around.
Add the – card.
Could this sum be written another way and still
be true?
How many ways can this sum be written in
total?
Let's do another one.
500 + 250 = 750

Put up the cards +, –, =, 1000, 150, 850
Ask a child to use these numbers to make
a statement that is true.
Ask another child to do a different statement.
How many are there altogether?
Is there always this number? Why?
Again with +, –, =, 899, 440, 459

Is there anyone who is still unsure of what
we have been doing? (If so, they could stay on
the carpet and work through exercises
together with support.)

Introduce independent work and explain how
it is to be written in their books/on PC
(do example).

Plenary:
Did anyone get onto the extension task on the chalkboard?

Can someone give me an example of the sum they gave their partner? (If not make one up.)

What other ways could this be written?

Do another one.

Extension activities:
Write a sum for your partner to solve adding 3 numbers. How many other ways can they write these numbers to make statements that are true using only + and –?

Use of ICT:
Top group do work on 3 PCs

Progression:
The relationship between multiplication and division.

Teaching

As you progress through your teaching practices, whether on a PGCE or teaching degree course, you will gradually be asked to teach more and more lessons, and with greater independence from the classroom teacher. However, you will be given a reduced timetable which should help you manage your time. There will also be no requirement for you to attend meetings or parents' evenings, and all the other bits of the job that permanent staff face. However, I would recommend that you take the opportunity to experience these aspects of the job if they are offered to you.

How and what should I teach in my TP lessons?

Above all, your teaching practices are a time when you can really enjoy and experiment with your teaching, so try to take full advantage of this. Put as much time as you can into planning and delivering exciting and interesting lessons, and think carefully about how well the children respond to this high quality learning experience. Here are some ideas about the type of approaches and activities you could use in your TP lessons, to really motivate and excite your students.

- *Use unusual teaching strategies:* Do take the opportunity to try out some original or unusual ideas with your classes. There is always a risk that these activities will fall flat, but it is actually more likely that they will really inspire and motivate your children. It's a great idea to experiment now, while you have the chance and nobody minds you 'getting it wrong'. However, it is probably best to save your wildest experiments for times when you are not being observed!
- *Keep it active and practical:* Try to incorporate active, practical exercises into

your teaching whenever you can (whatever subject you are teaching). Getting the children really actively involved with the learning is an excellent way to ensure that the work sticks with them. For instance, in a primary Maths lesson, you might tackle addition by asking the children to come to the front of the room as you 'add' more to your total. As well as being a good motivator and learning tool, practical exercises will also help you learn more about the logistics of managing a large number of young people in a confined space.

- *Think laterally:* Take the chance offered by TPs to think 'outside the box', for instance approaching a familiar topic in a lateral way. For example, if you are doing a piece of writing about the local area, you might do so from the perspective of a visiting alien. In addition, think about how you might incorporate some cross-curricular activities or ideas into your teaching. This might be writing, playing and recording raps in a foreign language lesson, or designing and building monsters in an English lesson on 'Frankenstein'.

- *Keep it topical and relevant:* In my experience, children are always well motivated by work that they see as topical and relevant to their own lives. For instance, you might find some way to incorporate the latest toy craze into your teaching, or use the format of a familiar television show to create a forum for discussion.

- *Plan for the future:* See your TPs as the 'information gathering' stage in your teaching career. As well as gathering information about how to become an effective teacher, you can also start to gather useful ideas and resources. For instance, you should begin to develop a 'bank' of useful games and short 'filler' activities for your subject. In addition, spend time making really top quality resources (such as board games) that you will be able to reuse later on.

Getting your class to behave

Behaviour management is a hugely complex aspect of teaching, and one that really concerns many student teachers (and indeed many experienced teachers as well). You may be lucky enough to find yourself in an 'easy' school, where the children are naturally inclined to behave well (although not necessarily all that well for a student teacher). Alternatively, you may be given the greater challenge of working in a 'difficult' school, where behaviour management concerns take up a great deal of your time and energy. Many of the issues faced by student teachers are also of concern to supply teachers, and it is worth looking at some of the ideas under the heading 'Tips for supply teachers' in Chapter 11 for some additional strategies.

It is well worth seeing your TPs as a chance to develop your behaviour management skills: an opportunity to make mistakes and learn from them, when you are just starting out. Here are some 'top tips' that you may find useful.

- *Be confident:* Yes, I do know how hard this is! However, do try to appear confident, no matter how terrified you feel inside. If you look like you know what you're doing (even when you don't) this really will communicate itself to the children and make them feel more secure about working with you. On the other hand, if you look scared and uncertain, the children will quickly notice this and try to take advantage. A lot of behaviour management is 'bluff', more about the strength and clarity of the verbal and non-verbal signals that you send, than the reality of your skills as a teacher.

- *Be well informed:* Many schools now have a whole school behaviour policy. Before you start working with the children, take time to study this and understand it as fully as you can. The key is knowing what is and what isn't allowed in the classroom, and what you should do if children do misbehave (i.e. what sanctions you can use, and when they should be invoked).

- *Make your expectations clear:* Children really do need to know what is expected of them, to be told where they stand (and what they can and can't get away with). The first time that they meet you, they will know as little about you as you do about them. Children seem to have an innate sense of when their teacher is unsure about what they expect, and they are usually aware of the (exciting) possibilities of getting one over on the supply or student teacher. So, talk to your class about what you expect, and give them as much clarity as you can. It's hard at first to do this, but it does get much easier with time and experience. Try giving at least three 'I expect you to' statements the first time you teach the class. Here are three suggestions that you might like to use:
  - *'I expect you to look at me and listen in complete silence when I'm talking.'*
  - *'I expect you to always work to the best of your ability.'*
  - *'I expect you to stay in your chair and put your hand up if you need to ask me something.'*

- *Don't get defensive:* It's the most natural thing in the world to become defensive if a student takes you on, or if a class is messing around and won't do what you say. The problem is, if the children manage to make the teacher defensive, they know that they are winning! If you start shouting and getting wound up, be aware that this is demonstrating your defensiveness to the class.

- *Stay calm:* In teaching, a calm approach really does pay dividends. For instance, it's very tempting at first to give the children work that will get them (over) excited, but until you are more experienced in classroom management this will often simply lead to chaos. Try to stay calm when you are managing children's behaviour, as well as their learning. A teacher who refuses to get wound up or angry will deal with behaviour issues much more effectively, and this will encourage the children to stay calm as well.

- *Be positive:* An assertive (not aggressive) and positive manner demonstrates that you are a confident and decent person. When you are in a bad mood, for whatever reason, or not feeling particularly well, try not to let this filter through into the way that you treat your children. Always think about how they are perceiving you from their side of the desks.

■ *Use your voice carefully:* Do think about how you use your voice when you first start teaching. Good modulation is very important, especially with young children: for instance being able to move between a happy and an annoyed tone. Avoid shouting at all costs: it can damage your voice and it is very rarely an effective means of discipline (see 'Don't get defensive' and 'Stay calm' above).

■ *Try to focus on rewards:* When you're finding behaviour hard to manage, it's tempting to dish out sanctions right, left and centre to try to regain the upper hand. Unfortunately, this can actually make the situation worse, by leading to a very negative atmosphere in your classroom. Instead of focusing on punishment, try giving rewards to those who are doing what you want, and ignoring low level attention seeking behaviour. A quick word of praise to a well behaved child can refocus the rest of the class very easily.

■ *A learning process:* Remember that learning to teach is difficult, a process that takes many years (and one, of course, which is never truly 'completed'). One of the best ways for us to learn is to make mistakes, to reflect on what went wrong, and to understand how to improve things for the next time. In fact, all the best teachers are still learning from day to day, even right at the end of their careers. As a student teacher you are just at the very start of that process: don't expect too much too soon.

■ *Keep a perspective:* It's very easy to lose sight of what really does and doesn't matter. At the end of the day, a few children messing around in your lesson is not a total disaster. The world really won't end if you don't get it right the very first time!

■ *Read a good book:* There are lots of excellent books out there which deal with behaviour management, so take the time to read them (preferably before you go on TP). Instead of the theoretical stuff that you might have been encouraged to read at university, look through a practical book on the subject. The next section gives some ideas.

Useful books on behaviour management

Getting the Buggers to Behave
Sue Cowley
ISBN: 0-8264-4978-6
Publisher: Continuum

A totally practical, best selling book on behaviour management, which deals with all different aspects of the subject, and gives a realistic overview. It offers you a huge range of useful strategies, tips and advice on managing your children's behaviour.

> *Cracking the Hard Class*
> Bill Rogers
> ISBN:0-7619-6928-4
> Publisher: Paul Chapman Publishing

This is just one of Bill Rogers' excellent, practical books on behaviour management. He has also made some helpful videos that may be available to watch in your school/university.

> *Surviving and Succeeding in Difficult Classrooms*
> Paul Blum
> ISBN: 0-4151-8523-8
> Publisher: Routledge Falmer

A practical, realistic and honest book about surviving and dealing with difficult behaviour.

4 Finding a job

This chapter deals with all the different aspects of actually finding a job in teaching. It may be that you are a young student teacher, just starting to look for your first post, or it could be that you've got a year or more of experience and now want to move on to another school, perhaps into a promoted post. Alternatively, you might be a mature entrant to the profession, moving into teaching from the commercial world, and wondering exactly what the job hunting process involves. You should find all the information, advice and tips that you need here.

Job hunting

The nature of schools means that teachers are required to give a relatively long period of notice (roughly a full half term before the teacher wishes to leave the school). Teachers are only allowed to leave at the end of a school term. This gives the school plenty of time to find and employ a new teacher. In addition, working to the end of a school term means that students are given reasonable continuity in their education. The actual deadlines for handing in your notice are:

- Autumn term: 31 October
- Spring term: 28 February
- Summer term: 31 May

This means that there are peaks in the number of job adverts around these times of the year. In fact, you'll notice this fact reflected in the size of the jobs section of the *Times Educational Supplement* (see below), which swells to the thickness of a small tree!

Publications

When you're hunting for a job, you'll find that the *Times Educational Supplement* (*TES*) becomes your bible. This is published every Friday and most schools (and universities) will provide at least one copy for their staff or students to browse. However, this single copy of the *TES* can prove like gold-dust (especially in a school where the teachers are keen to get out!) and the jobs section has usually done a disappearing act by the end of morning break. So, when you are job hunting it is well worth buying your own copy. Alternatively, use one of the internet sites listed below.

Jobs in education can also be found in the broadsheet newspapers, such as the *Guardian* and the *Independent* (see the 'Directory' section at the back of this book for details). If you're interested in a post in a single faith school, you could also look at the religious press.

The internet

The internet has made it very easy for teachers to access and search for jobs. The *TES* jobs website (www.jobs.tes.co.uk) is updated each Friday morning, and contains the same jobs as you will find in the printed publication. You can search for jobs in various different subject areas, age ranges, locations, and so on. You do not need to register any personal details to access the jobs. The newer ETeach website (www.eteach.com) also features jobs that you can access using a combination of various search criteria, such as subject, type of job, and so on. You will need to register your details to use this service.

The local authority

Depending on how efficient your local education authority is, it may be worth contacting them directly to check on the jobs situation locally. Many local authorities also send a booklet of current jobs to the schools in their area, so if you are already in post and looking for a new job in a nearby location, this could prove useful. Some LEAs actually advertise for NQTs in the *TES*. Your local authority will also have a 'recruitment strategy manager' (RSM) who may be able to help you in your search for a post. Again, much will depend on the efficiency of your local LEA. Look on the website of the local council in the area where you wish to teach to find more information, or contact them by post.

Supply agencies

If you are interested in working as a supply teacher, or if you need to take supply work until you find a permanent post, you will find a huge number of supply agencies vying for your services. Many of these agencies advertise in the publications listed in this chapter, and on the internet. Agencies range from the small, local operation, perhaps run by ex-teachers, to the larger national organizations with branches in many different locations.

You can find a list of supply agencies in the Directory at the back of this book. You will also find a lot more information about supply work in Chapter 11. It is also possible to register for supply work via your LEA. This route is in fact recommended by some teaching unions, but again the reality of doing supply via an LEA will vary a great deal across the country. In Scotland, applying to an LEA is the accepted way of finding supply work.

Working overseas

In my experience, working abroad as a teacher is a wonderful opportunity, and one that can only enhance both your personal and professional life. You have the chance to teach a very different group of students, to see a bit of the world and to experience another culture. However, there are pitfalls out there for the unwary, and do bear in mind that your employment rights will probably be less well protected than they are in the UK. Bear in mind too that the vast majority of international schools are looking for teachers who already have at least a year or two's teaching experience. For more information about what working abroad is really like, see 'Teaching overseas' in Chapter 10.

If you are thinking about working overseas, do be aware of the potential problems that exist. Your best bet is to find a job at a school which belongs to an accredited organization. The European Council of International Schools (ECIS) is the largest association of international schools. It has almost 600 international member schools. The ECIS organizes 'Recruitment Centres' across the world, to which schools looking for new teachers come to find recruits. The 'London Recruitment Centre' takes place in May, and you can find more information at the ECIS website (www.ecis.org). Overseas teaching jobs can also be found in the *TES* jobs section.

The independent sector

When you're looking for your first (or subsequent) teaching job, you may want to consider working at an independent school. If you are interested, a good starting point is to look at the Independent Schools' Council website (www.isis.org.uk) or to contact this organization for details (see the Directory for further information). When considering a job in the independent sector, there are a number of differences of which you need to be aware.

- Many private schools operate a different pay scale to those in the state sector. This may be more, or less, than the nationally agreed pay rates.
- Your working terms and conditions may differ to those agreed by the government with state sector teachers.
- Similarly, your pension arrangements may not be the same as for state sector workers.
- If you are just starting teaching, and wish to take induction, you will need to check that the school is able to offer this.

There are a number of factors both for and against working in private education. At the end of the day, the decision about which sector to work in will be an entirely personal matter.

For

- Smaller class sizes
- Better resources and more funding
- Generally speaking, discipline is likely to be better

- On the whole, higher academic standards (especially in schools that select by academic ability)
- Some independent schools will accept graduates without traditional teaching qualifications

Against

- There is often greater pressure from parents and the school to demonstrate academic success
- There can be a higher demand on teachers' time outside of the classroom, for instance in extracurricular activities
- It may be hard to move back into the state sector
- Personal considerations, such as your own stance on private education

Types of state school

State schools fall into different 'types' according to who runs the school and how admissions are handled.

- *Community schools:* These are provided by the LEA, which also decides on admissions. They do not adhere to a specific form of religious education.
- *Foundation schools:* These are provided by the LEA, but the school manages its own admissions, and can select criteria for this. As with community schools, they have no particular religious affiliation.
- *Voluntary aided schools:* These schools are partly maintained by voluntary organizations. The religious teaching will be based on the denomination of the school as originally set up.
- *Voluntary controlled schools:* As with voluntary aided these schools have a particular religious affiliation, but they are fully funded by the LEA.

'Specialist' schools

In England, a recent innovation has been the 'specialist' school or college. The first four types of specialist college have been in Technology, Language, Sport, and Arts. This is now being expanded to four new specialisms in Business & Enterprise, Engineering, Science and Mathematics & Computing. You can find out more about the scheme at www.dfes.gov.uk/specschl. When using a school's specialist status as a basis for taking a job, take time to discover how 'deep' the special interest goes. Anecdotal evidence suggests that some schools have applied for specialist status simply to attract additional funding for equipment, for instance extra computers.

Applying for jobs

Because the majority of teaching jobs are in the public sector, the application process is, generally speaking, very similar from school to school, or from LEA to LEA. Those of you who have previously applied for jobs and worked in the private sector may find the whole application process mystifyingly long-winded and complex.

Application forms

Most LEAs use a fairly standard application form, and you can see an example of this in the Toolkit (Chapter 14). You will probably be asked to provide a 'letter of application' or 'supporting statement' (see below) to accompany this. There is usually a small space on the application form where you can write your supporting statement. Normally, this is far too small to suffice, and it is fine to simply put 'see attached' in the box, and staple or paperclip your statement to the application form.

You should fill out the application form in black ink and, it goes without saying, take great care not to make mistakes. Filling out these forms is a frustratingly time-consuming process, but sadly there is no way around it! Some (more enlightened?) schools simply ask for a CV and a letter of application.

TOP TIP

I really wish someone had advised me to do this when I first started teaching!

Make sure you keep a note of all those little 'extras' that you do outside your normal job (perhaps in a small notebook). For instance, you might have acted as IT rep, directed the school play or organized a trip. Keep a note, too, of all the training courses you go on. All these things should be included with your application, either on the form itself or in your supporting statement. So, when you next have to fill out a job application, you can refer to your notebook rather than racking your brains trying to remember what you did a year or two ago!

Referees

When you apply for a teaching post, you will usually be asked to provide the names of two people who can give a reference. For a student teacher, this might be your university tutor and a TP supervisory teacher. For a working teacher, this will probably be your current head teacher and perhaps a head of department or other manager. Do, please, make sure that you ask your referees before naming them on an application. If you are lucky, your referees may show you a copy of what they have written about you, although this is by no means certain. Many schools will only apply for references once you have been shortlisted or actually offered a job with them. There will usually be an option on the application form to say whether the school may apply for references before interview. If you are already working as a teacher, but don't wish your school to know that you are job hunting, this lets you apply for jobs without alerting them to the fact.

Letters of application

The letter of application is peculiar to the teaching profession, and if you're a mature entrant to teaching who has worked in the commercial sector previously, you may find this aspect of the process rather puzzling. The letter of application allows the candidate to demonstrate how his or her experience, abilities and personality match the post being advertised. Your letter of application will normally be used, in addition to your application form, to decide whether to invite you for interview. You can find some sample letters of application in Chapter 14. Here are some thoughts and tips to help you write a successful letter of application.

- *Fit it to the job description:* Make sure you match your abilities and experiences to the post for which you're applying. Look carefully at the job description before you start, and ensure that what you say about yourself fits with what the school wants. This might call for some 'creative writing', but don't tell any outright fibs. You'll only get caught out at the interview!
- *Echo the language of the advert:* The language you use should echo that of the school's advert. They will have thought carefully about the wording, designing it to attract the appropriate candidates, and you should consider it closely too. Take the time to look under the surface at what they are really saying: for instance, a school that describes its students as 'challenging' will be looking for a teacher who is enthusiastic about working with more difficult children. In this case, you might comment that you 'relish a challenge'. A school which notes that its intake includes 'children with a wide range of abilities' will be looking for a teacher who is able to differentiate his or her teaching and planning, to suit students of varying ability levels.
- *Make the most of the experience you have:* If you're a student with little or no work experience, talk about your teaching practices and any other voluntary or part-time work you have done, especially if it involved working with children. Talk, too, about what you have contributed to university life. Perhaps you've been involved with the student union, or have helped to put on student drama productions? What have you learnt from these experiences? How might these help you contribute to the extracurricular aspects of school life, as well as in your day-to-day teaching? Which skills did you develop that might help with your classroom work?
- *Don't be shy!:* This is no time to be a retiring daisy. Describe your abilities and skills, and how they match the post. Talk about your talents, but try to

do so in a reasonably self-deprecating way. Use phrases such as 'I feel that I am' or 'I believe myself to be'. That way, you won't sound as though you're boasting.

- *Structure it properly:* Although you don't want the letter of application to be excessively long, do include a brief 'introduction' and 'conclusion', just as you would if you were writing an essay. Your introduction might give an overview of you and your style and philosophy as a teacher. Your conclusion could summarize the ways in which you meet the requirements of the post.

- *Check how it should be written:* Some schools like your letter of application to be handwritten, so check whether this is the case before you start. Unfortunately, hand writing application letters can be very time consuming, especially if you make a mistake halfway through. If you do have to hand write your application, it's a good idea to type it out on a computer first, to make sure that you have it word perfect before you start. In this way, you will also have a copy of the letter, in case you need to use something similar in the future. If you do get halfway through and make a mistake, remember that the excessive use of tippex is not going to go down well. Obviously, you should also make your handwriting as neat as possible (one of the reasons applying for jobs is so time consuming).

- *Create a 'standard letter':* Use a computer to create a standardized letter which you can then tailor to the different jobs for which you apply. This standard letter should include all the information about yourself and your skills/experience that you feel is essential to include. You can then add in some comments that are personalized to the particular job.

- *Make it readable:* If you do send a computerized letter of application, use a standard font such as Arial or Times roman. Ensure that the typeface is large enough to be easily readable. If possible, stick to one page of A4, or an absolute maximum of two pages. If you do use a second sheet, ensure that they are stapled together.

- *Identify yourself:* Schools are full of bits of paper, so write your name and the post being applied for on each sheet of your letter of application, in case it goes astray.

Job interviews

One of the drawbacks of a teaching job is that you only really find out what a school is like after you've started teaching there. Although this applies to all jobs in a sense, in education the ethos and management of a school can have a huge impact on the quality of your experience as an employee. In addition, if you do make a mistake, there is nothing you can do about it once you've agreed to take the job, and in most cases you will be looking at a reasonably long-term commitment to the post.

On the day of the interview you're likely to be nervous, and this could stop you from getting a realistic view of what the school is really like. In addition, the head teacher will want you to get the best impression possible. After all, they need to fill that vacancy! It's unlikely, therefore, that they'll take you to visit that nightmare Year Nine group who forced the previous teacher to quit. On the other hand, you may well be looking for a school which presents you with a challenge, rather than one at which all the children behave in an exemplary fashion.

Unlike some other professional jobs, teaching appointments are generally made on the basis of a single interview (although the interview may be only part of a long day at the school), along with references. Also unusual is the fact that teachers are typically made to decide whether or not they will accept the job on the day that the interview takes place. This puts you in a difficult situation if you're unsure about whether or not this is the job for you. In the following sections you'll find some useful checklists to help you make your decision.

Pre-interview checklist

Before you even attend the interview, make sure that you are well prepared. This will also help you feel more confident on the day, as you will be going into a situation about which you have some prior knowledge. Here is a checklist that gives some ideas for preparing yourself for the ordeal ahead.

- *Look at school information:* Read the school prospectus or brochure carefully, and any details sent to you with your application form. Try to read between the lines. Remember, a school brochure is designed to encourage parents to send their children to that school, and it will by its very nature be showing the 'best side'.
- *Look at inspection reports:* Check the school's latest OFSTED report (available at www.ofsted.gov.uk). Again, read between the lines, but do bear in mind that some of these reports will be a good few years out of date, and much may have changed at the school since the inspection was done.
- *Look at government information:* Look at the school's vital statistics in the government performance tables. These give you information about exam results, absence rates, and so on. They will also show you whether the school is improving or not. You can find this information at www.dfes.gov.uk/performancetables/.
- *Don't be too judgemental:* Having made the two points above, do remember that OFSTED reports can never tell you the full story about a school. Also, the children may be weak academically, or from disadvantaged backgrounds, but they may still be hard-working and rewarding to teach.
- *Check the school's popularity:* Find out whether the school is under or over subscribed. This will tell you whether the school is popular with its local community. Under subscribed schools may have to take on students who have been permanently excluded from their previous school, and this can have a serious impact on the overall behaviour and atmosphere.
- *Check the school's location:* Take a look at the local area, especially if you are not familiar with this part of the world. Are you looking for a 'cushy' job in a

leafy suburb? Or would you be more interested in a busy and vibrant multicultural community?

- *Visit the school if you can:* If at all possible, visit the school before your interview. This will give you the chance to take a realistic look around, at a time when you are not feeling quite so pressurized. It will also demonstrate how enthusiastic you are about the post, and could well have a beneficial impact on your chances of getting the job. If you are not able to actually spend time inside the school, it is worth visiting at the end of the school day to see what the atmosphere is like as the children exit the gates.
- *Ask around:* If you do live locally, ask around amongst your friends and family to get a general view of the reputation of the school. If you can find someone whose child attends the school, this would give you a good viewpoint of how things really are.
- *Prepare yourself:* Make sure that you have some questions prepared to ask in the interview. There is no harm in writing these down if you wish, and referring to your notes. There's no need to go overboard, but do show that you've thought about what you want to know in advance. See the section below ('The interview questions') for more ideas about this.

Teaching at an interview

Some schools will ask you to prepare a lesson, or an activity, to teach to a class on the day of the interview. In my opinion, this should be an essential requirement of teaching interviews — after all, we're being employed for our ability to teach, rather than how well we come across in an interview! Try not to panic if you are asked to teach at interview: it is unlikely that the school will give you a 'nightmare' class to work with — they won't want to put you off. Also, the presence of another member of staff observing you (probably a senior teacher) should ensure that the children behave themselves, which will allow you to teach to the best of your ability. When you're planning what and how to teach, take into consideration the following points.

- *Do what they ask you to:* Follow any guidelines that the school have given you very closely: for instance a primary school teacher may be asked to prepare a literacy lesson that fulfils the requirements of the NLS. Although a splash of inspiration will always go down well, this is not the time to demonstrate your individuality by deviating from the set task.
- *Give it energy:* Deliver your lesson with a good sense of pace and energy, and make sure that you show how enthusiastic you are about teaching and about children.
- *Make it engaging:* Find ways to really engage and interest the children (and the teacher observing you!). This might mean bringing in an unusual resource, or simply using a really irresistible activity.
- *Use the time effectively:* Don't plan to cram too much into the time you are allocated. It is far better to give a decent amount of time to each activity,

rather than feeling that you have to rush the students to fit in everything that you've planned. If you do have some time available at the end of the lesson, spend it reviewing how well the students have done and making sure you praise their work (if, of course, they deserve it).

- *Don't forget to show that you like kids:* Don't be so busy worrying about how the lesson's going, that you forget to show how much you like children, and enjoy working with them. At the end of the day, that's what it's all about!

The format of the day

Teaching interviews normally follow a reasonably similar format, although this will depend on the type of school, number of candidates, and so on. However, you are likely to encounter some or all of the following.

- a tour of the school;
- a visit to observe a (nice!) class;
- an introduction to the department or current Year group teacher;
- teaching a lesson;
- a lunch break;
- the interview;
- waiting for the results.

Pointers to a 'good' or 'bad' school

The pointers in this section cover factors that are reasonably easy to judge on the day of an interview, perhaps by keeping your eyes open as you're shown around the school. Alternatively, they are ones that you can assess for yourself by asking questions, either in the interview, or of the teachers you meet during the day. When using these pointers to assess whether or not this is the school for you, do consider the following factors.

- The school will be out to make a good impression, and you should try to look beyond your initial reactions.
- Even the most 'challenging' children will be far easier to teach in a school that is supportive and well run.
- A school with impeccably behaved children can still be a nightmare to work in if the management are useless.
- The actual structure and buildings of the school may be in need of repair, but the school itself could still be well managed.
- Be very wary of a school that does not allow you to observe at least one lesson during the day of your interview. What are they trying to hide?

The pointers and questions below focus on the structure, set up and staffing of the school, and on the attitudes of the students to their education. The way that your children behave and work in class will have a great deal to do with the overall 'ethos' of the school. These factors should help you discover what this is.

- *The environment:* The way that children and teachers treat the environment can be a powerful indicator of their feelings about and opinions of the school. Are the entrance hall, corridor and classroom displays colourful and reasonably neat (not just the front 'reception area')? Is there evidence that these displays are changed regularly, and that they relate to the learning that is going on in the school? Alternatively, does the school environment show evidence of vandalism, with graffiti on the corridor walls and in the toilets?
- *Staff relationships:* In my experience teachers can be incredibly supportive of each other, and positive staff relationships will make the difference between a good or bad working environment. Look to see how many teachers are in the staffroom at break and lunchtime, and how they interact with each other. If there are only a few staff there, why is this? It could be because they are giving detentions and dealing with incidents of poor behaviour. Alternatively, they might be busy running extracurricular clubs for the children, because they enjoy their work so much.
- *Movement around the school:* The way that the children go from lesson to lesson, or come into lessons from break and lunch, is a good indicator of their attitude to the learning. Is there a sense of urgency (but not aggression), or do you notice pushing or a total lack of enthusiasm? Is the focus on getting to the learning, and do the children have smiles on their faces and look keen to start work? Or do groups of students hide in doorways and toilets or linger in the playground and have to be chased into class?
- *Treatment of staff:* When they interact with teachers or other staff, how do the students treat them? Are all staff treated with respect by the children, including learning assistants, office workers, lunchtime supervisors, caretakers and catering staff? On the other hand, do the students only show deference to the head teacher and other senior staff?
- *Student relationships:* The way that the students mix with each other, both inside and outside the classroom, can be a good indicator of the ethos of the school. Is there evidence of bullying or gangs? Do the children play together cooperatively in the playground or not?
- *Staff turnover:* This is a tricky one to check up on, but well worth doing if you possibly can. A high turnover of staff does tend to indicate a school with low morale or poor support structures.
- *Extracurricular activities:* If the school has a high level of after school clubs or other extracurricular activities, this does tend to suggest that the staff are enthusiastic and keen to get involved.
- *Support for NQTs:* If you're joining a school for your induction year, do ask how NQTs are supported and developed. Promises made in the formal setting of an interview are more likely to be kept!

The interview

The interview itself will probably take place in a formal setting, such as the head's office, or a meeting room. You are likely to be interviewed by a panel made up of a number of people. This might include the head teacher, a school governor and a manager (probably the head of faculty or department for a secondary post). Depending on the job that you are being interviewed for, the interview may last around half an hour to an hour. If you have already decided that this is definitely not the school or the job for you, then it is best to tell the panel that you are going to withdraw right at the start of the interview.

The interview questions

Below are just a few of the questions that you could be asked in your interview. It's worth considering what your answers would be if you were to be asked any of the questions below. Although there's no point in preparing an 'off pat' answer (which you're unlikely to remember anyway), it is certainly useful to have some familiarity with the types of points that you might raise. If you're asked a question that you don't understand, get the panel to clarify what they mean, rather than waffling vaguely around the issue.

- *'How would you describe yourself as a teacher?'*
- *'What do you feel are the most important attributes of an effective teacher?'*
- *'What skills and abilities would you bring to this school?'*
- *'What would you do if you witnessed one child bullying another?'*
- *'What can you offer our school outside the classroom?'*
- *'Please describe a lesson that you felt was particularly successful.'*
- *'How do you incorporate the National Literacy Strategy into your teaching?'*
- *'How do you differentiate work for different children and abilities within your class?'*
- *'How could you contribute to extracurricular activities in our school?'*

At the end of your interview, it is highly likely that you will be asked: 'Is there anything that you'd like to ask us?' At this point, you may well find that your mind goes completely blank because of the stress of the interview situation. For this reason it's a very good idea to work out in advance some questions that you do want to ask. You might want to actually write these questions down, then refer to your notes in the interview. There is nothing wrong in referring to some brief notes: in fact, it shows that you are well prepared and professional.

On the other hand, don't overdo things at this point in the interview. It's best to stick to what you feel are the really important issues, and not to ask too many questions just for the sake of it. Bear in mind that queue of other nervous interviewees waiting in the staffroom! It's unlikely that the panel will have scheduled loads of extra time just to sit and answer your long list of queries.

The final interview question will often be: 'If we offered you this post, would you take it?' This makes it easier for the panel to decide whether or not to offer you the job. It can be very tempting to accept any job that you're offered, and so you may feel like saying 'yes' despite any misgivings you have. However, it does pay to be honest — if you're not sure at this point what your answer would be, then say so. If you would turn the job down, admit this and you can then go home!

Questions about salary

If you do have experience outside the teaching profession, or in another role within education, you might feel that you want to ask whether additional money would be available, should you be offered the job. This is an awkward one. The school will have to find extra money for your salary out of their budget, and this can make a 'cheaper' teacher seem a tempting option. On the other hand, if they employ an experienced teacher, he or she will automatically start at a higher point on the scale. So, it is a difficult balancing act between actually getting the job and being paid what you know you're worth.

Do feel free to check on your salary at this point, before making a verbal agreement to take the job. It is relatively easy for schools to go back on a vague discussion during the day, but far harder if you have actually specified what you expect in the interview, before accepting the post.

Succeeding at interview

Success at teaching interviews relies on a whole range of factors, some of which will be outside your control. If you're not successful in getting the first job you apply for, don't assume that this is because you're 'not good enough', or that you're 'rubbish at interviews'. Bear in mind, too, that every interview provides useful experience for the next one (and the one after that, if required). If you don't succeed, it could be that the school was looking at factors that you had no way of influencing, so console yourself that an unsuccessful interview may have been as a result of one (or more) of the following.

- *Your previous experience:* Unfair as it might seem, a school could invite a few student teachers to interview alongside more experienced candidates, perhaps to 'make up the numbers'.
- *How much you 'cost':* A teacher with a good length of service will be far more expensive than an NQT, and consequently the newer teacher might prove tempting.
- *An internal candidate:* It is sometimes the case that interviewees are put up against an internal candidate, who has already practically got the job in the bag.
- *The competition:* Some subjects are simply more competitive than others. This is both as a result of the number of people with that subject entering the profession, and also the number of posts actually available (i.e. a school will have more English teachers than Art teachers). If you are qualified in a

shortage subject, such as secondary Physics, you are likely to have the pick of the jobs.

- *The area:* Similarly, some areas of the country have far more jobs than candidates. This is especially the case in the costly inner cities such as London.

On the other hand, it is well worth considering the areas that will make a difference to the likelihood of you being offered a job, and doing your best to come across as well as you can.

- *Your appearance:* Teaching is a graduate profession, despite the relatively low pay levels compared to areas such as law or accountancy, and that means you should aim to look as smart as possible at interview. There is no doubt that the way that you dress will affect your chances. In fact, studies have shown that interviewers make snap judgements about people because of their appearance, and this will have a strong influence on your chances of getting the job. It might sound blatantly obvious, but do wear a smart suit, put your hair into a neat style, and remember to polish your shoes!

- *Your body language and facial expressions:* The way that you use your body is a crucial part of being a teacher. You will already have learnt how to appear confident in front of your children, and you need to transfer this ability to the interview situation. Sit up straight, with your head held high, and try not to fidget nervously throughout the interview.

- *The way you use your face:* Similarly, the way that you use your face and eyes is all part of the skill of the teacher. So, put some animation in your face while you're talking, and look the interviewers in the eye, both when they question you and when you answer.

- *Your responses to questions:* Nerves can play a huge part in making you clam up, or alternatively waffle on endlessly! Make sure that you answer the question that you've been asked (surprisingly hard when you're under stress). Try to keep your responses reasonably brief, although with sufficient detail to make your points clear. Give specific examples from your own school experience whenever possible. Remember too that with practice you will find it easier to judge exactly how much to say.

Choosing the right job

With only one day to get a feel for the school, it is often very difficult to decide whether or not this is the right job for you. Make sure you take time *before* the interview to get some background information and ideas about the school (using the 'Pre-interview checklist' on p.64). During the day, use the 'pointers' given earlier in this chapter to get a better feel for the school. Finally, go with your gut instincts about the place, bearing in mind that you are committing yourself to this job for a substantial period of time.

After the interview

When your interview is completed, you will probably be asked to wait in a room for all the other interviews to take place. After this, the panel will discuss the relative merits of all the candidates, and this can take a long (and very nerve wracking) time. In some schools, the candidates will be sent home after they have been interviewed, and a telephone offer will be made either later that day or on the following day. When the panel have reached their decision, one of them will come back to the room and ask one of you to come with them. In most cases, this is the person who has got the job! Do ensure that, if you don't get the post, you ask for feedback if this is not freely offered. This feedback may take place on the day, or may be by telephone after the event.

Job offers

Job offers in teaching work in a rather unusual way. If you've worked in the commercial sector before moving into teaching, you will find this a very different approach. Basically, you will be invited into the room, offered the job, then asked for a response on the spot. Once you have accepted a job, you must go through with your acceptance. You will have made a verbal contract and you may be sued or even 'blacklisted' from all the schools in the area if you do decide to pull out. You may decide that you are unsure, and tell the panel this. In some situations (perhaps where there are no other suitable candidates), you may be given 24 hours to come to a decision.

Police checks and medicals

After you have been offered the job, you will be asked to take a police check. These police checks are organized via the DfES. You will also be checked against 'List 99', which is a list of teachers who are barred from employment because of medical or misconduct issues. If you do have a criminal conviction, much will depend on what the offence itself was. For instance, it's probably unlikely that a school will refuse you employment because of a speeding offence. Some schools and LEAs also insist on a medical examination.

5 Your first year

This chapter gives you advice, information and strategies for getting through that crucial (and difficult) first year as a teacher. It looks in detail at the induction arrangements, including answers to commonly asked questions. You can also read some interviews with NQTs about their own experiences of the first year in teaching.

What's it really like?

I can still remember vividly the days leading up to the start of my own first year in teaching. After the academic pressures of qualifying to be a teacher, and the stress of searching for my first job, I was filled with a mixture of overwhelming excitement, alongside a feeling of almost total dread. There really is nothing that can truly prepare you for that first day in front of your very own class: that first moment when you really become a proper teacher. Hopefully, though, you'll find answers below to some of the biggest concerns that face you before you start work, and in your first few weeks in the job.

> What if I've forgotten how to do it?
> Will the kids riot?
> Why is it so hard?
> What if I can't cope?
> How do I fit everything in?
> Will I pass my induction?

- *What if I've forgotten how to do it?:* Many of us experience that awful feeling that we might have somehow 'forgotten' how to teach. This feeling often strikes just before the start of a new term, or at any time when you've been away from the classroom for a while. But teaching is like riding a bicycle – once you've done it, you'll never really forget how. As soon as you stand in front of the children, it will all come flooding back to you (honestly). And after a few days (or perhaps even hours or minutes) it'll feel like you've been doing it forever.
- *Will the kids riot?:* Managing behaviour is, for many of us, one of the biggest concerns in our professional lives. You can find lots of advice and information on dealing with behaviour in this book (see Chapters 3 and 8). I'm not going to promise you that your kids won't misbehave, because this simply might not be true. On the other hand, it is unlikely that there will actually be a full

scale riot in your classroom on your first day of teaching, and this is as much to do with external factors as it is to do with your own classroom management. As you first start out in teaching, bear the following points in mind to give you some comfort.

- On the whole, children do look up to teachers as figures of authority (at least to some extent).
- Generally speaking, your class or classes will give you a few lessons' grace in which they decide whether or not to behave for you.
- Although a small minority may make life hard for you, the vast majority of children in your classes will not be badly behaved at any one time.
- Students who have been at a school for a while will be aware of the school rules, and what might happen to them if they do mess around.
- There are plenty of people ready and willing to support you in achieving good discipline.
- If things go badly wrong, your school will have some sort of emergency procedure in place. If the worst comes to the worst, send a 'nice' child to go and get another teacher to help you.

- *Why is it so hard?:* Unless you're some kind of superhuman, you will find the first few days and weeks in teaching incredibly hard. One of the main reasons for this is that your body is adapting to the life of a working teacher, and the intellectual, physical and emotional demands your new job is making. You might find yourself physically exhausted at the end of the day, or emotionally drained by poor behaviour. Hopefully, you'll also be enthused and excited about finally becoming a 'real' teacher. When things seem particularly hard in your first year, do bear in mind that it'll never be this difficult again.
- *What if I can't cope?:* The feeling that you simply 'can't cope' is actually quite normal for a teacher. This state of affairs can be brought about by a whole variety of things: difficult behaviour, excessive workload, trying to mark all the books. As an NQT, learn to turn for support to other members of staff – we were all new teachers once, so we know exactly how you feel. Teachers really are wonderful at supporting each other. Please don't suffer alone.
- *How do I fit everything in?:* Prioritizing, and knowing when to stop work, is perhaps one of the hardest tasks that faces the teacher, whether he or she is new or experienced. You want to do the best that you can possibly can, but the job expands to meet the amount of time that you're willing to devote to it. The answer to this problem is that you must work out what really matters, and which bits of the job you can spend less time on. In your first year, put 'teaching well' right at the top of the agenda, followed by 'getting to know the kids'. Writing overly detailed lesson plans and doing filing really is not all that essential.
- *Will I pass my induction?:* If you're a good teacher, the answer to this question is 'yes'. Instead of worrying about induction, try to focus on doing the job to the best of your ability. Find out the facts about the induction year

(see the sections on induction below) but don't let thoughts of passing or failing prey on your mind.

Top tips for surviving your first year

Pace yourself: Don't use up all your energy at the start of the term or year.

Don't take on too much: Make your classroom teaching the main priority.

Balance your planning: Give yourself 'quiet times' during the school day/week.

Don't reinvent the wheel: Use pre-existing plans and resources.

Don't suffer alone: Ask for help and support when you need it.

The first week

The first week of any school year is always a busy and exciting time, and of course your very first week as a 'proper' teacher is bound to be a stressful experience. You should have at least one INSET day at the start of term when the staff are at school before the students arrive. Much of this time may be given over to training and meetings, but you should also be given some time to yourself to get prepared. Use this opportunity wisely. The following tips and advice will help you prepare for, and survive, the first week in your new job.

- *Make an impact in your room:* The children will be making judgements about you as a teacher from the first moment that they meet you. The way your room appears is vital in making that important first impression a good one. Making changes to your room (or rooms) helps you mark out the room as 'your' space, and can increase your confidence. Bear in mind that the children will often have had a previous experience of this space. It is now yours, and it will help indicate to the children the type of learning experience they can expect. For more thoughts on setting up your room, see Chapter 7.
- *Get your room organized:* Aim to be an efficient teacher, who knows where everything is and can access resources, equipment and materials easily. This will help you appear well prepared, and ensure that you do not waste time or get flustered when the children need something and you cannot find it.
- *Keep important papers together:* In your first week, it's inevitable that you'll be given lots of bits of paper. Some of these will be more important than others. A good idea is to have one folder in which you keep every piece of

paper that you need to refer to on a daily basis. This might include class lists, lesson plans, timetables, and so on.

- *Don't be too organized:* This might seem like a strange tip to give you. It is all too tempting to start writing your class lists or timetable into your teacher's planner or mark book during the first week, but being this organized is actually a mistake so early on. Bear in mind that the information you've been given may not be fully accurate yet, or that there may be changes to the school roll in the first week or so. It's far better to wait for a couple of weeks before you write up all this information.
- *Get hold of resources early:* Exercise books and paper can be like gold-dust at the start of term, especially if orders have not yet arrived. If possible use the INSET day or days to collect the resources that you need. Don't feel guilty about this – I can assure you that the 'old hands' will have made sure that they have the resources they need early on too.
- *Don't aim to do too much in your lessons:* There tend to be lots of administrative tasks to take care of in the first week, such as handing out exercise books, checking names, and so on. There will often also be changes to the timetable, for instance special assemblies, that will eat into your class time. In addition, it's crucial to spend some time talking through your expectations, rules and boundaries with your class or classes. Although it's important to have lessons planned, don't feel any pressure to get through huge quantities of work in the first week of school.
- *Set the standards now:* In the battle to get good order and discipline, the first week is a really crucial time. Think carefully, in advance of meeting your students, about how you are going to run your class and your lessons. What expectations do you have of the students' behaviour? What standard and quantity of work do you want to see? What will happen if misbehaviour does occur? Take time out in the first week to talk all this through with your children. Show them that you know exactly how your class will be run, and that you have high expectations of what they can achieve.

'First lines' for greeting a class

One of the biggest stresses for new teachers is often that very first few minutes with the class, while you are setting the tone for what will follow. Here are a few useful and tactical 'first lines' for the meeting and greeting of your students at the start of school, with a brief explanation of how and why each one might work.

The triple command

- 'Before we go in the room I want you all lined up, facing front and standing in silence, please.'
- 'I want everyone sitting in their seats, completely silent and looking at me, please.'

Using a command or statement ('I want') rather than a question lets the children know exactly what is required of them. Focus on what is really crucial: three instructions seems to be the maximum amount of information that children can take in at any one time.

The target + reward

- 'Let's see who's sitting silently, ready to work and deserves a merit mark.'
- 'That's fantastic, Jimmy, you're obviously ready to work because you're sitting silently in your seat. Well done!'

By giving the children a target, and a reason for aiming to achieve that target, you can set a very positive atmosphere about the lesson right from the start. In the second example, the teacher focuses on one individual who is doing what she wants, thereby setting a target for the others to follow. The 'reward' in this case is her verbal praise.

The target + avoided sanction

- 'Let's see who's ready to work and wants to go to break on time?'
- 'Hmmm, I'm a bit surprised that so many of you aren't silent yet. Can it *really* be that you want me to give you a detention?'

The great thing about this approach is that the sanction is only hinted at vaguely, rather than threatened. It is almost as though the children will be 'rewarded' for good behaviour by missing out on the sanction, rather than being 'punished' for bad behaviour by receiving it. In the second example, the teacher's surprise that the children might 'want' a sanction makes his wishes very clear.

Survival tactics

In your first year, it can often seem as though your first priority is to actually survive each day, let alone enjoy your success as a teacher. The tips below will help you survive as an NQT: physically, emotionally and psychological. And please don't worry, in your second and subsequent years as a teacher, life really does become much, much easier.

Physical survival

Teaching is a surprisingly physical profession. This is true not just for teachers of physically active subjects such as PE and Dance, but for every classroom teacher. Teachers are communicating with their students verbally, and this can put a considerable strain on your voice. We also move around the classroom helping individuals, handing out books, and so on. For some teachers, for instance those without a classroom of their own, there can be a lot of carrying equipment around the school.

Looking after your voice

The following tips will help you take care of your voice, in the first year and beyond. If you get the chance, it really is well worth undertaking some INSET training in voice use, for instance from an acting coach.

- *Avoid shouting at all costs:* As well as putting a terrible strain on your voice, and potentially doing long-term damage, shouting simply doesn't work as a strategy in the classroom. Teachers who resort to shouting are demonstrating a loss of control to their students. Stay calm, and keep the tone and volume of your voice low as far as is humanly possible.
- *Be a 'quiet' teacher:* The quieter you are as a teacher, the quieter your students will have to be to hear you. This method really does help in getting children to be more attentive to what you are saying. Think of the image of a volume control button on a stereo, and learn to lower the volume of your own voice just as you would with a piece of music.
- *Learn to 'hear' yourself:* I can remember listening to my mum teaching her students when I was a child, and thinking that she sounded very different to the mum that I knew. Often our voices will betray the tension and strain of controlling a class, but these are the very messages that we don't want to send, because we want to appear calm and in control. Take a moment on occasions to 'step back' and actually hear yourself as you must appear to others. You may be surprised at how loud or tense your voice actually sounds.
- *Don't rely on 'chalk and talk' methods:* It can be tempting to focus on teacher led work in your first year, as this gives a sense of control over the class. However, this type of strategy is very heavy duty in terms of voice use. Let your children do the talking whenever possible, for instance during group work or question and answer sessions. Ask a child to 'be teacher' and explain the work to the class when your voice needs a rest.

Looking after your body

As well as taking care of our voices, we also need to limit the strain we put on our bodies. Here are some tips to help you.

- *Delegate!:* Many physical jobs can be delegated. For instance, if you've got books to hand out or equipment to carry between rooms, ask for a couple of student volunteers to help. (Ensure, though, that you don't put a child's health and safety at risk when you do this.) It's very worthwhile fostering a good relationship with the school caretaker. That way, if you need the chairs set out in the hall, you can get help with the task.
- *Dress sensibly:* Nurses spend much of the day on their feet, and the shoes that they wear reflect this. The same applies for teachers: if you do decide to wear that pair of high heeled stilettos, your back and feet are bound to suffer for it.
- *Sit down sometimes!:* As an eager new teacher, you will probably find yourself bounding around the classroom, explaining work and enthusing about the subject. Don't forget to sit down occasionally to give yourself a rest, perhaps getting the children to come to your desk for help, rather than you going to them.
- *Take your breaks:* I can't stress enough how important it is to go to the staffroom at break and lunchtime if at all possible. The chance to sit down and have a quick cup of tea or coffee will help you relax. It may seem like a hassle at the start of term, but in the long run taking your breaks will really pay off.
- *Pace yourself:* If you know you've got a particularly 'heavy' and physical lesson or activity during the week, then balance this out with some opportunities to sit and rest. This 'rest' might be setting a class test, or watching a video.

Emotional survival

As well as the physical demands teaching makes on you, there will also be many times when you feel emotionally drained and exhausted. Again, long-term survival as a teacher is about learning how to cope with the emotional stresses of the job, such as dealing with students who are abusive towards you.

- *Learn to deflect insults:* An insult from a child is only a problem if you allow it to get to you. Of course, the natural reaction to being insulted is an emotional response. If you work with difficult children you will need to find a way of overcoming this, if you are not to end up in floods of tears every other lesson. My suggestion for deflecting insults is to simply agree with everything that the child says, because this leaves the student with nowhere to go, and no reaction to feed off. So, if a child says 'you're really fat/ugly/stupid, miss' simply answer 'yes, I know, isn't it wonderful/awful/ amazing?'
- *Put up a 'wall':* If you can learn to put up a metaphorical wall between yourself and poor behaviour, this will help you keep your emotions in check. Like the deflector shield on the Starship Enterprise in *Star Trek*, try to simply let the rudeness 'bounce off' your defences.

■ *Remind yourself that it is the child who has the problem:* A child who is rude or abusive towards an adult generally has a problem of some sort. After all, this really is not normal behaviour. Try to remind yourself that it is the child who has the issue – perhaps his or her parents are unable to keep control and set boundaries in the home? Feel sorry for, instead of angry with, the child.

■ *Don't be afraid to let it out:* Having said that you should try to 'block out' your emotional responses, there will be times when you are tired or fed up and you cannot simply intellectualize the situation. When this does happen, get yourself to the staffroom or somewhere else private, find a sympathetic shoulder and have a good old cry or rant.

■ *Don't get overly involved:* Some of the children with whom you work may have very unhappy personal lives. Although you will obviously become emotionally involved with these young people, if you are to survive teaching in the long term you need to keep a separation between your working life and your home life.

■ *Build up your support networks:* There are many people who can support you: your colleagues, family, friends, the unions, and so on. Build up a network of support to get you through the tough times, especially during your NQT year. If possible, spend time sharing your worries with other NQTs – having a good old moan with others who are experiencing the same as you can provide a very useful safety valve.

Psychological survival

To survive psychologically as a teacher, one of the main criteria is that you simply cannot be a perfectionist. The job really is as big and as difficult as you allow it to be. Even the teacher who worked 24 hours a day, seven days a week would still not be able to do the job perfectly. Here are some tips that will help you keep in top psychological condition.

■ *Learn to prioritize:* One of the crucial factors in finding a balance as a teacher is learning to prioritize. You must accept that you simply cannot do everything, and instead you will need to work out what you feel is most important. This applies both in terms of the parts of the job that you see as vital, and also in finding a balance between work and your 'normal' life. For instance, on a Friday night is it more important to get that set of books marked, or to go home and have a break?

■ *Know when to say 'no':* The temptation in your first year is to agree to do everything that you are asked. It can be very difficult to say 'no', especially when you are full of enthusiasm for the job. However, a teacher who spreads him or herself too thinly may be able to do a little bit of everything, but will do nothing properly, especially the teaching.

■ *Keep a home/school divide:* Teachers do have a tendency to take their work home with them, both literally and metaphorically. It can be incredibly difficult to switch off at the end of the school day, especially when you've been through a particularly difficult incident. However, achieving this home/ school divide is crucial for your own sanity, especially if you hope to stay in the profession long term. As you become more experienced, you will find your own ways of making this divide. Some people stay late after school, refusing to take any marking or other work home; others use the holidays to take a complete break from school-related tasks; while some teachers find they need a sabbatical after a few years in the job to recreate the balance between home and school.

- *Don't expect to always get it right:* Even the most experienced teachers will have days when their classroom or behaviour management falls apart. If you set your own standards too high, you are setting yourself up for failure. Accept that you will make mistakes, try to learn from them, and then put them behind you.
- *Develop your confidence:* The most effective teachers are very confident in what they do, and this confidence communicates itself to the students. Build up your confidence by celebrating your own successes: in a 'difficult' school simply getting the children to stay in their seats may be a huge achievement. Learn to pat yourself on the back: use a positive philosophy of rewards rather than sanctions on yourself as well as on your students!

The induction process

Although you will have spent a good deal of time on teaching practice, your first year in the profession is the time at which you really 'become' a teacher. It's during this tough time that you learn about the reality of life at the chalkface: the ups and downs, the stresses and strains, the shortcuts and strategies essential for survival. Not so long ago, the first year was known as the 'probation year'. Along with the name change to 'induction' has come a more rigorous and rigid system of testing. This induction is described in detail in the sections below.

Although the 'guidelines' are fairly clear-cut in what should happen during your induction year, schools will vary in how good they are at following them. Much will depend on how effective (or not) your induction tutor proves to be. It can be hard as a new teacher to make a fuss if things aren't progressing as they should, but do make sure you know what your rights are. After all, it is you who passes or fails at the end of the year.

At the most basic level, induction is made up of both support and testing. The idea is both to help you become the most effective teacher you can be, and to test whether you are 'good enough' for the profession. As an NQT, you will (or should) receive:

- Support from experienced teachers.
- Non-contact time to help you cope with and adapt to the workload.
- Observations of your work.
- Informal and formal assessments of your teaching.

- Target setting and objectives on which to work.
- Further professional development.

Induction arrangements vary from country to country within the UK. It's important to understand the particular requirements of the place in which you find your first job. The following sections will help you do this.

Something to remember

In the darkest hours, don't forget:
- Nobody expects you to be 100 per cent perfect yet;
- Induction is designed to help, not hurt, you; and
- The overwhelming majority of teachers do pass

Induction in Wales

At the moment there is no official 'induction period' in Wales. However, the Minister for Education and Lifelong Learning recently announced new arrangements that will come into place shortly. From September 2003, an induction year will become a statutory requirement for new teachers in Wales. There are also plans to begin a pilot induction programme from September 2002.

Induction in Scotland

Previously, the induction period in Scotland was two years of teaching service. However, there were often problems for teachers in completing their probation. From August 2002, all eligible teachers working in Scotland are entitled to a one year 'training post' with a Scottish LEA immediately after they qualify. During this year, they undertake probation or induction. In a similar way to arrangements in England (although slightly more generous), NQTs will have to teach only 70 per cent of a full timetable, and will have non-contact time of 30 per cent in which to work on professional development. They will also have an 'induction tutor', an experienced teacher within the school where they are working. Once the probation year has been completed successfully, teachers will qualify for full registration with the GTCS.

Induction in Northern Ireland

Northern Ireland has an 'induction stage' in teacher education. Teachers who have completed this are exempt from induction in English schools.

Induction in England

In this section, you can find straightforward and easy to understand answers to some of the more common questions about induction. It really is well worth equipping yourself with all the information you can about induction – that way if something goes wrong, or if your school is not meeting its obligations, you will know about it. You will also know who you are meant to turn to for help. You can download the current Induction Guidelines from the internet at: www.dfee.gov.uk/circulars/5_99/index.htm.

Please note: In most circumstances, the 'appropriate body' referred to in the Guidelines is the LEA, and I have used the term 'LEA' to indicate this. In certain situations (see the Induction Guidelines for details), the 'appropriate body' will be different.

Q. Who has to complete induction?

A. All teachers who gained QTS after 7 May 1999, and who want to work in a maintained (i.e. state) primary or secondary school (or non-maintained special school) in England.

Q. How long is induction?

A. Induction takes one academic year, which in most cases is still three terms, although at some schools it may be four or five. If you move schools during induction, and your new school operates a different term structure, the induction period becomes one calendar year. If you are working part-time, the induction is done on a pro rata basis. In other words, if you only work half a full timetable, your induction will take two academic years. *Note*: The induction period does not have to be continuous.

Q. Do I have to start induction immediately on qualifying?

A. No, there is no time limit for starting induction, although you would normally be expected to complete induction within five years of starting it. Of course, it's probably best to get it over and done with straight away.

Q. Where can I do my induction?

A. You can complete your induction at any state school or non-maintained special school. Sixth form colleges are also able to offer induction if the LEA agrees. It is also possible to take induction at an independent school if the school fulfils certain criteria and liaises with the LEA.

Q. Who is responsible for my training during my NQT year?

A. Responsibility is shared between:

- the head teacher
- the induction tutor
- the 'appropriate body', usually the LEA. (You should be provided with the name of someone you can contact at the LEA if you have any concerns about your induction.)

As well as being responsible for your training, these people are also expected to provide you with the support that you need to pass induction. Your induction tutor is responsible for keeping records of your lesson observations, meetings and so on. At the end of induction, the GTCE is sent lists of those who have passed and failed induction. Any appeals are made to the GTCE.

Q. How much teaching should I be doing during my induction year?

A. You should be teaching for no more than 90 per cent of normal average teaching time. It is a statutory (i.e. legal) requirement that the head teacher ensures this, so make sure you get your entitlement! The time created by this reduced teaching load is meant to be a proper part of your programme, and not just viewed as 'non-contact' time.

Q. Who will my induction tutor be?

A. The guidelines say that this should be your line manager, a senior member of staff, or other experienced teacher with whom you have considerable contact. Your head teacher may also act as your induction tutor, although in reality this is probably relatively uncommon.

Q. What about my Career Entry Profile? What role does that play?

A. You should show your CEP to your head teacher and induction tutor as soon as possible after you start your job. It remains yours, but it is meant to be used when setting your objectives.

Q. What should I expect in terms of who and what I have to teach?

A. In theory, you should be teaching within the age group and subject that you trained to teach. You should not be given a class or classes that have particularly bad discipline problems. You should teach the same class or classes on a regular basis, and undertake the same type of planning, teaching and assessment as other similar teachers at your school. Finally, you shouldn't be given extra, non-teaching responsibilities without being properly prepared and supported.

Q. What other help can I expect?

A. You should also be given advice on various aspects of your role as a teacher. This would include being given a formal schedule of when your assessments will take place, and being given information about sick pay, salary and pensions. This sort of advice and information is similar to what any new employee would be given.

In addition, you should receive information about the school itself, and how your induction programme will work. You should have the chance to take part in any training that is going on at your school. You might also get the opportunity to spend time talking to the school's SENCO about SEN issues, and this can be a very valuable and worthwhile experience for an NQT.

Q. What will the induction programme be like?

A. The programme is meant to be 'tailored to your individual needs'. It should also be designed to actually help you pass induction. The programme should build on your ITT training and your CEP, setting objectives and giving you regular assessment of your progress. It should also help you develop your self-evaluation skills and prepare you to develop your career further.

The guidelines suggest that you are actively involved in planning the programme. You should also have complete access to records of observations and the outcomes of meetings about your progress. In reality, the quality of the programme you receive will vary widely from school to school. Much will depend on how effective, efficient and supportive your head teacher and induction tutor prove to be.

Q. How often should I be observed and receive reviews of my progress?

A. You should receive at least one observation in your first four weeks in the job. You can then expect to receive one observation every six to eight weeks, which basically means every half term. The same applies to reviews of your progress, which should take place once every half term. You'll find an overview of the observation, review and assessment process in the following section.

Q. What sort of things will my tutor be observing?

A. The observations should focus on specific aspects of your teaching and will be linked to the requirements for passing induction, and the objectives that have been identified for your development. You can find out more about the 'induction standards' at the end of this section.

Q. What should happen after the observation?

A. You should have a discussion with your induction tutor about the lesson, and you should also have access to a short written report on the observation. This is meant to focus on your objectives, showing where any action needs to be taken, and whether any changes have been made to the objectives. Schools are busy places and it may be that you need to 'chase' your tutor to ensure that the discussion takes place, and that you receive the written report.

Q. Do I get the chance to watch other teachers in the classroom?

A. Yes, you are meant to get this opportunity. These observations might take place in your own school, or they could take place in a school nearby that has been shown to be a particularly effective one. If nobody offers you the chance to observe, then ask! Watching other teachers in action really is an invaluable way of learning.

Q. How many formal assessment meetings will I have and when will they be?

A. You should receive three formal, or 'summative' assessments during your induction year. In a school that works on the three term system, these will probably take place towards the end of the term. In other situations, such as a five term school or a teacher working part-time, the formal assessment meetings should be spread evenly over the induction period. Again, see the overview in the following section to see how this works.

Q. What will happen at these formal meetings?

A. The meetings will be with either the head teacher or your induction tutor. At the first meeting you will look at how you are beginning to meet the induction standards; the second meeting will look at how well you are progressing; the final meeting will confirm whether or not you have actually met the standards required. In this final meeting, if you've been successful, you might set some objectives for your second year in teaching.

Q. What evidence will be used to check on my progress at the assessment meetings?

A. A variety of forms of evidence should be used. These will include notes from at least two observations and progress review meetings that have taken place during the term. The meetings might also look at your assessment records of students (including exam results) and your lesson planning and self-evaluations. You should be given copies of all written records about your induction.

Q. What happens after the summative assessment meeting?

A. After the meetings, you will be asked to sign the summative assessment forms. There is also a space on the form for you to write any comments of your own. The forms are then returned to the LEA within ten days of the meeting (or at the end of your induction period after the third meeting).

After the final meeting, your head teacher will write to tell the LEA whether or not you have completed induction satisfactorily. You should receive a copy of this notification.

Q. What happens if my progress is unsatisfactory during the induction period?

A. There should be early intervention and you should be given support and advice to help you improve. Your weaknesses should be identified, and a programme of support should be put in place to help you. If your head teacher is not your induction tutor, he or she should come in to observe some of your lessons, to check that the induction tutor's evidence is correct.

The head teacher should also formally notify you that you are at risk of not passing induction, and he or she should send you a copy of the formal report identifying where your weaknesses are, what objectives have been set, and what support will be given.

If you feel that your progress is being impeded because the school is not fulfilling its responsibilities, you should notify the named person at the LEA. This information may be important if you fail induction and then decide to appeal the decision.

Q. What do I do if I'm not happy with my induction?

A. This is an awkward situation in which to find yourself. According to the guidelines, your first line of action should be to make use of your school's internal procedures, including going to the governing body. If that doesn't work, you should then contact your LEA. In practice, though, this might prove very hard for an NQT to do. Your best first step is to try and talk things through with your induction tutor, assuming that you get on with him or her. As an experienced teacher, your tutor may well be able to advise you further.

Q. What if I'm working as a supply teacher?

A. If your supply post is going to be longer than a term, the head teacher must agree that it will count towards induction. If you're employed for periods of shorter than a term, you are exempt from induction. However, this only applies for the first year and one term that you're working as a teacher. It's not possible to 'collect' short term periods of supply (of less than a term) and add them together to make up your induction.

Q. What if I don't pass my induction?

A. If you don't pass induction, you won't be able to teach in the state sector. However, you will be given the chance to appeal against the decision, and if you do go to appeal, your school does not have to dismiss you. If you're going to appeal you should do so by sending a 'notice of appeal' to the GTCE within twenty working days. Details of what must be included in this notice can be found in the induction guidelines.

Q. What if I'm off school for a long time during induction?

A. If your absence is due to sickness, and this is for more than 30 days, the induction period will be extended by the total of your absences. If you are off school because you're on maternity leave, you do not have to have your induction period extended, unless you want to. In this situation, your final assessment won't take place until you return to work, and have been given the opportunity to receive an extension.

Q. What if I did my probationary period outside England?

A. You don't have to do induction in England if you completed the equivalent probation period in Scotland, Northern Ireland, Wales, Isle of Man, Guernsey, Jersey or Gibraltar.

Q. How is my induction paid for?

A. Schools are given money within the Standards Fund to pay for the costs of your induction. Bear this in mind if you're not being properly supported!

Q. What are the induction standards?

A. As well as continuing to meet the standards for QTS, you'll also be expected to meet the 'induction standards' in your NQT year. These cover all the 'basics' of being a good teacher, such as planning, teaching, classroom management, assessment and so on. You can find a detailed outline in the induction guidelines. The standards cover a range of areas.

- Target setting
- Teaching strategies
- Planning for all abilities
- Getting good behaviour
- Dealing with SEN
- Multicultural approaches
- Assessment
- Liaising with and reporting to parents

- Implementing school policies
- Professional development

Induction – a brief overview

A brief outline of the timings of observations, reviews and formal assessments in your induction year

TERM ONE

Show the school your CEP
Objectives set
Observation and follow-up discussion
Review meeting

WEEK 5

Observation and discussion
Review meeting
Formal assessment (1)

TERM TWO

Observation and discussion
Review meeting

HALF TERM

Observation and discussion
Review meeting
Formal assessment (2)

TERM THREE

Observation and discussion
Review meeting

HALF TERM

Observation and discussion
Review meeting
Formal assessment (3)

Career Entry Profile

On qualification, student teachers are now given a 'Career Entry Profile' (CEP). This profile gives information about the strengths that a teacher already has, and also about the type of professional development they might need. The profile is given to the induction tutor and head teacher by the NQT, and is then used to help in setting objectives for induction and in creating a suitable action plan.

Starting out

The interviews that follow give you a glimpse into the lives of three newly qualified teachers as they tackle the ups and downs of their first year in the profession. From each of my interviewees comes a sense of determination and dedication: two factors that have a huge influence on your success in the job.

Newly Qualified Teacher

Primary (Reception Class)

Coleford Infants School, Forest of Dean

Emily Scriven

Q. What made you decide to become a teacher?

Emily – It was something that I'd always wanted to do after being inspired by many teachers who had taught me through my school life.

Q. Tell me about your training.

Emily – I did a three-year degree in Primary Education with QTS. I felt that the three-year route really displayed my commitment to teaching, rather than doing a one-year course on top of an ordinary degree. It was a very intense course that would otherwise have been completed in four years. I trained in Wales, and now that I'm teaching in England there are many differences that I've faced, particularly with induction arrangements. The relationship between you and your supervisory teacher on teaching practice is essential – I did not have a good relationship with mine, this made an already stressful final practice a real uphill struggle. Luckily I dug my heels in and battled on through. However, other trainees I am aware of quit the whole course as they couldn't cope with the added stress.

Q. And you're just completing your first year of teaching?

Emily – That's right. I teach a Reception class in the Forest of Dean in Gloucestershire.

Q. How have you found it, being an NQT?

Emily – The first term, when I was teaching on supply, was a nightmare! But since finding a permanent job, my mentor has been fantastic and provided me with a lot of support and advice. My non-contact time has been valuable, as I use it a lot to observe other teachers in their classrooms. I do feel frustrated slightly, as I am constantly paranoid and wonder if I have made the right decisions, set the right work simply because I am working with teachers a lot more experienced than me, but I know this will stop in time as I grow in confidence in my new career.

Q. What's been the best thing about teaching for you so far?

Emily – My best moment in teaching was on my first day with my own class. There was no one there watching me and grading my teaching. I was on my own and it felt great! Also, the sense of achievement you feel when a child has been struggling with a concept and it finally clicks, with your input.

Q. And what about the worst thing?

Emily – My worst moments in teaching were during my first term of teaching on supply through an agency. I was really thrown in at the deep end in really tough schools, having to travel 60 miles in some cases. The agency offered no mentoring system and I felt totally isolated. I wanted to throw in the whole thing until I got my own class – now I wouldn't do anything else.

Q. What's the best thing about teaching Reception?

Emily – The fact that you really are laying the foundations for the rest of the child's school life. The children seem so much more willing and interested in new concepts. They are mostly all very innocent and frequently come out with 'little gems' that I enjoy hearing.

Q. And the hardest thing?

Emily – The worst thing about this age group at the moment is the new Early Learning Goals and Stepping Stones that really do seem to isolate Reception from the rest of the school, as things are done so differently. I feel, talking to colleagues experienced in Reception, that there has not been enough guidance given to schools and teachers on the new system.

Q. What about classroom planning – how is that different now that you're a 'proper' teacher?

Emily – The main difference between planning as a student and planning as a 'real' teacher is that the planning is very much for your information rather than there to be scrutinized and put under the microscope by lecturers. I use a format that runs throughout the school – we all use the same planning sheets. I much prefer it this way as nobody can become confused with other people's plans.

Q. How about longer-term planning? How does this work at your school?

Emily – I plan very closely with Year group colleagues – we complete medium-term planning together and then together plan one week in advance from this. This ensures that all the objectives are met. For Foundation subjects this is relatively simple as we follow QCA units of work. Many teachers have different methods but I prefer a topic based approach which can be taught through the literacy hour in many cases, such as using non-fiction Big Books to teach Science.

Q. Any thoughts on the Literacy and Numeracy strategies? How have they affected you as a classroom teacher?

Emily – The literacy and numeracy hours came into effect as I began my training, therefore I have never really known anything other than teaching the subjects through the strategies given by the DfES. As an NQT I enjoy teaching the strategies as they provide very obvious methods of teaching. It is all outlined in the document and so I feel that I am doing it correctly when I follow it! I am aware that many more senior colleagues have very mixed feelings about the strategies as they feel they are constricting. It did help whilst on supply having a detailed knowledge of what is meant to be covered – this proved invaluable, as I was able to arm myself with suitable work when entering a totally unfamiliar year group.

Q. Have you been promoted yet? How do you feel about it?

Emily – I've been given the curriculum responsibility for Geography. I enjoy this greatly. My major subject is Literacy, which in the future I would like to coordinate in a school where I have deputy head status. But, obviously this is in the very far future!

Q. What about support for you as an NQT?

Emily – I had no support during my first term of teaching, and it was difficult to talk to friends about it as they mostly had their own classes, whilst I was on supply. However, my main sources of support now are from other NQTs, teachers in school and my mentor who has been a great source of inspiration for me. I feel that it is essential to share your experiences with other teachers to prevent a feeling of inadequacy as an NQT!

Q. Can you recommend any good resources for NQTs?

Emily – The Handbook for NQTs published by the Stationery Office is fantastic. Also, the Eteach website is good for talking to other teachers. The 100 Literacy and Numeracy Hour books published by Scholastic are very good.

Q. Would you recommend a teaching career to others?

Emily – Yes, I would, but you must be very aware of what you are getting into. I would advise 'would be' teachers to do a lot of research and to be sure that it's what they really want to do.

Q. What could be done to improve teaching as a profession?

Emily – Raising the profile of teachers as professionals and reflecting this in our pay. Also, giving schools more power in disciplining poor behaviour and making parents more accountable for their children's actions.

Q. Finally, in your opinion, what makes someone a good teacher?

Emily – I think a good teacher is someone that is able to combine high expectations of behaviour and work with that of a friendly and caring approach. I feel taking an interest in what the children have to say and taking time to listen is an essential quality, turning the classroom into a happy environment rather than a production line is also important! Also you must have the ability not to take yourself and other colleagues too seriously. The ability to admit mistakes and to learn from them is important. Above all, if you're on final teaching practice – *don't give in*! It is a struggle but it's very near to the finishing post so hang on in there.

Newly Qualified Teacher

Primary (Year 3)

Bentinck Primary and Nursery School, Nottingham

Tracey Nightingale

Note: You can learn more about Tracey and her work in Chapter 12 'Planning in the primary school'.

Q. What made you decide to go into teaching?

Tracey – I always admired teachers when I was at school and originally wanted to teach RE in secondary school. To me, teachers had a good status in society at the time. I looked up to my teachers and respected them (oh, how times have changed!). I always got on well with my teachers and had good relationships with them so teaching seemed to be a rewarding and challenging career. Then I went through the usual teenage changes of mind but eventually ended up applying for primary teaching courses at university. I'd done some work experience in my old primary and I kind of liked it. I decided against a pure teaching degree (BEd was being phased out according to a few universities) as I wasn't 100 per cent sure teaching was for me. I ended up doing a four-year BA Religious Studies degree with QTS so if the teaching didn't work out I'd still have a good degree to fall back on.

Q. Did you go straight into teaching without a break from the education system?

Tracey – Yes, I did, but I don't regret it. If I wanted to take time away from teaching and travel then I could. If I wanted to change career then I could. I knew what I wanted and I went for it. No regrets!

Q. And what made you decide to go into primary rather than secondary teaching?

Tracey – I wanted to teach a range of subjects, not just one or two, so that I was personally challenged. I felt younger children were more receptive and eager to learn and that I could build closer relationships with children who are in my class all of the time.

Q. What was the hardest thing about a BA/QTS degree?

Tracey – The long hours! Not that the hours are anything compared to the reality of teaching full-time, but it was hard in comparison to non-teaching students who were doing about eight hours a week. We had 17 hours of lectures and seminars, plus one day in school every week. Also, the essays and assignments added to the stress.

Q. Did other (non-teaching) students feel that you were working much harder than they were?

Tracey – I lived with a modular studies student in my second year of uni who was doing the same degree subject as me. We had the same tutor for lectures and, apparently, he used to complain about the lack of dedication we (QTS students) had to the subject and 'reading around the subject'. I wasn't impressed with this and I felt it made us look bad. It devalued how hard we were really working, plus it undermined the status of teaching.

Q. Was there any conflict between the subject side of your degree and the teaching side?

Tracey – Yes, it definitely caused difficulties. There was a lack of liaison between the two sides – for instance our degree subject tutors would set essay deadlines for the same time as our QTS deadlines or teaching placements. It wasn't until the fourth year of my degree that there was someone appointed to be the liaison between the two departments. This made things a lot better as it gave us someone who understood the pressures we were under, and gave us someone who would listen to our point of view.

Q. What about the more positive sides of doing this type of degree?

Tracey – I think a positive aspect was definitely the opportunity to study a subject to degree level. I went to university to train to be a teacher, but equally importantly to further my own knowledge of a subject I enjoyed. The combination of degree and QTS enabled me to do this. If it had turned out that I didn't want to go into teaching, or if in the future I decide I want a change of career, I still have my degree which stands alone from the QTS. I'm not pigeon-holed as 'a teacher'; I am a person too.

Q. How about teaching practice? How did you find that side of things?

Tracey – At the time, the planning, routines, assessment, differentiation, the general juggling act, was a little difficult but it was all new. It got easier and now I look back, most of it has become second nature (well, almost!).

Q. What about the interview for your current job? What was that like? And why did you decide to accept the post?

Tracey – The interview was relaxed and friendly. The head, deputy and one governor asked questions about experiences, teaching styles, etc. I had to do a short presentation on a lesson that went really well. I took the job because I asked around about the school, everyone I'd spoken to said it was a good school with an excellent reputation. I'd visited the school and the staff were friendly. I think you can cope with just about anything if the staff is supportive (and they are!).

Q. Could you tell me a bit about your current teaching job?

Tracey – I teach at Bentinck Primary & Nursery School. It's an inner city primary school in Nottingham. I've just finished my first term there with a class of 32 Year Three children, the majority of whom have English as a second language and three who hardly speak English at all. I also had one child in that class with severe ADHD. I'm now four weeks into the autumn term with a class of 26 Year

Three children. Again, many of them have English as a second language, and approximately eight are on the special needs register.

Q. Are there any tips that you've got for teachers working with children who have English as a second language?

Tracey – Do make use of any support staff you have, they usually have specialist knowledge and specific skills which many class teachers don't. Also, stick to routines as far as possible. A good idea is to make a 'picture timetable', which is a basic timetable with words replaced by pictures, for example a picture of children playing outside for breaktime. Make sure you speak to the child, for example saying 'good morning', etc. Use common phrases when giving instructions, for instance I always say 'Stop, Look and Listen' when I want the class's attention. They soon pick this up. Also, use gestures, point to things and hold things up if you're talking about them.

Q. And is this your first teaching job?

Tracey – No. Before this I did two terms of supply teaching. My first week was at a school in a rural village on the Nottinghamshire/Leicestershire border, then my second week was at an Infant school in the town where I live. After that I did six months at a large school near the centre of Nottingham. They streamed children from four classes of Year Five and Six into five groups for Numeracy and Literacy, so I was the fifth teacher. In the afternoons I supported the two Year Six classes (each with 42 children in them!).

Q. It must have been hard dealing with such a huge class. Are there any tips that you've got about working with such large numbers of children?

Tracey – Stay calm! It is different teaching such a large group on supply, then full-time. I guess you need to be ultra-organized and on the ball. And have a large classroom!

Q. Could you describe one of your best moments as a teacher?

Tracey – I had a boy in my class who got himself quite angry when someone upset him or he was asked to stop doing something. He would often refuse to come in from the playground if there had been an incident during break. Sometimes, because of his anger, he would have to be physically removed from the classroom. I had tried really hard to build up a relationship with him over the term. On the last day of term he was sat at his table with a piece of paper and crayon, scribbling away. I just let him sit there and carry on while I did the register. At the end of the day he came up to me and gave me a picture he had drawn of himself and me, with a message on the back saying 'Dear Miss Nightingale, thank you for being a good teacher. You are a nice teacher.' I carry it around with me in my diary. Like a reminder of why I do this job.

Q. And how about your worst moments as a teacher?

Tracey – It's that feeling of total helplessness when you have a class of children who are trying to be as badly behaved as they can manage and not knowing what to do about it. During my supply teaching experience I was working in a school where there wasn't a whole school behaviour policy (well, there might have been on paper but it wasn't evident). I had a group of 30 Year Five and Six children in a small room for Numeracy. They'd had three other supply teachers before I arrived (in the fourth week of term!) and had basically got away with behaving how they liked. By the end of my six months with them every day I was worn out, physically and mentally and had tried every trick in the book. I remember standing at the front of the classroom one morning, looking around me at total disarray of noise, disruption and disobedience and just shrinking. I didn't know what to do.

There have also been a couple of times when I've been in physical danger. During my first week at my current school I was taking my new class swimming. One boy had been misbehaving most of the day. He had pushed into the line so I asked him to go to the back. He refused so I told him again or he'd have to stay behind. He marched past the rest of the class and crossed to the central reservation of the main road! I went to get him, and as I did he went to run across the other side of the road, just as the lights were changing! I had to hold him to prevent him crossing the road, with him struggling and cars whizzing past.

The second time the same child had been having some difficulties at home. On this occasion he had been to stay at his father's for the night and had been in a bad mood in the morning. When he came in after lunchtime he was still drinking a drink his mother had given him. He was due to go into the hall to be part of the choir for the school performance. During the register I had given him a chance to finish his drink. When it was time for him to go to the hall I asked him to leave the can on my desk. He refused, so I told him again. At this point he swore at me. I said he was to sit outside the head teacher's room. Again he refused to do as he was asked and began to slap, punch, kick and scratch me. Luckily there was another teacher there to restrain him while I took my class into the hall and fetched his mother who was there to watch the performance.

Q. How did that make you feel, being physically attacked?

Tracey – Shocked mainly, especially as it wasn't the usual kind of behaviour I got from this child. At the time I was upset as I thought we had built up a good relationship but soon after I realized it was nothing personal.

Q. What's the best thing about teaching Year Three children?

Tracey – I think it has to be that they are still eager to learn and to please. Older children, especially in the social climate of my school, tend to become more resistant to school and learning as they get older. At Year Three they still seem to hold on to the idea that education affects your life, they want to have the good things in life and that this takes hard work when you're at school. I like to think I help them get a solid grip on this belief.

Q. What about the induction process? How has that gone for you? Did you understand what was going to happen during your first year of teaching?

Tracey – No! The induction process seemed a little bit of a mystery when I first left university. It wasn't explained very well. All I knew was I have to fill in the Career Entry Profile and take it with me. When I started supply teaching after uni I did not get any non-contact time. That was tough, going from being a trainee teacher to full-time, no break, no non-contact time was hard work, but I'm glad I did it. Sink or swim. It also made me appreciate the non-contact time I have now.

Q. And how does your current non-contact time work?

Tracey – I get Tuesday mornings off timetable (I'd recommend any NQT to ask for a morning slot – I arrive at work about 8 a.m. and get a good four or five hours that way). We're lucky in our school that we have a Community Teacher who covers the NQT non-contact needs. It means you're not relying on unknown supply teachers and you can discuss the work and class beforehand and afterwards.

My NQT courses have been a little disjointed because I didn't start my induction at the beginning of the academic year, so I got the last session of the previous year's NQT induction and will start from the beginning this term.

My mentor is the deputy head which has meant I've not had as much support from him as I might have done, as he is busy with other responsibilities. Last term was also the school production and his first term as NQT mentor, so it was really a learning process for the both of us, in amongst the time-consuming demands of him organizing and rehearsing the school production. We ended up reviewing my CEP during the summer holidays! I think we're just about straight now.

Q. What about support for you as a new teacher? Who has helped you out most?

Tracey – Support from other trainee teachers is the most valuable. Just the 'you are not alone' feeling. I remember when I finally got my current job after doing two terms of supply teaching, my mum said, 'You're a proper teacher now!' Like supply teaching was just 'pretend' and it didn't count as a proper job.

Q. Would you recommend a teaching career to other people?

Tracey – I wouldn't recommend it to someone who is expecting a 9 a.m. to 3.30 p.m. job with 13 weeks' holiday, because it isn't. It's a five or usually six day week, 8 a.m. to 5 p.m. (or later) with thirteen weeks of planning, organizing, and paying extortionate rates for holidays. On the other hand it's also the most fulfilling and satisfying job when you see children grow physically, mentally and spiritually.

Newly Qualified Teacher

Secondary ICT

Welshpool High School, Welshpool, Powys

Deborah Williams

Q. Could you tell me a bit about why you decided to go into teaching?

Deborah – Basically my interest in teaching stemmed from my interest in IT. I was initially frightened of secondary teaching and thought about a career in primary. However because I was keen to teach IT I realized I would need to be in secondary for it to be at the level I desired.

Q. And what route did you take into the profession?

Deborah – I did a BSc (Hons) in Business Information Systems Management, before continuing with a PGCE in Information Technology.

Q. Could you give me some impressions about your teaching practices?

Deborah – I felt my teaching practices went extremely well. The first school had an extremely supportive senior mentor. I really jumped in at the deep end and feel better for having done this. I encountered some bad behaviour, but the teachers generally supported each other with disruptive pupils. My second placement went fantastically well; the subject mentor was really helpful. I sailed through the remainder of the course and still managed to maintain my enthusiasm!

Q. And could you tell me a bit about what you're teaching now?

Deborah – I currently teach at an 11 to 18 school, I teach GNVQ ICT, AVCE ICT and GCSE ICT. I also teach Key Skills ICT to Year Twelve at the moment, although I'm not sure what will happen in the future. Mostly I teach upper school, but I also teach two Year Eight classes and three Year Seven classes. I particularly enjoy teaching lower school, as this is where I find you get the most positive feedback from pupils. Pupils are extremely keen and the amount of work some of them get through never ceases to amaze me. I'm sure this isn't the case at all schools, I remember Year Eight at my first practice school – unenthusiastic, cheeky and generally annoying! I feel the ethos and support at this school plays a major role in the behaviour of pupils.

Q. Any difficult moments during your training or teaching so far?

Deborah – During my training it was dealing with confrontational pupils. At present it is dealing with pupils who are unenthusiastic about a subject they have chosen to take for GNVQ/GCSE. However, the support network at school means that I've not yet been faced with a confrontational pupil as such.

Q. And any subject specific problems?

Deborah – Although I have the added bonus of a PC to keep pupils happy it is difficult to control what they actually do. Pupils will quickly check email, tune into radio stations on the internet and check out their favourite sites when they think you're not looking! Also lots of pupils see IT and the internet as one. If they're in an IT class they think they should be using the internet, in reality this is rarely the case.

Q. How about the induction process as you've found it so far?

Deborah – My school has helped significantly. I am only taken for cover when necessary (not often), and I also have a named person responsible for my professional development. She provides help and advice and will come to observe lessons if required. I have been able, with her help, to identify areas for development during this year in order to keep my Career Entry Profile up to date. I can honestly say, within school I have not faced particular difficulties as an NQT. What is sometimes hard is being a mature NQT with family commitments, that extra financial burden to cope with and missing my daughter's first Christmas play at school!

Q. Would you recommend a teaching career to other people?

Deborah – Yes, of course. Having worked before coming into teaching I feel that I can compare it with the other jobs out there. Yes the hours are long, but in the past I worked an 8am to 5pm day without having lunch most days. Yes there is paperwork, but go into any office and mention paperwork – unfortunately it's a fact of life today! Yes the pupils can be a challenge – but I've worked in customer service and I've dealt with equally challenging customers using the ethos 'the customer is always right!'.

Q. Any ideas about how teaching could be improved as a career generally?

Deborah – What I have found difficult is the financial burden training to teach has left me with. A fellow student also studying IT didn't go into teaching and started on two and a half times my salary! I am also paying out a quarter of my monthly wage in childcare fees. The government should offer non-contributory pension for the first year and help with childcare if applicable. It would certainly make my life more bearable. Also the government would attract more students into teaching if they offered payment of outstanding student loans after three or five years of teaching.

Q. Could you tell me a bit about how you got your current teaching job?

Deborah – My interview arose after the school contacted me and asked me if I was interested in a post there. The interview was quite informal and I was given the opportunity to look around the school before going back to teach. I liked the fact that the head was extremely positive and open and that I was left to look around freely. Although the job entails quite a journey to and from school, the environment and atmosphere impressed me – I was sure (and still am) that I could not have found a better offer.

Q. And how has being a mature entrant to the profession affected you?

Deborah – I feel mature entrants are in a better position to see the benefits of working in teaching. However, I feel there are more commitments outside school and this makes being an NQT a little bit more difficult. Also, as most NQTs start on the same number of points the starting salary is not as attractive as it would be to people coming straight from education.

6 Anatomy of a school

This chapter offers you the 'anatomy' of a school: details of the wide spectrum of different people, jobs and roles that go to make up the whole. For each post you will find a brief description of what the role involves, along with some sample interviews from people who do these jobs. Schools vary greatly in their size and structure: from the secondary school with thousands of students and literally hundreds of staff, to the small village primary school with only a few employees.

Typical school management structures

Typical management structure of a primary school

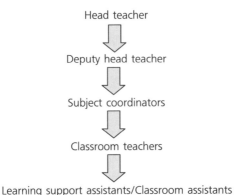

Head teacher

Deputy head teacher

Subject coordinators

Classroom teachers

Learning support assistants/Classroom assistants

Typical management structure of a secondary school

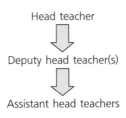

Head teacher

Deputy head teacher(s)

Assistant head teachers

Curriculum	Pastoral
Heads of faculty/Heads of department	Heads of year
⬇	⬇
Deputy HODs/Subject coordinators	Deputy heads of year
⬇	⬇
Classroom teachers (subject specialists)	Form tutors

Head teacher

The role of the head teacher can seem a bit of a mystery to normal classroom teachers. In a large school you may have little contact with the man or woman at the top, and little real idea of exactly what it is that your head teacher does on a day-to-day basis. Although you will not necessarily be aware of what is actually involved in being a head teacher, you will certainly feel the impact of a good (or bad) leader at your school.

If you're interested in moving up the promotion ladder, you can find a great deal more information about school leadership from the National College for School Leadership (see the Directory for contact details). The DfES publishes 'National Standards for Head Teachers' and within these are 'key areas' of headship which give an outline of the key roles involved in being a head teacher.

- Strategic direction and development of the school
- Teaching and learning
- Leading and managing staff
- Efficient and effective deployment of staff and resources
- Accountability

> Head teacher (secondary)
>
> Tuxford School, Nottinghamshire
>
> Chris Pickering

Q. Why did you become a teacher in the first place?

Chris – Because we didn't get any formal careers guidance in school, and I fell into it. Fortunately, I took to it like a duck to water, and now I wouldn't do anything else.

Q. And how did you originally qualify and in what subjects?

Chris – I did a teaching certificate which took three years, followed by a BEd for one year. Then I took two diplomas in education after I'd been teaching a couple of years. I trained as a Geography/PE teacher originally. I taught both on teaching practices, but I've never taught PE since.

Q. What are your feelings about the way that teachers are trained nowadays?

Chris – I think we've got some much better trained teachers, because the training establishments have got their acts together. Student teachers are being trained to teach, and trained in the art of teaching, as opposed to being trained academically.

Q. And what are your thoughts about a teaching degree versus the PGCE route?

Chris – I think we have better trained teachers who come through the specialist teaching degree course. That's not to say that you don't get good teachers with PGCEs, but I would far prefer to see somebody trained to do the job than be swayed by the offer of money after doing a first degree.

Q. How would you describe yourself as a teacher, when you were a full-time classroom practitioner?

Chris – I was determined to get the best results out of those children, but I was not necessarily the greatest risk taker. 15 years ago, that wasn't high priority on people's lists. I was quite didactic. Essentially in those days it was about getting people through their 'O' levels. Things have changed away from knowledge based learning to the development of skills and concepts, which needs different methods of teaching. In the classroom now I'm completely different to what I was like as a full-time teacher. I've had to adapt like everyone else.

Q. Could you tell me about the route that you took to become a head teacher?

Chris – My first teaching post was in Doncaster in a large comprehensive school. I was there for five years. I went for my first promotion after two years, to become a second in the Geography department. I left there to become head of Geography at a school in Derbyshire. After two years there I was promoted again to head of upper school and head of department. After five years there I went to a boys' school in Buxton. When the boys' school amalgamated with the girls' school, I got the deputy headship. In my last year there I was acting head, before getting a permanent headship at a school in Sheffield. After three years there I got the headship at Tuxford and this is my sixth year here.

Q. When you originally came into teaching, did you plan to become a head teacher?

Chris – No. I've not actually had a plan in my career at all. I basically tried to do my best at every level and that's how I get satisfaction, by doing my best and people recognizing that what I do is good. Then the opportunities just came along, or I suddenly felt that it was time to go for something else.

Q. As a head teacher, how are you involved in the classroom now?

Chris – I'm intimately involved in all the different initiatives and developments that impact in the classroom. I do a little bit of teaching, but I don't think it's absolutely essential for head teachers to teach in the classroom. I think it's essential for head teachers to keep in contact with the classroom and have the ability to teach, but I find that every hour that I spend in the classroom has to be matched with an hour for marking and preparation which basically reduces my working week. We're moving into an era now where it's increasingly hard to combine classroom teaching, leadership and management responsibility with quality delivery in the classroom. I would always ensure that I had the skills to step into the classroom and do a good job, if ever I was called on to do it, though.

Q. Would you recommend your job to teachers just starting out on their careers, or would it be too stressful for some?

Chris – The stresses and strains of headship are immense, but there are stresses and strains at all levels. When people say, 'I could never become a head, it's too stressful' then my response is 'well if you find that you can cope as a teacher, then you'd be able to cope with headship too'.

Q. What sort of person does a head teacher need to be?

Chris – It takes the sort of person who is happy never to be praised, who is happy to carry the can, and to bail people out, and who can bite their tongue, and still remain positive and enthusiastic. You also have to be the sort of person who doesn't wear their heart on their sleeve. No matter how frustrated or angry or stressed I am, that has to stay with me. Otherwise you can have a terrible effect on other people.

Q. What skills does a head teacher need to have?

Chris – Multi-tasking, having many things on the go all at once. Having the capacity to switch from something that is very mentally demanding, which is high powered in respect of the impact the decisions you make will have, to something which may be very trivial to you, but which to other people is very important. You get that all day. I don't think you get that sort of pressure in industry. You can never be sure that things are going to go well for any longer than a few minutes. I can come in and something will happen which is a real success, then in the next five minutes something happens which brings you straight down into the trough. It's crest, trough, crest, trough, that sort of roller-coaster ride all the time.

Q. What's your approach to dealing with your staff?

Chris – My attitude is that teachers are your most valuable resource and therefore they need to be treated as such. My philosophy is to invest as much as I possibly can in the staff – in their training, their morale, their working conditions, in the way I treat them personally. I think that time and money invested in that way reaps its rewards in terms of good work. That's why this school puts its Investors in People status at the heart of things. I'm talking about all staff, too, not just teachers.

Q. What sort of person would be your 'ideal' teacher?

Chris – Someone with energy, enthusiasm, a desire to make a difference with children. A really first class classroom practitioner with a sense of humour and a sense of perspective.

Q. And how do teachers keep that energy up in the long-term?

Chris – A lot of how teachers react isn't just about life in the classroom, it's about how the school as a whole is managed and run. The stresses and pressures on teachers can be multiplied many fold if the working conditions and the atmosphere in the school is not good. I passionately believe that. The morale here is such that for 90 per cent of the teachers it alleviates the downsides of the job, and helps them to retain the energy and enthusiasm.

Q. When you're looking to promote someone, what sort of person are you looking for?

Chris – Somebody who has vision, who appreciates what it is to plan, set targets, achieve targets. Somebody who can manage people – who can challenge poor performance, who monitors and evaluates, analyses and brings the best out of people. Who can build and lead teams. Someone with initiative, vision, ideas and the capacity to carry them through and make a difference. There's not many people around in middle management positions who've got those qualities. There are lots of middle managers who believe it's all about the administrative aspects, and who shy away from the real, hard-nosed bits of the job.

Q. And finally, could you describe for me one of the best moments of your career, something that really sticks in your mind as making it all worthwhile?

Chris – It's difficult to pick one out. I doubt that one moment would make it all worthwhile. I have received some excellent feedback from parents on a number of occasions. People who have bothered to put pen to paper and pass on their thanks and gratitude. Achieving the best ever GCSE results, gaining technology status and perhaps above all the accolade paid to the school after our last Investors in People assessment stand out above most things. Our assessment report began 'Tuxford is a model organization, one which has people (staff and pupils) and their development at its core'. This tells me that we are on the right lines.

Deputy head teacher

The role of the deputy head teacher, and the type of management responsibilities that he or she may have varies widely from school to school. Some large schools may have a number of deputy heads, whilst others may only have a single deputy, and then a number of assistant head teachers. In a school with a number of deputies (perhaps two or three), one may perhaps be responsible for curriculum issues, another might look after the pastoral aspects of school life, whilst another might deal with timetabling and behavioural issues. Again, the way that these responsibilities are organized varies very widely between schools.

The 'professional duties' of a deputy head teacher include taking over the role of the head if he or she is away. The deputy is expected to carry out the duties of a teacher and also any management responsibilities that the head assigns. Deputy heads are expected to play a major role in working out the aims and policies of the school. As with the head teacher, there is no limit on the number of working hours that the deputy head teacher must do.

Deputy head teacher

Tuxford School, Nottinghamshire

Geoff Lloyd

Q. Could you tell me about why you originally became a teacher?

Geoff – It was a combination of a number of factors, the main ones being a desire to work with young children and a wish to transmit my knowledge and love of chemistry to others. Also, the flexibility that teaching offers in deciding where to live and the holidays.

Q. And how long have you been in the teaching profession now?

Geoff – 27 years.

Q. What subjects have you taught?

Geoff – I've taught Science at Key Stage Three, Chemistry at GCSE and 'A' level, and Psychology at 'A' level.

Q. Why did you choose to move into management?

Geoff – I initially wanted to lead and manage a department, especially to develop the area of teaching and learning and other ideas. Also, we needed the money because we had a young family and a 'normal' teacher's pay was poor. Once I had been a head of department I then wanted another challenge, in particular to influence colleagues and formulate policies and vision. I was interested in my professional development and the appreciation that I needed to move forward or my view of forward.

Q. And how did you move up the scale to become a deputy?

Geoff – I started as a head of Chemistry, then I took on the additional role of TVEI coordinator. After that, I was promoted to senior teacher, and from there I became a deputy head.

Q. Could you tell me a bit more about your role as a deputy head?

Geoff – I'm the single deputy in the school and my main role is curriculum, although since Christmas this is being transferred to another and younger member of staff! I've undertaken most roles at senior level although not the budget. I support the pastoral system as a generic responsibility. However, I'm renegotiating my role with Chris, the head. He's keen to expand some of the areas I already undertake, for example self-review, including data analysis and target setting. Also, Key Stage Three manager and technology status manager and no doubt one or two more.

Q. What are some of the positive aspects for a teacher of moving into management? Do you find it's possible to combine classroom teaching with a management role?

Geoff – When I was head of department my main focus was the classroom and I enjoyed the development side of the job. I still try and maintain this as much as possible, but because of the number of initiatives and other responsibilities I'm less effective as a teacher. However, I appreciate the demands made on my colleagues and I also experience the rhythm of the school. I enjoy being part of the leadership team: helping to develop a vision for the school and being able to guide, implement, support, change, counsel and innovate. The pressures are great but so are the rewards.

Q. What would you say are some of the best things about being a teacher? What gives you satisfaction personally?

Geoff – Any good lesson gives me a buzz. It's good to give a well paced lesson, with the youngsters on task, well motivated and enjoying the learning. Also, it gives me satisfaction to see young people going on to study Chemistry at a higher level, or feeling they can do Chemistry. I like to see understanding developing in the students.

Q. And what about the downside?

Geoff – The opposite of the above really, especially mishandling an incident with a youngster in terms of their behaviour.

Q. In your opinion, what makes a 'good' teacher? What do you look for in applicants to the school?

Geoff – I feel that it's important to focus on personal qualities, what do the pupils rate as important? Kindness, support, fairness and firmness are vital. Someone who is well organized, with a sense of humour, who is energetic, positive and motivated. It's also important that these qualities are shown under pressure, especially when a teacher is tired. After all that is in place, we can focus on the knowledge and the teaching skills. Even if someone doesn't have these, there is the potential for these to be developed. For a promoted post, a teacher needs to have management skills and leadership or the potential for it.

Q. What could be done to make teaching a better, more attractive profession?

Geoff – The status of teachers has been undermined by the media and politicians, anything for a cheap point. There's no trust between the parties. We need less initiatives, or at least better thought out initiatives. We also need joined-up thinking from the politicians. There needs to be an appreciation of the job and the pressures that come with it. Also, more respect from the public and from the growing number of pupils that don't respect us. There needs to be less of the 'blame a teacher' culture that exists at the moment.

Q. What about in the past? Were things better then?

Geoff – There were certainly less initiatives and less interference. There was more time to do the job in the past. Also, there were more 'characters' in the profession. However, teachers overall were less professional and I do feel that standards of teaching have improved now.

Q. And finally, what about the future for you? What does that hold?

Geoff – We have a strong vision for the future of Tuxford and the surrounding rural areas, and I'd like to continue playing a key part in implementing this vision. I think this will take five years and then I'll look for a move. Perhaps into part-time teaching or a secondment onto a project. Maybe I'll go to the DfES and tell them what for! I hope that if I lose my drive and enthusiasm then I'll be able to move with dignity, and with the support of others, to another stage and ensure progress continues at Tuxford.

Assistant head teacher

The position of 'assistant head teacher' is a fairly recent innovation, and is basically designed to replace the previous post of 'senior teacher'. As with the deputy head teacher, the assistant head may take responsibility for a particular area within the school (see Tina's comments below).

Assistant head teacher

Tuxford School, Nottinghamshire

Tina Powell

Q. Could you describe for me the route you took into teaching, and how you became an assistant head teacher?

Tina – I did a degree in Zoology with Chemistry, then I did a PGCE. After teaching for three years, I stopped to have a family. Six years later I got back into teaching. I started back as a supply teacher, and because I was a Science teacher I used to pick up lots of contracts – a term, two terms, a year. I came to Tuxford as a Maths teacher originally. They had an opening for a Science teacher and I said 'well actually, I'm a Science teacher' so I transferred to that post.

As far as promotion goes, I started running Key Stage Three Science, then I just applied for jobs that came up. I organized the SATs when they first came in, just off my own back. I just asked whether they needed somebody to organize it. I got that job, then I sort of bolted jobs on. I've probably been quite ambitious. When I was young I didn't want to stay as a standard teacher all the time so I would see an opening and take it. This school's been very good because they allow you to do that.

Q. So now you're an assistant head teacher. Could you tell me about what the position is, and the type of role you have?

Tina – It's like the old post of senior teacher. There are five assistant heads at the school, we've got a big leadership team. Each of us is in charge of one particular area. There are managers in charge of Key Stage Three, Key Stages Four and Five, curriculum, pupil progress (that's me) and personnel.

Q. And what does your own role involve?

Tina – I'm in charge of pupil progress, assessing and tracking. I manage everything to do with assessment – reports and so on. I talk to heads of department to ensure that they're tracking pupil progress.

Q. Could you describe an aspect of the job that gives you satisfaction?

Tina – I like the fact that my ideas can help to take the school on, it's not just the pupils anymore, but it's moving the school on as a whole. And we have a staff who are very willing to do things, who are keen to go along with new initiatives. One of the things that I started a long time ago was mentoring for Year 11 students. We put this idea to the staff that they might give up their lunchtimes to mentor the Year 11's, and they agreed. So they give up their lunch hours to talk to the pupils about revision, from February through to study leave. That's the busiest time, and they give up that time voluntarily for one-to-one mentoring, about 40 staff. That's the sort of willingness people have.

Q. Why do you think the staff here have such a positive attitude to the school? Is it to do with the way that the school is managed?

Tina – There's the feeling that staff can progress through, the school is very encouraging to staff, they're allowed to take initiative. You don't get a promotion because you've been here 10 years, but you do if you've got good ideas. There's a feeling of opportunity and I've certainly benefited from that. We have a wacky walk which happens every year, and the staff give up their time to go and stand in a field. They're happy to do that because there's a good team spirit here. As managers we give them reasons why they have to do things. Generally we get everybody on side and people muck in.

Q. What about one of your best moments as a teacher? What would that be?

Tina – It's when I teach somebody all the way through from Year Seven to GCSE and 'A' level. This particular boy I'm thinking of struggled at 'A' level, but he passed and got his certificate. He said to me 'Look what I've got, this is absolutely brilliant'. When they succeed it gives you such a buzz.

Q. Would you recommend a teaching career to other people?

Tina – I think so, if they're the right sort of person. Your colleagues are always interesting, always on a par with you. When I talk to people who work in other fields, they don't have that. Okay, you've got the bad kids, but the good kids are great, or even the bad class who you have a good lesson with, you do get satisfaction out of that. There is a huge amount of work, you take a lot of stuff home with you, but there are more goods than bads. What I like is that it's about relating to people, and that keeps you young. On the down days, when you're really tired, that's when it gets to you and you feel like you haven't got the energy. I usually manage to keep going very well in school, then I flop when I get home.

Q. How has it been for you combining teaching with having a family?

Tina – My daughter was six and my son was four when I started doing supply work. I wanted to be able to take my children to school, and the agency would be quite flexible. It was difficult organizing childcare, although it's easier nowadays. Once it got past that early stage it all got much easier. They both came to this school, but that was alright. I taught my daughter for GCSE and 'A' level and we had very much a pupil–teacher relationship. I taught my son for 'A' level, and he used to call me 'mumsie' as a joke.

Q. What do you believe makes a good teacher?

Tina – You've got to be honest, and have a sense of fun. You have to lay down your rules – the limits of where you're prepared for things to go. I tend to listen to the children – are they interested in what I'm saying? And if they're not, I've got to be flexible. Good teachers are flexible, they listen to what's going on and are willing to change the lesson if needed. You've got be adaptable and think fast.

Q. And finally, what advice would you give other teachers about staying in the profession for a long time and avoiding cynicism?

Tina – Perhaps it's down to personality. I do enjoy mixing with people, and that's important. As a teacher, you also need to get a sense of control. If you haven't got that, it probably gets you down. I've been lucky that I've been able to progress through, as well; that has helped to keep things fresh for me. What you have to remember is that you're there for the children, to help them succeed. I enjoy being in the classroom, so although I've gone into management I do still fight to stay in the classroom.

Head of department or faculty

In the secondary school, the different subjects are divided into departments or faculties. A department is a smaller unit, in which each subject or subject area has its own management, meetings, area of the school buildings, and so on. In some cases, a single department might have responsibility for more than one area: for instance an English department might also take care of Media Studies and Drama; a Humanities department would include both History and Geography teachers. In many cases, teachers in a single department which covers different curriculum areas would teach each of those subjects.

With the faculty system, each faculty includes a number of different but related subjects grouped together. These groupings vary from school to school, depending on management decisions about which subjects 'work best' when placed together. For instance, in one school Art, Music, Dance and Drama may be grouped together as a 'Performing Arts Faculty', whilst in another school Dance, Drama and PE may be put under the same umbrella.

Alongside the responsibilities of the 'normal' classroom teachers, as listed in the section 'Classroom teachers', managers also have a huge range of other duties, including those listed below.

- Organizing the planning and delivery of the curriculum.
- Managing assessment, recording and reporting within the subject.
- Helping to select and interview teachers and non-teaching staff for the department.
- Helping to provide professional development.
- Helping with the induction and assessment of NQTs.
- Managing the work of other teachers.
- Taking part in reviewing, developing and managing activities related to the curriculum and to whole school issues.

Head of English Department

Caroline Forgeron

Q. Why did you decide to become a teacher?

Caroline – It was something I'd always wanted to do. To start with I wanted to teach abroad. That didn't work out, but I found teaching in England was just as good. It's probably more of a challenge too, which is very rewarding.

Q. Could you tell me about your career so far?

Caroline – I started out in London as a classroom teacher of English and French. I did that for two years. Then I dropped the English to teach 'A' level Psychology. After that I took a promotion as assistant exam secretary. Finally I moved to my current post of head of English which I've been doing for four years now.

Q. Why did you decide to move into management?

Caroline – It seemed a logical step for me. I wasn't satisfied with the way things were being organized in my department when I was a classroom teacher. I constantly felt I could do things better. To me there wasn't enough emphasis on basic skills or continuity within the department so moving to head of department meant I could choose how I organized schemes of work, etc., and allowed me to develop the ethos I wanted. I've been lucky at my current school in that the department has grown a great deal since I've been here. We started with only three English teachers and now there are seven full-time teachers and also several part-timers. Most of these teachers were NQTs which meant although they didn't have lots of experience they had lots of new and exciting ideas. This also meant I was able to do lots of the training within the department myself. We are now a very strong and united team.

Q. What do you see as the main roles and responsibilities of a head of department?

Caroline – The role of HOD means you have to be very organized – that was the first thing I learnt when I took up the post. You have to manage all the stress of exams – SATs, GCSEs, the new 'A' levels. In addition there are further exams such as the Year Seven Progress tests and internal school exams to deal with. Another responsibility which seems to take up lots of time is schemes of work – especially with the new Literacy Strategy which means all our current schemes of work need to be reorganized! The GCSE syllabus also has this effect. Then there are things such as stock, stationery, discipline issues, coursework moderation, exam moderation, evaluating baseline data to predict next year's results.

I really enjoy deciding on schemes of work and finding new resources which I know will motivate the boys. I've always been interested in reading so this tends to influence me, I suppose. Being a Head of English also means I'm involved in whole school literacy initiatives and so I've had to deliver INSET to the whole school on training days about reading, writing and spelling. Although this was quite nerve wracking it was also quite exciting knowing you could be helping the whole school take on a more consistent approach to basic literacy skills.

Q. What sort of advantages and disadvantages are there in running your own department?

Caroline – I think this is a very personal thing. For me lack of time is always a disadvantage. I only get one extra free a week for running a large department – other smaller subjects get the same which has always seemed unfair. Advantages are things like having more power and control over issues in the school. As an HOD you are asked for your opinion (sometimes!) about new initiatives. As a classroom teacher your voice would often go unheard.

Q. And what are the best and worst things about the role?

Caroline – I have always liked the fact I'm in charge! The trouble is that also means carrying the can when things go wrong. I'm very lucky in that my department are a good team – we all get on really well, not just in school but socially, too. Making decisions about things is never hard work – the main problem is usually that we have too many ideas!

Q. What sort of qualities do you feel make a good teacher? What do you look for in applicants to your department?

Caroline – For me the main ingredients for a good teacher have to be enthusiasm and confidence. They need to have a sound knowledge of their subject but more importantly love what they are doing.

Q. Could you describe one of your best moments as a teacher?

Caroline – The best moment for me is when a student who has always seemed very weak or under-confident makes some monumental step. It might be a very small step but they suddenly realize that they can achieve it. That is very rewarding.

Q. And what about your worst moment?

Caroline – That's a very difficult one. It's probably not anything to do with the teaching in the classroom. It would have to be something like watching a very ineffective teacher giving INSET on a training day and thinking the whole time about what you could be doing with your time instead.

Q. Finally, what sort of changes do you feel need to be made for teaching to become a more attractive career choice?

Caroline – More time and more money would definitely give anyone a bigger incentive to join the profession. Also the constant bombardment of new initiatives doesn't really inspire anyone – as soon as you think you've got it all organized they change it again. It used to be every few years, which was acceptable – now it seems to be every year. Most of us just can't keep up with it all – however hard you work.

Subject coordinator

Subject coordinators are found at both primary and secondary level. In the primary school, a subject coordinator would help with planning the curriculum and delivery of their 'own' area (often their specialism at degree level). The coordinator might help create lesson plans and resources for the whole school, and could also hold seminars or training sessions covering the latest ideas and developments within their subject. There may also be coordinators with special responsibility for literacy and numeracy.

In the secondary school, a subject (or key stage) coordinator might work within a department or faculty, focusing on one smaller area of that subject. For instance, within a Science department there might be subject coordinators for Biology, Chemistry and Physics. Alternatively, there could be key stage coordinators, one for Key Stage Three and another for Key Stage Four.

Head of year

In a secondary school, the head of year is responsible for the pastoral care of an entire year group. This might mean, in a large school, the responsibility for 200 or more students. Often, the head of year 'stays with' his or her year group as they progress up the school, getting to know the students in that year very well in the process. There are sometimes separate posts for the heads of Year Seven and sixth form, to take into account the additional responsibilities that these jobs might entail (for instance the induction of new students into the school for a head of Year Seven).

A head of year undertakes a wide range of pastoral and administrative responsibilities, just a few of which are listed below.

- Ensuring that registers are taken correctly, absence notes received, and so on.
- Meeting with form tutors on a regular basis to discuss relevant issues.
- Dealing with the behaviour issues within the year group. This would include meeting with individual students, keeping records of incidents, meeting with parents, and so on.
- Taking year assemblies.
- Planning trips and rewards for the year group.
- Dealing with examination related issues, e.g. SATs in Year Nine, GCSEs in Year Eleven.

> Head of Year
>
> Tuxford School, Nottinghamshire
>
> Barry Wolff

Q. How long have you been teaching?

Barry – 15 years.

Q. And what route did you take to qualify as a teacher?

Barry – I did a BA in German, then a PGCE at Glasgow University.

Q. What was the PGCE like?

Barry – It was excellent. I loved every aspect of it. I loved all the theory and the teaching practices. I did three TPs, one in a middle class school, one school that was 'half and half' and one 'down amongst the dead men'.

Q. And what was that last experience like?

Barry – Well, because I had no point of reference to compare it to, it seemed fine to me. The school was in an extremely deprived area in Glasgow. The kids were from disadvantaged backgrounds, and had all the social problems that come with that. But my experience was all positive, the head of department gave me lots of support and I enjoyed my TP there. It was very exciting, putting all my ideas into practice.

Q. Why did you decide to become a teacher?

Barry – When I finished university I went to Berlin for a year. I wasn't sure what I was going to do, but I'd always been involved in youth work and there was nothing else that appealed to me. I thought I might as well give it a go, it certainly wasn't a vocation at that time. I'd always got on quite well with children.

Q. Can you describe one of your really good moments in teaching?

Barry – I suppose my highest moments in teaching are out of the classroom. I've directed about six school productions over the years and starting from nothing, over a short space of time, you get a bunch of people to create something together. You work with pupils of all ages and all abilities on a project which you see through to the end. The whole school's buzzing, everybody wants to help. The feel good factor is quite incredible.

I was called into my line manager's office last year, and he told me how impressed he was. I basically got all the naughty kids in that year and involved them in the play. He said to me, 'I've only just realized what you've been doing this term. We haven't had any problems with this one and that one like we did in Year Seven because they've been with you doing rehearsals.' I had people who'd never said a word before on stage in that production. It's all about positive relationships.

Q. And would you recommend a teaching career to other people?

Barry – Yes. I say to everybody, it's certainly worth it. Give it a go and see how long you can last. It's never dull, something different happens every day because you're dealing with people. It can be extremely enjoyable – the highs that you get from teaching are certainly as high as you might get in a workplace. When something goes well, a lesson for instance, it's wonderful. You know you're alive when you work as a teacher.

Q. What about your role as head of year? Could you tell me a bit about that?

Barry – This is my fourth year in the job, and I'm currently head of Year Nine. I picked them up when they were in Year Eight. There's a cyclical system in the school, although the head of Year Seven stays the same.

Q. Could you tell me about how and why you went for the post of head of year?

Barry – I was originally deputy head of English, then head of English for a term, in a school that was deep into special measures. I left that school shortly before it closed to come to Tuxford. I didn't enjoy all the admin and paperwork of being a subject manager and I'd always wanted to do pastoral work. Speaking personally, I find that the pastoral work keeps me going, because I got a bit bored with classroom teaching after 15 years of doing it. Also, with all the new restrictions and guidelines coming in, English teaching is a lot more prescriptive now. When I came to Tuxford School I said I was interested in pastoral work and Chris, the head teacher, got me shadowing an existing head of year. She got promotion, and within a short space of time I got promoted to head of year.

Q. What aspects of the job of head of year really appeal to you?

Barry – The relationships with children and with parents. I have 195 children in the year group. I'm always on the phone to parents – they trust me, so the children know that they can't get away with things at home. Sometimes I feel a

117

bit like an overgrown tutor, because all the pupils come to me, they all know me. I like to see them all, I'm very inclusive, whether they're A* students or whether they're always naughty it makes no difference, I treat them all the same. I also have extremely good relationships with a huge number of parents. I took my whole year group to France on a week's residential, it was a team building exercise. It was absolutely wonderful.

Q. What are your feelings as a teacher and a head of year about dealing with behaviour issues?

Barry – One of the things that I really enjoy doing is conflict resolution, because a school is a human place full of human beings. I am totally anti punitive measures. I'm very much against any sort of sanctions. Of course I employ sanctions, and I try to stick to the school's policy as much as I can, but I do bend it. I don't think that punishment works 99 per cent of the time. It can be extremely damaging. I'm very much into counselling and getting people to sort out their problems. I want to fight disaffection, and sanctions create disaffection because people get membership of a club. They get a reputation and they live up to that reputation. They join the 'naughty club' and they get a great deal of kudos from it. I try to keep my pupils well away from that sort of culture. One of my ambitions is not to have any disaffected pupils in my year group. I'm determined to do that.

Q. And what about the downsides of the job?

Barry – It's very difficult to measure success in tutoring. A lot of staff don't regard tutoring very highly, they regard it as register taking. The feeling is, if you've got a problem, give it to the head of year and the problem will disappear.

Q. Any tips about teaching that you would like to pass on to other people?

Barry – When I started teaching, in a wonderful school in Corby, there were seven probationers. The head took us into his office and he said to us, 'the sweetest sound to any child is the sound of their own name'. It's one of the few things that has stuck in my mind, and I always say to my tutors, 'learn people's names'. It's the crucial thing. Until you know somebody's name, you're running uphill and you can't complain when things go wrong. You're saying to that child that you don't consider them important enough to use their name.

Advanced skills teacher

Becoming an advanced skills teacher (AST) allows teachers who want to stay in the classroom, rather than moving into management, to further their careers (and get paid a higher salary). The government provides various 'signs of excellence' for those wishing to become ASTs. These include high level teaching, classroom management and behaviour management skills, as well as quality of planning and assessment, and relationships with students.

An AST is expected to spend 80 per cent of time teaching his or her own classes. For the remaining 20 per cent, additional 'outreach' responsibilities would be undertaken, so that good practice is shared with the wider community. Typically, the AST would spend four days a week in his or her own school, then one day working with others.

Advanced skills teacher

Additional responsibilities might include:

- giving demonstration and 'model' lessons
- helping schools in special measures
- supporting lessons of other teachers
- helping with induction and mentoring
- developing quality resources

ASTs are paid on a separate pay spine from normal teachers, and they are not awarded additional management points, or money for recruitment and retention. The AST also works under different conditions to the normal classroom teacher, for instance the specified number of working hours do not apply. For a teacher to become an AST, they must first have reached point nine on the teacher's pay scale, then passed the threshold.

Form tutor

In a secondary school, the form tutor is responsible for the pastoral care of his or her form or tutor group. Although not every teacher in the school will necessarily be a form tutor as well, in the majority of cases a secondary school teacher will, at some point, also be expected to fulfil this role. The form tutor undertakes a number of responsibilities, some of which are listed below.

- Giving out various routine paperwork, such as school diaries (at the start of the year), parents' evening timetables, detention reminders, etc.
- Managing the form group during registration (some schools set specific activities to be done during form time, such as private reading).
- Taking the register.
- Chasing up notes for absence.
- Checking that students are wearing the correct uniform, and dealing with them appropriately if they are not.
- Passing on information to the tutor group.
- Assisting with option choices in Year nine.

- Helping with other career or further education decisions.
- Checking school diaries on a regular basis.
- Collating information on tutees from subject teachers, e.g. about behaviour and rewards.
- Talking to individual students about problems/issues.
- Meeting with parents as necessary.
- Preparing presentations for year assemblies.

In addition to the responsibilities listed above, the form tutor might also undertake a number of additional jobs under their own volition. These could include activities designed to cement a positive feeling within the tutor group, such as those listed below.

- Creating a 'form notice board' for the group, which might contain
  - the names of the tutees
  - pictures, messages or other personal contributions
  - jobs rota (e.g. collecting the register).
- Keeping a chart of merits/commendations received.
- Giving birthday cards.
- Giving individual 'tutor certificates' for good work or behaviour.
- Collecting money for presents, and getting cards signed, e.g. when a member of the tutor group leaves the school.

Year 9 Form Tutor

Second in Maths Department

John Bentley Secondary School, Calne, Wiltshire

Chris Smy

Q. Could you tell me about how you trained to be a teacher?

Chris – I did a BSc degree in Maths with Statistics, then a PGCE, both at Bristol University. I wanted to do a maths degree because I enjoyed doing the maths. There were also more options than if I'd done a BEd, if I'd changed my mind about teaching.

Q. And what teaching practices did you do?

Chris – In the first term we did two days a week, plus a four-week block. Then the whole of the spring term we were in school, right from January to April, on a two thirds timetable. That's certainly enough as a student, when you're spending an hour planning every hour's lesson. Then we had a three-week block in the summer.

Q. What made you decide to go into teaching in the first place?

Chris – That's a difficult question. I went to an independent boarding school, and I decided in the sixth form that I wanted to teach. I had some really good maths teachers. My Year 10 and 11 teacher was very good: her teaching style and my learning style matched. She was very traditional, she gave us notes and it all made sense. I really enjoy the subject. I enjoy doing maths all day, it's great.

Q. How long have you been teaching now, and what's your current job like?

Chris – I'm in my sixth year of teaching. I love it here at Calne. The support here is brilliant, especially in terms of behaviour management. You can ask the management to come and do something and they will. I haven't had to use that, but it's nice to know that they're there if you need them. You can say to a kid, 'if you continue doing that, I'm going to have to get a member of management', and they usually stop, which is nice.

Within the department, I'm getting really good support. I can chat to the year teams and management, if I have any problems. They're approachable, that's really important. We're a Phase One school for the Numeracy strategy, so there's lots of interesting stuff going on.

Q. Could you tell me about one really good experience you've had in your career as a teacher so far?

Chris – It's just a small thing really. I've got a Foundation Year 11 group, which is quite hard work. You can't get a 'C' at Foundation level, so the students think 'right we can't pass, so there's no point', which makes it hard going. We were doing some stuff on area, an investigation that's one of my favourites. Anyway, there were three girls sitting at the back of the class, working collaboratively. With a bit of help they managed to prove the result algebraically, which is basically the proof of Pythagoras' theorum. I said 'that is absolutely fantastic'. They got a real buzz from that, a real sense of having achieved something.

Q. And what about a bad experience that you've had as a teacher?

Chris – OFSTED. It was in my second year of teaching. They were doing half lesson observations, so they couldn't get a full picture. I was teaching a Year 7 mixed ability group, period five, right after they'd had PE. The whole situation was just set up for problems, and all the Year Seven Maths classes that they saw got 'unsatisfactories'. The beginning of the lesson was good, and OFSTED didn't see that. I felt hard done by. It didn't bother the head, or the head of department, or even me particularly. I actually felt I had been getting somewhere with those kids, but it just happened that OFSTED came in when the lesson had degenerated.

Q. Could you tell me about your experiences as a form tutor in your first year of teaching?

Chris – In my first school, I had a Year 11 tutor group in my NQT year, and that was horrible. I had a lot of support from my head of year, but it was very very hard work. The support was brilliant, but it was very hard work in terms of discipline. That was probably my weakest area, and it probably still is. I didn't have the experience to deal with it. I was thinking, 'that's great, they'll leave and I'll get a Year Seven group, and I'll know where I'm at'. All the other new teachers had a Year Seven group, and that was great for them, because it's the blind leading the blind.

Q. And what happened at the end of that year? Did you get a Year Seven form at that point?

Chris – No! The deputy head came up to me and said 'would you like a sixth form group next year?' and I said 'yes please'. So I had three years of sixth form tutor groups. That was good, because I was relatively new out of university, I knew the systems, I had a good idea of what university was like.

Q. What about your tutor group at your current school? What are they like?

Chris – My current tutor group can be an issue. They're Year Nine. They just can't be quiet during tutor time and PSE. They tip back on their chairs and wander around the room. At first, they tried to wander in and out of the room, although I've stopped that now. They'll do things like flicking bits of paper, and that sort of low level disruption. It's difficult, because it's not a 'get out go to head of year or senior management' issue.

Q. What methods have you used to cope with them?

Chris – At first, I tried waiting for silence, but 20 minutes later I was still waiting, so obviously that didn't work. Then I sent one of the nice kids to go and get the head of year, but I didn't feel like a failure doing this, I didn't feel that I couldn't handle it. I felt that I was handling it the right way. In fact, it was only six kids who were causing problems, but that was enough to mean that it was hard to deal with. The head of year is great, he's very supportive.

We've now introduced a behaviour policy with the tutor group. They might lose their break times, or we have a time out room, which is a fairly major sanction. It's easier to deal with discipline within the department, because we can move kids between classes for an internal time out. For instance, we might put them in with a top set or sixth form group.

Q. What about the other aspects of pastoral work, such as dealing with students' emotional concerns?

Chris – I don't really feel qualified to deal with people's emotional issues. When a child comes to me and says 'she's not my friend anymore', it's hard for me to deal with it.

Q. How about actually teaching your tutor group? What's that like?

Chris – I teach them for PSE every three out of four weeks and I also teach some of my tutor group in my Maths group. In that situation, they're the worst behaved in the class. They feel that they can behave like they do in tutor period in my class.

Q. So is it harder to discipline the kids who are in your form? Is discipline harder as a form tutor?

Chris – I know where I am within the Maths department, we're all together. I know where the head of department is, I can find him. But the Year Nine tutor groups are scattered throughout the school. I don't necessarily know where the head of Year Nine is – he may be in his office, he may be visiting a tutor group. Although we meet as a year team, we tend to congregate as a department. I think if you get a tutor group in Year Seven, you can be horrible to them for a term, and they're innocent enough to be scared of you. It's harder starting with a group higher up the school.

Q. I understand you have a young child. What's it like combining a full-time teaching job with being a parent?

Chris – Very busy! Our baby is in nursery full-time, and she's loving it. The daily routine is hard: we have to get up very early, wake up our daughter, get her ready, take her to nursery, then get into school. So, there's no time to do any school stuff before staff briefing. Then it's teaching all day, a short lunch break, maybe helping sixth formers after school. I like to leave promptly and pick up my daughter, then we're with her until 7pm and after that it's have dinner, start marking, then straight to bed!

My wife and I are both teachers, but my wife has given up her responsibility. She was a second in department for three years. Of course, our priority is our daughter. The summer holidays are fantastic, though. We're both off work, so it's brilliant, we can have a great time.

Classroom teacher

Unless you are a non-teaching member of senior management, your main professional role on a daily basis will be as a classroom teacher. The list below gives a summary of the main duties of the classroom teacher.

- *Teaching*
  - Planning and preparing lessons.
  - Teaching students according to their educational needs.
  - Setting and marking work for school and homework.
  - Assessing, recording and reporting on how the students are progressing, and what their attainment is.
- *Other activities*
  - Looking after the students' progress and 'well-being'.
  - Offering advice on issues related to students' education, social matters, further education and careers.
  - Recording and reporting about students' personal and social needs.
  - Liasing with parents and other bodies outside the school.
  - Taking part in meetings related to any of the above.
- *Assessment*
  - Giving or taking part in spoken and written assessments about individuals and groups of students.
- *Appraisal*
  - Taking part in appraisal (of yourself and others) as set out in the regulations.
- *Review*
  - Reviewing your teaching methods and planning.
  - Taking part in training or other professional development.
- *Educational methods*
  - Working with others to prepare and develop plans, schemes, resources, etc.
- *Discipline, health and safety*
  - Keeping discipline and looking after your students' health and safety, both at school and during school activities (e.g. trips) elsewhere.
- *Staff meetings*
  - Taking part in meetings about the curriculum or about the running of the school as a whole.
- *Cover*
  - Supervising and, if possible, teaching students whose teacher is away (with some exceptions).

- *Public exams*
  - Preparing your students, and assessing them for exams.
  - Recording and reporting on the assessments you have made.
  - Helping supervise exams (i.e. invigilation).
- *Admin*
  - Doing admin and organization as required for the tasks described above.
  - Organizing equipment and resources.
  - Going to assemblies, registering and supervising students.

Teaching assistant

There has been much discussion recently about exactly what the role of the 'teaching assistant' should be. The following interview with Janet Kay clarifies exactly what a classroom assistant does, and should be of great interest both to the classroom teacher working with an assistant, and also to those interested in working in classroom support.

> Programme Leader, BA (Hons) Early Childhood Studies
>
> University of Derby
>
> Author, *The Teacher Assistant's Handbook* (Continuum, 2002)
>
> Janet Kay

Q. First of all, could you tell me a little bit about your background and current work in education?

Janet – I'm a qualified social worker and I worked in social services for children and families for many years, specifically in child protection. My second career was in Further Education, teaching and managing in the early years, health and social care programme areas. I'm currently the Programme Leader for the BA (Hons) Early Childhood Studies course at the University of Derby.

Q. Could you explain exactly what a 'teaching assistant' is?

Janet – It depends on the definition used. The DfES use the term 'teaching assistant' to describe a whole range of classroom support roles. Under the DfES definition, teaching assistants can support individual pupils, or support the teacher, the curriculum or the whole school. In LEAs the term is used to describe more specific roles, but these can vary between LEAs. Overall there are literally dozens of terms used to describe the roles of non-teachers in the classroom.

Q. What sort of things would a teaching assistant do on a daily basis?

Janet – Teaching assistants may be employed to work with an individual child or children, usually with SEN. They might support a class in more general ways, such as working with small groups, or supporting specific core curriculum subjects. They could also be helping a teacher with routine tasks such as escorting children, setting up materials and equipment or demonstrating activities.

Some teaching assistants are also involved in planning and assessment, and devising differentiated activities for individuals or small groups. They may work with one class or a range of classes, groups or individual children. They are also involved in school-wide activities such as organizing events (sports day, trips out) and contributing to whole school developments. Many teaching assistants have a number of varying roles throughout the week. For example, they might be supporting a single child for part of the week, supporting the Reception class for another period of time, and supporting literacy and numeracy hours at Key Stage One for the rest.

Q. What sort of qualifications do teaching assistants have?

Janet – Not all teaching assistants have qualifications. Some have childcare qualifications such as NNEB, CACHE Diploma in Childcare and Education, BTEC National Diploma in Early Years or relevant childcare and education NVQs. Others have qualifications gained 'on the job' such as the CACHE Specialist Teaching Assistants Award or NCFE Initial Training for Classroom Assistants qualification. There are now a whole range of different types of qualifications for teaching assistants including NVQs for Classroom/Teaching Assistants and the newly introduced Foundation Degrees, which can lead to Senior Practitioner status in the early years, where they are sector-endorsed. Sector-endorsed means that the Foundation Degree meets the 'Statement of Requirement' for Early Years Sector-Endorsed Foundation Degrees published by the DfES Early Years and Childcare Unit, and as such, the Foundation Degree confers Senior Practitioner status on those who pass it. This denotes a higher level of competence in the practitioner. Six per cent of teaching assistants have degrees.

Q. Could you tell me a bit more about what the CACHE Specialist Teaching Assistants Award involves? What subjects are studied?

Janet – This course looks at areas such as supporting core subjects at Key Stage One, behaviour management, professional practice, working in teams and good practice issues.

Q. What kind of qualities does a person need to make a good teaching assistant?

Janet – They need knowledge and understanding of a wide range of children's needs, including SEN, child development and how children learn. Also, strategies for promoting learning and supporting the growth of confidence, independence and good self-esteem. Patience, good teamwork skills, excellent interpersonal and communication skills are very important. Also, the ability to work flexibly and to learn new skills and knowledge as required. The ability to recognize parents as partners and work with them is vital, as is good knowledge of the curriculum, how schools work and health and safety issues.

Q. Can a teacher's assistant become a qualified classroom teacher? How would they go about doing this?

Janet – Yes, they can, and there are different ways that they might achieve this. The graduate registered teacher programme (GRTP) is a an employment-based route into teaching which particularly suits mature experienced students who wish to work while they train. It has two strands. The graduate teacher programme (GTP) lasts one year and is for graduates who are working in schools. The registered teacher programme (RTP) lasts for two years and is for students who have completed the equivalent of two years of higher education and have a place to complete their degree while training, and who are also working in a school. For example, a teaching assistant who had considerable experience and was employed in a primary school started a part-time BA in Early Childhood Studies. After completing the equivalent of two years higher education, she applied for the RTP and over the next two years completed her degree and the RTP to become a qualified teacher. In both strands of the GRTP the student needs to be supported by the school and by a recommending body, for example a school, university or LEA.

Other routes include the PGCE, which requires a degree in a relevant subject and one-year full-time or two-years, part-time study including teaching practice. Teaching assistants with Level Three qualifications such as 'A' levels, or BTEC or CACHE Diplomas can use these as entry to a BEd, which will lead to qualified teacher status, or to get onto a BA Early Childhood Studies, which could be used to go on to a PGCE. Access courses can be used as entry to teaching in some cases, especially where they offer English, Maths and Science GCSE equivalence.

Q. What are the main differences between being a teaching assistant and a qualified classroom teacher?

Janet – At present, teaching assistants do not have sole responsibility for classes. They may have a role in planning and assessment, but the overall responsibility for this lies with the teacher. The teaching assistant works within plans developed and agreed with the teacher and they have responsibility for some of the learning and assessment within these. However, they work under the direction of the teacher to achieve their agreed aims. Basically, the class is the teacher's responsibility and the teaching assistant works under his or her direction.

Q. Could you tell me a bit about your new book The Teacher Assistant's Handbook. How would it help people training to be or already working as teaching assistants?

Janet – The book is a very practical guide to the sort of knowledge and skills a teaching assistant may need across the range of roles. It's designed to support teaching assistants doing the CACHE STA award specifically, but it also provides the knowledge base for the NVQs and other relevant courses. It provides a clearly written introduction for new teaching assistants, and a handbook for reference for those already doing the job.

The book covers a whole range of issues: the role of the teaching assistant in supporting core curriculum subjects at Key Stage One and in supporting groups and individual children; how children learn and the role of the primary school; assessment; working with others; behaviour management; professional development; and good practice issues including child protection, equal opportunities, health and safety and bullying. The book includes case studies, discussion points and exercises to promote reflective practice and deeper understanding or to be used as teaching tools on relevant courses. The style is simple and straightforward, in order to be accessible to a range of readers, including those who have not accessed training courses as yet.

Q. What do you think about the proposal that classroom assistants take on some whole class teaching to allow teachers more time for paperwork and planning? Is it a good idea?

Janet – Like all such ideas, it depends! There are many skilled and experienced teaching assistants who could contribute a great deal more, given the opportunity. However, the training, qualification structure and pay should reflect any new duties and responsibilities, and new and existing routes from teaching assistant to teacher should continue to be developed. Also, the role of teachers needs to be carefully considered – is it a step forward for them to be spending more time on paperwork or is the real issue whether the quantity of administration needs to be reviewed? In the end, does this plan actually improve children's experiences of learning or is it an ill-thought out response to teacher overload? A lot more wide-ranging debate is needed before any such plan is developed further or implemented.

Q. Finally, any other comments that you'd like to add about the work that teaching assistants do?

Janet – Only that during my research for *The Teacher Assistant's Handbook* I spent a lot of time talking to and looking into what teaching assistants actually do and I am filled with admiration for this group of workers who have a huge range of skills and talents, who don't always get paid much or have much status or recognition outside their school, but who really are the 'glue' that keeps many a primary school together. They deserve wider recognition, and more opportunity and support for their contributions, rather than some of the negative comments that occasionally come their way. There are some new and exciting developments coming their way and, hopefully, their role will be developed and extended in ways that benefit schools, children and the teaching assistants themselves.

Special educational needs coordinator (SENCO)

The role of the SENCO (in Scotland the Principal Teacher, Support for Learning) is a complex and crucial one within the school. You can find a huge amount of information about SENCOs, and about SEN, from the National Association for Special Educational Needs (see the Directory for contact details). It really is worth getting to know your special needs staff properly, and turning to them for expert advice when you need it, especially if you are working in a school with 'challenging' children. An experienced special needs teacher may be able to give you some background information, or make a simple suggestion, that transforms your relationship with a particularly difficult child. SENCOs have a number of different responsibilities within a school, and these include the following roles.

- *Entitlement:* Making sure that students with SEN get full access to the curriculum.
- *Inclusion:* Making sure that students with SEN can access the same opportunities as others.
- *Meeting with parents:* For instance, agreeing targets for the student and ways that the guardians can help at home.
- *Working with other agencies:* Helping to encourage links between different types of support for the student with SEN.

Educational psychologist

Educational psychologists are highly qualified individuals. To become an educational psychologist, you must have a degree in Psychology (or equivalent), at least two years' teaching experience, and also a postgraduate degree in

Educational Psychology. Schools have a 'link' with a named educational psychologist, who will help with assessment of children who have SEN, for instance in diagnosing dyslexia.

The psychologist would normally be called in after the child's IEP has been drawn up, and if the SENCO feels that additional help or advice is required for the individual. The educational psychologist may observe the child in class, work with the child individually, and use tests to check on his or her skills. A consultation meeting may also be held, at which various professionals discuss how best to proceed. As well as working with children, educational psychologists also help with training work, advising teachers about SEN, and so on.

Educational welfare officer (EWO)

The EWO deals with issues connected to the educational welfare of the children, ensuring that they benefit fully from their education. The EWO helps with areas such as truancy and absence, for instance checking registers, monitoring attendance, talking with children, and making home visits. Some schools have an EWO who works 'on site', while many others have a visiting EWO from the LEA.

School librarian

The role of the school librarian, or learning resource centre manager, is being seen as increasingly important within schools. He or she may be a 'chartered librarian', which involves a graduate or postgraduate level training, and membership of the Chartered Institute of Library and Information Professionals (CLIP). School librarians undertake a number of different responsibilities.

- Helping school managers to create policies about providing learning resources.
- Assisting students in accessing the resources they need for their learning.
- Teaching core skills, such as ways of accessing knowledge.
- Managing and promoting the library resources, which include books, ICT, and so on.
- Helping to promote literacy skills and to increase students' enjoyment of reading.
- Managing the library environment.
- Managing the library budget.
- Passing on relevant advice and information to teaching staff.

School Librarian

Clevedon Community School

Melanie McGilloway

Q. How did you become a librarian?

Melanie – To become a qualified chartered librarian, you can either do a degree, or a masters. I did an English degree in France, then I did a Masters in Library and Information Studies in Aberystwyth.

Q. And why did you decide to become a librarian?

Melanie – I knew I wanted to work with books and it was either publishing or librarianship.

Q. What are attitudes like towards school libraries? Are they generally well funded, and run by well qualified staff?

Melanie – It depends on what they think of the library. If the head is interested in the library, they give it money. The same goes for the librarian's wages as well. Some librarians are on a scale 1, which is like a technician, while some librarians are on what we call SO1 which is about £20,000. It really depends on what people think of their librarian and the library. I've been lucky in my jobs, where I've been paid reasonably well and I've always been treated well. A lot of school libraries employ non-qualified librarians. It doesn't mean they can't do the job, but it makes it easier not to pay them much money. In Scotland, though, all the school libraries have a qualified librarian.

Q. What was your first post as a librarian?

Melanie – It was in a secondary school in Glasgow. The kids were rough but nice. There were a lot of social problems, they really had a hard time, and you did feel sorry for them. It was my first job and I learned a lot, but it wasn't too daunting because the numbers at the school were quite small.

Q. What sort of resources did you have there?

Melanie – Hardly anything. Everything was over 20 years old, because there wasn't any money. There were no computers, and I had a budget of £50. The kids were enthusiastic, and I managed to do some things, like having an author in.

Q. What about your second post? What were things like there?

Melanie – I worked at a big secondary school in Berkshire. There were about 1300 children including a sixth form. The school had quite a big library, and I had an assistant. There were loads of computers in the library. That was the year when the government gave extra money to schools to buy computers. There was a big stock and a reasonable budget of about £6000 a year. I was there for three years. I did things like writing a whole reading unit, and organizing all the lesson plans and activities. That's the part of the job that I really enjoy.

Q. And your current job?

Melanie – I'm at Clevedon Community School which is another big comprehensive, with a sixth form, in the South West of England.

Q. What sort of different things do you do in your current post?

Melanie – I manage the budget, I run library inductions for Year Seven and Year Ten, and I organize things like Book Week. We've got two visiting authors, and I also run reading promotions. I've just started doing the information retrieval part of the literacy progress units. Those kids who come for that, they might never come to the library, so it helps you get to know them. It was nice spending time with them.

Q. What sort of things do you spend your budget on, and how do you decide where the money goes?

Melanie – When I started in the school I did a stock evaluation. I had a look to see what different areas of stock were like, and I found a few things where the books were really old. I try to tackle a few subject groups every year. For example this year I'm going to buy some poetry books. Then, when you get reps in, you see books that are good and you know that the kids will use them, so you buy those too.

I buy a lot of fiction, obviously – there are always authors who are popular. I subscribe to a few magazines that do reviews to keep in touch with things. There are so many children's books published now. It's the new thing, since Harry Potter it's just gone mad. I also buy newspapers. We get the *Telegraph* free – they give it free to all schools who've got a sixth form. We also get the *Guardian* and the *Daily Mail*.

Q. What ideas do you have for getting your students more interested in reading?

Melanie – I'm planning to get more magazines that they'd be interested in, like *Heat*, which are not necessarily educational. If you want the kids to come and read you have to give them what they want to read. With fiction, there are some excellent authors around who write really well, but if the kids prefer to read a Point Horror surely it's better for them to read that than nothing? I tend to be open-minded. They love series, the comfort of knowing what they're reading, of knowing what they're getting. Of course, there are also some really good readers at my school, and they'll read anything you give them.

It's a matter of how you present it as well. That's one of the things I'm going to spend some money on this year. I'm going to buy some display carousels and categorize the fiction by genre. If there's a place with all the horror books, they'll go to that. If there are just shelves of books, they don't pick up anything. A lot of the students pick up books that are much too easy for their reading level. They read in tutor time once a week, and a lot of them just want something quick to read, especially boys, something quick and painless!

We're also doing the shadowing process for the Carnegie Medal. The students read the books and shadow the real judges. That's a good way of introducing new authors. The kids act as judges, although it doesn't have any effect on the real judging. It's good for keen readers. They have a website where you can send reviews, and there's loads of scope for different activities. You have to buy the books, though, and that's a big problem, because most of them are hardbacks.

Q. Do you enjoy the teaching aspects of your role?

Melanie — Yes, I do. Being a school librarian is a good alternative to being a teacher. It's hard at first — behaviour management, how to conduct a lesson, things like that. But when you feel you've really grasped it, and the kids actually listen to you, that's great. The first time I actually said 'quiet' to a Year Eight and the kids actually listened to me! — I was like 'wow'. I love that bit. I'd also love to design textbooks, and school books in general.

Q. How do you go about getting teachers more involved with the library?

Melanie — There are teachers I can go to, and they'll always be open-minded about things. It's really hard to get to the ones who are not interested. A lot of the time teachers haven't got time to get involved, but I try to push it. Every so often I put stuff in their pigeon-holes, like lists of websites or lists of books I have bought that might interest them. Teachers ask me for information, and I do research for them, for instance on the internet.

Q. If a teacher is planning a visit to the library what can they do to help you, and what do you do to assist them?

Melanie — It's important for me to know the year group and subject, and if you're in a school with sets, to know what level the kids are at. A lot of the time I do a book box, so if the teacher wants the kids to get on with their work straight away, I can have the books ready. I also need to know whether or not they're going to use the computers, and if they are, whether they want me to find some websites. The kids get 'lost' on the internet and sidetracked very easily. If you give them a list of websites they get on task more quickly.

If a teacher wants to use the resources, but they don't want to come to the library, I do them a book box which they can take away. They can then use these in the classroom. Sometimes they book the computer room and the kids have the computers and the books as well.

Q. What sort of hours is the library open?

Melanie – We're open all day, including breaks and lunch. We start at 8.15 a.m. and go through until 4.15 p.m. My assistant works in the mornings until just after lunch.

Q. How do your students view the library? What sort of behaviour do you see, and how do you deal with misbehaviour?

Melanie – Some of them see it as a place to hang out. A lot of the kids do come just for the computers, which is annoying. I was thinking about doing a non-computer day at least once a month. When the computers don't work, it's amazing how the atmosphere changes in the library. Then the pupils that come in are the ones that want to read or study. When it's raining, it's particularly busy. If the weather's nice, the kids go in the field to sit down. We're much more popular on a rainy day!

The pupils are usually quite good. They're noisy, but not really bad. I don't think in a normal comprehensive it's possible to have complete silence. I don't think you can expect 13 year olds to be totally silent. On the other hand, during lesson time, if it's only the sixth formers or small groups of students in, I expect them to get on with their work quietly. If students do misbehave, we can send them out and they do go when they're asked. We like to keep the use of the library as a privilege, rather than as a right.

Q. And finally, do you also have books for teachers?

Melanie – At the moment there's a library in the staffroom for the teachers. I want to bring it down to the library, because that would make the teachers more likely to come down and use the library. We've got the *TES* in the library, and that's a big attraction!

Office staff

In my experience, it really is worth spending time getting to know the office staff in your school. They play an invaluable role in the day-to-day running of the school, although their work is not always understood or acknowledged by hard-working teachers. Having the office staff 'on your side' will make life much easier for you, in small but numerous ways. For instance, when the photocopier breaks down in the middle of that vital run of exam papers, the office staff will often be far more knowledgeable and skilled in fixing it than you are. Alternatively, when you're waiting for that important phone call from a particularly troublesome parent, a receptionist who likes and respects you is far more likely to ensure that the call gets through, or that a proper message is taken and passed to you.

The head teacher's secretary is often one of the most powerful people in the school. She (or he) has access to a surprising amount of information, and will generally have a very good idea of exactly what is going on. Again, keep on the right side of the head's secretary, and he or she may ease your path when you do need an emergency meeting with the head!

Bursar

The school bursar is responsible for the accountancy functions of the school, and he or she will report to the head teacher. Some bursars are also given additional administrative responsibilities. The bursar's job might include areas such as maintaining financial records, paying invoices and staff expenses, preparing contracts for teachers and other staff, and reporting to the school governors about the finances of the school.

In smaller schools, the bursar may take on the whole range of administrative roles, in addition to the finance function. In larger schools, the bursar may have other administrative staff working for him or her. In the very large secondary school, with a complex budget, there may also be a finance manager.

Caretaker

The caretaker is responsible for running and maintaining the physical environment of the school. This might include general upkeep and repairs, dealing with the boiler, managing the setting up of chairs for assemblies, keeping master copies of school keys, organizing the school for lettings, and many other jobs. It really is well worth the classroom teacher getting to know the caretaker, and taking the time to thank him or her for any help, for instance in setting up the hall.

School governor

School governors come from a huge range of backgrounds. Some governors will be parents of children at the school, who are appointed by the parental body.

Others will be teacher governors, appointed by other teachers at the school. There may also be governors from the non-teaching staff of the school, lay governors, people appointed by the church to be governors in a religious school, and so on.

Governors work as a team, attending meetings perhaps once or twice a month. They will play a variety of roles in the running of the school, including agreeing the budget, helping to interview new staff, appointing the head teacher, ensuring that the curriculum is broad and balanced, and so on. You can find lots more information about school governors from the DfES, at www.dfes.gov.uk/governor.

Inspector

General Inspector (Primary Links)

Nottinghamshire County Council

Advisory & Inspection Services

Gordon Wallace

Q. Could you explain to me what your job as an inspector involves?

Gordon – My main role is that of 'linking' with 17 primary schools with a brief to 'challenge and support' them. The main purpose is to give the LEA a full picture about how well the schools are doing in terms of attainment, teaching and learning, and leadership and management. I do this through regular visits, analysis of outcomes data, target setting, classroom observations, analysis of school documentation and discussions with staff and children. I also support governing bodies in the appointment of head teachers and deputy head teachers.

At the moment I'm supporting a school in 'special measures', which is particularly time consuming because of the high level of monitoring, training and support activities. I also look after training and development activities. I organize conferences, organize courses and manage our head teacher induction programme. I also deliver training to individual schools, groups of governors or on open access courses. I'm a trained and experienced OFSTED inspector, although that element of my work is currently taking a back seat. Needless to say there are never enough days in the week or weeks in the term to get all the work done.

Q. How does a teacher get into advisory/inspection work? How did you move into the job?

Gordon – Most inspectors, particularly at primary level, come through the route of having been successful head teachers. My route was a little different. I started teaching in a middle school, then moved to a high school, then I looked for a job which would involve development and training, but which would also get me into a wide range of mainstream schools. I ended up opening a new teachers' centre just outside Nottingham, then moved to run the main teachers' centre in the middle of the city. After that I had a succession of jobs which involved developing training and support activities for schools in different areas of Nottinghamshire. In 1993 I was appointed as Inspector for Consultancy and Training. In 1998 we were reorganized and all inspectors had to take on a 'link' function and as most of my previous work had been with primary schools I became a primary link inspector but still hung onto some of the training and development function.

Q. What are some of the best things about working as an inspector? What really satisfies you about your job?

Gordon – The best things are working with enthusiasts and seeing improvements in schools as a result of things I've said or done. Also, the variety in the job. There's a significant amount of personal autonomy within an agreed structure. I get satisfaction through knowing that I've done a good job – people tell you! I also enjoy seeing children getting a better deal as a result of my work. Plus, people saying things like, 'You know that course you ran two years ago which I thought was crap! Recently I dug out the notes and it has been really useful.' Also, knowing that, sometimes, I make a difference.

Q. There must be difficult parts to the job as well. What's hard about your job as an inspector and how do you deal with it?

Gordon – The most difficult things are giving hard messages and the frustration of knowing what is needed without the power to insist. I deal with this by constantly reminding myself that *schools* carry the responsibility for what they do. My responsibility is to know about the quality of what they do and advise. I can't do it for them!

Q. How do the teachers you meet react to you, especially in your work as an OFSTED inspector?

Gordon – Reactions vary. In the OFSTED context teachers react in many different ways – defensive, assertive, aggressive, crying, compliant, cooperative, uncooperative, etc. I always respond by being polite, pleasant, understanding, showing a sense of humour, but not prepared to accept or condone a situation where children are not receiving their entitlements. In my link role where I've developed long-term relationships with schools I usually get very friendly and positive reactions.

Q. What do you feel makes a good teacher?

Gordon – Qualities like empathy, patience, humour, sense of fun, understanding, resilience, optimism, intelligence, self-knowledge, credibility, etc., are crucial.

Q. What about a good head teacher?

Gordon – The National Standards for Head Teachers suggest that heads need a number of qualities. Personal impact and presence; resilience; adaptability to changing circumstances and ideas; energy, vigour and perseverance; self-confidence; reliability; enthusiasm; intellectual ability; integrity; commitment. I would suggest that teachers need all these as well! Is it any wonder we have a shortage?

Q. And what makes a good school?

Gordon – I would say that a good school has dynamic leadership, and the staff are valued and developed. A school with good teaching which challenges *all* children and provides enjoyment, where children are cared about, respected and their views taken into account. Also, where children learn effectively and enjoy coming to school.

Q. What tips or advice would you give to an NQT just starting out in the job?

Gordon – I'd suggest that they read a good book on the first year in teaching! Plus, be highly organized, but not afraid to ask for help and advice. Set yourself small steps as targets – you can't change the world in a day. Also, remember to listen and contribute. Make the learning challenging and enjoyable – a sense of fun is crucial. And of course, get to know all the children well.

Q. Would you recommend teaching to young people making decisions about a career?

Gordon – Probably not, unless they exhibited the personality and attributes mentioned above and were prepared to work harder and earn less than most graduates! If they met these criteria it would be a great profession for them!

Q. What could be done, then, to make teaching a better and more attractive career?

Gordon – I have a theory about primary schools. One of the biggest problems is finding time to do the job properly. If every primary class teacher had a four day contact week with a day for planning, records, assessment, monitoring and evaluating, their lives would be changed overnight. Also, if every class had a classroom assistant to support the teacher with learning, behaviour issues and time-consuming classroom chores, the job would also be improved significantly. These developments would be very difficult to initiate because there are not enough teachers at the moment, but progressively introduced would make doing a good job much more manageable and rewarding, and also give time for a life outside of school.

7 Preparing to teach

Lesson planning

As a student teacher, lesson planning plays a central role in learning how to become an effective practitioner. However, once you take on a 'proper' teaching job, and become more experienced (and busy), you start to realize that it is not important or indeed possible to plan every single lesson in the kind of detail that you used to when you were a student. As you gain experience, you will start to work out for yourself exactly what you want and need to include to create a successful lesson plan that works for you. In some cases your school or department will provide you with 'ready made' formats for schemes of work and lesson plans that you can (or must) use.

At times, for instance when your school is being inspected, or when managers ask you to produce paperwork, you may find yourself returning to a more detailed format. However, the majority of the time you will want to focus on finding a lesson plan that is simple, effective and not too time intensive to prepare. For an experienced teacher, or for one who has taught a particular topic before, it may not even be necessary to have a plan at all. In fact, some of my most successful lessons ever have been ones where I entered the classroom with a topic in mind, but without any clue about how I was actually going to teach it.

This kind of spontaneous approach allows you to react to the particular children and their specific responses and mood right at that moment. It also allows for the kind of individuality and even (dare I say it?) inspiration that seems to have been knocked out of the teaching profession by the constraints of the National Curriculum. Of course it's not an approach that I would recommend using on a daily basis.

You can find lots more information about planning in Chapter 3 which deals with teaching practice, and in Chapters 12 and 13 which show case studies on planning in the primary and secondary school. In addition, Chapter 14 of the 'Toolkit' offers you some blank lesson planning formats to use or adapt.

'Good' and 'bad' lesson plans

What makes a 'good' lesson plan?

- It makes you feel happy and confident about what you're going to teach

- It's easy to refer to and use in a real life classroom situation

- It's flexible enough to adapt 'on the spot' if you find that the activities aren't working

- There's enough information for you (or someone else) to reuse the plan at a later date

---

What makes a 'bad' lesson plan?

- It is excessively prescriptive, and does not allow the individual teacher to have any input

- The layout is complicated and cannot be easily referred to and read in a real life classroom setting (this can lead to a situation where the teacher spends more time reading the plan than teaching!)

- There is little flexibility and the teacher tends to stick to the plan, even though it isn't working

- Alternatively, the plan is too vague or lacks sufficient detail

Planning time savers

Planning lessons can be as quick or as time consuming as you want, and there are plenty of things that you can do to save yourself some time, without compromising your teaching. The tips below should give you some ideas for keeping the paperwork to a minimum.

- *Don't reinvent the wheel:* There are now a huge range of different sources from which to find 'ready made' lesson plans. Your colleagues at school, the internet, textbooks, and so on, can all stop you from repeating work that has already been done, and thus offer you a way of saving time.
- *Adapt what you've already got:* Many of us have lesson plans (for instance from our student days) that sit mouldering in a file. Take a look through what you've got at the moment, and see which bits you can adapt to use again.
- *Repeat work from year to year:* As the years go by, you'll find that you can repeat work that you have done in previous years, perhaps making small alterations to improve things, or simply to keep the teaching fresh for yourself.
- *Think on your feet:* When there simply isn't time to plan a lesson properly, the more experienced teacher is usually able to go into a lesson with a general 'idea' about what he or she might teach, then simply respond to the children when working out exactly what activities to use.

- *Use a project:* Giving your students a project on which to work means that a single sheet of tasks or activities can be spread over a number of lessons. Projects are also an excellent way of motivating disinterested children, and can help you stretch those of higher ability as well.

The teacher's planner

Some schools provide their teaching staff with a 'planner' – a useful spiral bound notebook that allows you to keep all your records and important notes in one place. If your school doesn't automatically provide you with a teacher's planner, do ask if you can order one. The advantages of keeping all your information in one place really cannot be overemphasized. The teacher's planner comes in two sizes – A4 and A5. There is a huge range of information that you can keep in your teacher's planner:

- Yearly diary
- Daily diary with space for lesson outlines and homework
- Class registers
- Class assessment and marks
- Weekly timetable

The National Curriculum

The National Curriculum is organized in four Key Stages, the first two of which cover the primary and middle school years, the second two of which occur at secondary school.

Key Stage One	Ages 5–7	Years 1–2
Key Stage Two	Ages 7–11	Years 3–6
Key Stage Three	Ages 11–14	Years 7–9
Key Stage Four	Ages 14–16	Years 10–11

The 'core subjects' within the National Curriculum are English, Maths and Science. The other subjects are Design and Technology, Information and Communication Technology, History, Geography, Modern Foreign Languages, Art and Design, Music, Physical Education and Citizenship (from August 2002, at Key Stages Three and Four). Within the National Curriculum subjects, there are also details of programmes of study (which say what pupils should be taught), and attainment targets and level descriptions (which set the expected standards that the students will achieve). You can find the National Curriculum online at www.nc.uk.net. For further details, see also www.dfes.gov.uk/a-z/CURRICULUM.html

The National Literacy Strategy

Having originally been implemented in primary schools, the NLS has now reached secondary schools as well, with the 'Framework for Teaching English'. The idea behind it is (obviously) to improve literacy standards, and this applies to all areas of the curriculum. Teachers are given word, sentence and text level work, and specific areas are set that must be covered with each year group. The 'Literacy Hour' is a daily literacy lesson that is divided into four fairly rigidly defined areas:

- Shared reading/writing (approximately 15 minutes)
- Word level work (approximately 15 minutes)
- Guided group/independent work (approximately 20 minutes)
- Plenary (approximately 10 minutes)

You can find more details about the NLS on the DfES 'Standards Site' at www.standards.dfee.gov.uk/literacy/.

The National Numeracy Strategy

Similarly, the NNS provides a framework for helping children with Maths work, initially at primary level but now moving into secondary schools. Students in Years R to Six are given a daily numeracy lesson of 45 minutes to an hour. As with literacy, a mixture of different strategies are to be used, such as individual and pair work, group work, whole class work, and plenaries. The framework provides teaching programmes for primary school children, and again you can find much more information at the DfES 'Standards' site: www.standards.dfee.gov.uk/numeracy/.

Special educational needs

The number of children identified as having SEN will vary widely from school to school. It is important to bear in mind, too, that not all children who actually have a special need will already have been identified when you meet them in the classroom. The students that you teach will have different levels of severity in their SEN. It might be that some of your children are 'statemented' (see 'What happens to children with SEN?' and 'Statements' below). If this is the case, it is possible (although by no means guaranteed) that you may be given additional support for that child.

There will be a register of special educational needs within your school (kept by the SENCO). You would normally expect to be informed about the children in your class or classes who do have a special need, although this is not necessarily always the case. If you are not given this information, do ensure that you ask for it. It is helpful to make a (coded) note of this on your register or mark book. Bear in mind that all SEN information is highly confidential, and take account of this when dealing with the children, and with the paperwork.

The classroom teacher and SEN

Although formalized assessments will play some part in identifying students with SEN, the classroom teacher also plays a hugely important role. Some children do slip through the net, perhaps because they develop a special need later on in their school career, or alternatively because they have simply not been identified by their previous teachers or schools. If you suspect that a child has SEN, you should notify your school's SENCO or other relevant person as soon as possible, so that testing can take place.

What are special educational needs?

There are a huge range of different special needs: some which the classroom teacher may come across on a fairly regular basis, others for which children would often attend a specialist school. The National Association of Special Educational Needs is an excellent source of detailed information on identifying and dealing with children who have SEN (see the Directory for contact details). Some of the more commonly experienced difficulties are explained below.

- *Emotional and behavioural difficulties:* This is often one of the major areas of concern for the teacher. The term 'EBD' is a catch-all name for a whole range of issues. Children with EBD might present the teacher with confrontational, angry attitudes, or even with violence. The term also covers those students who are withdrawn, or who have social problems.
- *ADHD:* A condition that has only been defined in recent years. Children with attention deficit hyperactivity disorder can appear very clumsy and disorganized. They may have problems interacting socially with other children. Inattention to work is often a problem. Children with ADHD are sometimes treated with the drug Ritalin.
- *Specific learning difficulties:* This term covers special needs that involve a particular area of learning. If left unidentified, a child with a SpLD may exhibit poor behaviour, as they struggle with a particular area of the curriculum. Special needs such as dyslexia come under this heading.
- *Physical needs:* Some children will have an SEN with a clear physical origin, such as the child who is partially or fully deaf or blind.

What happens to children with SEN?

The sooner that a special need can be identified, the better it is, both for the child and for the teacher. Once a problem has been noted, the teacher, SENCO, other specialists and also the parents will work together to try and help the child in learning. The Code of Practice for SEN gives full details about how teachers,

SENCOs and other agencies can work together in identifying and meeting a child's needs. Until very recently, five different 'stages' were used to show where a child was in the process of identification and support (these are shown below). These stages may still be in use in some schools, where you could be told that a child has SEN and is 'at stage three'. The latest SEN Code of Practice can be obtained from the DfES, by emailing dfes@prolog.uk.com.

- *Stage One:* The child is identified as having a special need.
- *Stage Two:* The SENCO and teachers work to develop an individual educational plan (see below for more information on this).
- *Stage Three:* Support is given to the teachers and the SENCO by outside specialists.
- *Stage Four:* The LEA decides whether a statutory assessment is necessary.
- *Stage Five:* The LEA decides whether a statement of SEN is required.

Individual education plans

An IEP is basically a plan that shows what is going to happen to help the child with SEN, and how this help will occur. When you teach a child with SEN for the first time, it is well worth getting hold of a copy of any IEP that the child has. This will help you deal with the child's specific needs, whether they are to do with behaviour or learning. The IEP should include a range of information, as listed below.

- What the child's SEN is.
- What is going to happen to help deal with the child's needs.
- Who will be involved in the process.
- Details about the type of activities, resources, etc., that are needed.
- How the parents or guardians can help.
- What targets the child should aim to achieve, and by when.
- Any particular pastoral or medical needs.
- How the progress is going to be monitored and assessed.
- When and how reviews are going to take place.

All children at stages two and three of the model described above should have an IEP. After a review of the IEP, the child might stay at the same level, or might move up or down.

Statements

Only a relatively small number of children with special educational needs will be given a statement. The 'Statement of SEN' is given to children whose needs are such that they cannot reasonably be met by the resources available within the mainstream schools in that area. The school might consequently be given additional resources by the LEA, or the child may be entitled to provision in another, more specialized educational environment. The child with a statement may also be disapplied from certain aspects of the National Curriculum. You may find that you teach a child with a statement within a mainstream classroom, but that there is a specialist working alongside him or her to help facilitate learning.

Inclusion

Inclusion is about ensuring that all children, whatever their needs or background, have their entitlement to the same standard and quality of education fulfilled. In the past, children with special needs were often removed from the mainstream classroom. The 1981 Education Act began to move the emphasis towards educating all children within the mainstream state system. The National Curriculum (introduced in 1988) was designed to ensure that all children's needs were met with a broad and balanced curriculum. During the 1980s and 1990s there was also a great deal of legislation designed to help students with SEN to be effectively catered for within mainstream schools.

Schools and teachers have a responsibility for providing an inclusive education. This might involve adapting the way your classroom is set up, for instance ensuring that children with visual problems are able to see the board properly. It will also mean that you need to adapt the way that you teach, and the way that your lessons are organized, in order to allow all children to learn. You can find information on differentiation in Chapter 8.

Schemes of work

A scheme of work provides a medium-term overview of the work that is planned. It details the lessons that will take place to cover an entire topic or subject area, perhaps over a half or even a full term. Schemes of work do not include as much detail as lesson plans, but give a general outline of how the subject or topic will be approached, with a series of lessons listed in (usually chronological) order. You can see some examples of schemes of work in the case studies on planning (Chapters 12 and 13). You can also find a blank medium-term plan in Chapter 14 of the Toolkit (page 274).

For the experienced teacher a scheme of work may provide sufficient detail to actually teach the lessons. This is especially the case when you have taught the lessons before, and in these instances the scheme of work acts simply as a reminder of the content. Bear in mind that primary (and some secondary) teachers will be working from a number of different schemes of work simultaneously, in a variety of different curriculum or topic areas.

Resources and equipment

Finding, setting up and organizing resources and equipment can be a time-consuming business for the teacher. This is especially so for the primary school teacher, dealing with the whole curriculum, or for the teacher of a secondary school subject that is resource or equipment intensive (such as Art or PE).

On the other hand, the use of resources in the classroom can be an extremely effective tool for learning. They can help you motivate your children to work hard; provide a reward to encourage good behaviour; and also allow a tired teacher to step back from teacher led work and take a well deserved rest. The tips below will help you in finding and managing resources within your own classroom.

- *Everything in its place:* Schools are full of *stuff* (planning documents, worksheets, textbooks, exercise books, pens, pencils, etc.). If you want to avoid complete chaos, try to find a suitable and set place for each type of resource or equipment. For a Drama teacher this might mean organizing a costume and props cupboard. For a primary teacher it could mean labelling drawers that contain pencils, felt-tip pens, rulers, and so on.
- *Be well organized:* It really is best, if at all feasible, to get your resources or equipment organized before the lesson begins. This is especially so for the student teacher, as it helps avoid last minute panic. It is also crucial with resources that may cause problems, such as the TV and video (see below).
- *Give the children responsibility:* I can remember 'tidying the stock cupboard' being viewed as a real treat when I was at junior school. Take advantage of your children's natural willingness to help out with adult tasks. At a signal from you they could divide into 'teams', each one responsible for tidying up or sorting a particular resource area.
- *Think laterally:* A resource is basically anything that the teacher (or student) brings into the classroom to inspire or assist the learning. When you're considering what resources you might use, do try to think laterally, and come up with some more unusual and exciting ideas. The sections that follow give some more original suggestions for resources, in addition to the traditional worksheet.

Using paper based resources

Worksheets are a real boon for the hard-working teacher. They can be created on a computer and are consequently easy to differentiate for a variety of abilities. They are also a good 'cop out' when, for whatever reason, you feel that you just can't cope with any whole class or teacher led work. Of course, we do need to be wary of using too many worksheets, because students will quickly become bored with lesson after lesson of them. If you're inexperienced in using computers, you can find a useful section about creating computerized worksheets in Chapter 18.

Although on the face of it a simple task, when making or adapting a worksheet for your class you do need to think carefully about factors such as presentation, readability, and so on. There are various things that you can do to ensure that the resource is as effective as possible.

- For students with low levels of literacy, it can difficult to read a worksheet that is heavily text based, so keep worksheets for these students clear and simple.
- It is a good idea to use a text box or other highlighting device for important instructions.
- If there are a number of tasks or activities for the children to complete, you could put a quick summary of these at the top of the worksheet, then a more detailed description below.
- Pictures and other visual aspects are important. These will help motivate your children in their work, and can also help with the clarity of the tasks.

The joys of photocopying

With the worksheet comes the joy of having to make photocopies, and one of the main factors to be aware of here is the stress involved in actually getting enough copies for your class. The following thoughts and comments about photocopying are based on my own experiences as a teacher. They are designed to be both helpful and also slightly tongue in cheek.

- School photocopiers are not necessarily top of the range machines, and the copies you receive will not always be good quality. A badly copied worksheet which the children find hard to read is likely to lead to disinterest and confusion.
- The school photocopier is a busy machine. Sod's law says that it is likely to break down, jam or run out of toner when you are most in need of it. Alternatively, there will be a queue of five people ahead of you, all with equally urgent work to copy.
- Trying to photocopy a worksheet for the lesson following break at break time really is asking for trouble. Always try to do your photocopying well in advance of the actual lesson time.
- Bear in mind that most schools have some sort of budgetary or other constraint on the amount of photocopying you're allowed to do. You may be given a code or a photocopying card, which will keep a check on the number of copies you or your department makes. It is best not to use up your allocation too early in the year, and to save some copying capacity for when you're exhausted and need a lesson off.

As a useful alternative to photocopying, you could try a sneaky tip that I worked out early on in my teaching career. (If you're an ICT teacher or librarian responsible for buying printer cartridges, please do not read any further in this paragraph.) The tip is simply to open the document on a school computer, then send the number of copies you want to the school printer. That way you don't 'buy' the photocopies from your copying budget. In addition, each copy is clean and easily read. All this assumes of course that you don't have similar breakdown problems with your school printer.

Some sensible schools employ a technician to do photocopying, although you have to remember to order copies in advance. If this is the system at your school, it's well worth getting 'in' with the relevant person, in case you do have a situation where you require a last minute emergency copying job. There will be (or should be) a copyright notice posted above your photocopier. As someone whose livelihood depends on copyright, I would urge you to read this notice, and to take account of it.

Using media resources

The basic rule with electronic equipment seems to be 'if it can go wrong it will'! This is perhaps particularly so in schools, where the machines are subjected to a lot of usage, as well as being moved around from room to room, and generally mistreated by students (and teachers) alike. It can prove a real nightmare if you are teaching a difficult class and they have to wait for you to repair the video, so do check that the equipment you propose to use is working before the lesson begins.

On the other hand, watching a video offers the teacher a real time out from the hard work of proper teaching, although it is of course important to ensure that the video is one that will actually interest, engage and educate your students. Media resources such as video cameras can be incredibly motivating for students and the stress involved is usually more than worth the effort in terms of the enthusiasm it will elicit from your children.

If you are going to use a video camera with your class, it is well worth framing this as a treat, and one that must be earned by good quality preparation work leading up to the videoing itself. For instance, your students might work for a number of lessons on scripting a piece of drama, finding costumes, props, and different locations in which to film. The actual videoing then becomes a reward for completing this work properly. If you are brave enough, and if it's appropriate with your children (that is they are old enough and well behaved enough), it is an excellent idea to let the students actually do the filming themselves.

Using the computer as a resource

Using computers and ICT in your teaching has a number of important benefits. As well as being a key aspect of a modern child's education, using computers also makes for a nice, easy child centred lesson for the teacher (and there's nothing wrong with that!). In my experience, children's behaviour is always better when they are sat in front of a computer. In addition, you can use the privilege of using a computer as a motivating factor to encourage hard work. There are, however, a number of important factors to be aware of when using computers as a resource for your class.

- There will not necessarily be sufficient computers to go round the whole class, and you will need to find strategies for dealing with this issue.
- Some children will be far more advanced in their ICT skills than others (and more advanced than many teachers for that matter).
- There is a tendency for children to stray off task when faced with the myriad temptations of computers and the internet.
- Crashing computers can cause real heartache for children who have not learnt to save their work.
- If using the internet, be aware that high traffic levels at certain times of the day can lead to a frustratingly slow experience.
- In some situations and schools, the children may treat the machines with a complete lack of respect, and you will need to deal with this problem.

You can find lots more useful information about using computers as a teaching resource in Section 4 of this book 'ICT'. Look too at my book *Getting the Buggers to Write* (published by Continuum), which gives helpful hints about the practicalities of computer use within the classroom.

Using people as a resource

When thinking about the type of resources you might use in your classroom, don't forget to consider other people as a source of information, entertainment and motivation. Bringing somebody new into the classroom always seems to go down well with the children. For some (highly irritating) reason, children who normally tend to misbehave often become little angels when confronted by an adult who they've not met before.

The work inspired by a visitor to the classroom can be a surprisingly powerful motivator for the lessons that follow. And of course another useful side effect of inviting other people into your classroom is that you get a chance for a lesson off. Here are just a few ideas for using people as a resource which you might like to try.

- *The parent/guardian as 'expert'*: Many of your children's parents or guardians will be experts in a field of their own so, if they are willing, invite them in to share their interests and expertise. This might be connected to the work they do (for instance a poet or astronomer); it could be to do with their hobbies (the keen amateur painter or potter); it might also be part of their cultural background (the Indian dancer or Welsh harpist).
- *Specialist agencies*: Some schools have an arrangement with local police officers who come in to do work with the children about drugs related issues. If not, consider setting up this type of scheme yourself, especially if you teach PHSE. Specialists may also come in to offer sex education lessons, and so on.
- *Theatre groups*: For some children, who have perhaps never had the opportunity to go to the theatre, watching a drama group perform (and even do a workshop) is a wonderful experience. Although there will be costs

involved, the experience is usually well worth the money. Some secondary English departments bring in a group to perform an abridged version of a Shakespeare play near SATs time.

- *Visiting artists:* There are opportunities to organize visits from many different types of artists – sculptors, musicians, poets, authors and so on. For instance you may like to work with your school library in making contact with an author and organizing a visit as a wonderful way to inspire children with their reading (and writing).

Unusual resources

It is often the case that the more unusual a resource is, the better the children will respond. For some reason, seeing something in the classroom that would not normally be there can inspire high levels of interest and motivation in your students. You can find ideas for some unusual resources below.

- *Objects:* You might bring in a beautiful shell to inspire some creative writing. A sealed cardboard box could prompt interesting discussions about exactly what is inside. Work on the senses will be much more inspiring with a range of different objects to smell, touch, taste and so on.
- *Props:* A prop that the children can use while pretending to be somebody else is a great way of stimulating the imagination. For instance, a handbag containing different objects that a character might use.
- *Costumes:* All children love dressing up (and this includes those disaffected teenagers in your Year Nine class, I promise!). There is no need to limit the use of costume to a Drama lesson. For instance, if you're teaching Geography you could look at different clothes worn around the world or in Art you could do some work on different fashion or shoe designs.
- *Living things:* Bringing a plant or animal into your classroom can motivate and educate your children, and also teach them about taking responsibility.
- *Food:* Any child is going to be motivated by the idea of something as 'naughty' as eating in class. Using food in a lesson is especially good for subjects such as Modern Foreign Languages. For instance, the children could set up a café and learn how to buy different types of food and drink.

Setting up your room

Whether you are a primary or a secondary teacher, the way that you set up your room will have a big impact on how your children behave and learn. In teaching, there can be a tendency to maintain the status quo in terms of the way that classrooms are set up. If you are an NQT, it's only natural for you to feel cautious about rearranging furniture in a room that has only just become your own. In addition, you may feel that you simply don't have the time or inclination to be shifting desks, chairs and bookcases around. However, changing the way your room is set up can have a number of important consequences, especially for a teacher who is new to a school or a class.

- It helps you take charge of the space, to mark your territory and feel more confident within it.
- It will help you stamp your own personality on the room, and start to feel as though you belong there.
- It's actually good fun setting up the classroom exactly as you want it.
- Taking personal charge of the space in this way shows the children that you mean business.
- When the class first arrives at the room, it will be clear that this is a fresh start, with a new teacher who has different ways of doing things.
- It will allow you to organize resources, equipment, etc., in a way that best suits you.
- You can become familiar with what is actually in the room. You will know where everything is, having moved it around yourself.
- You can take the opportunity to chuck out old papers, books, or anything else that is not of use to you, thus freeing up space within the room.

If you are nervous about rearranging things in your room, ask your line manager or induction tutor to see whether this is okay. You will probably find that they are more than happy for you to do this, and that they view it as a very positive sign of initiative.

One final tip about rearranging a room is to do it before the term starts, when you have a little time on your hands. Alternatively, a mid-term rearranging session can inject a fresh impetus and atmosphere into your classroom and your teaching, for instance if you are having behaviour problems.

Primary and secondary classrooms

There are a number of important differences between primary and secondary classrooms, and the way that they might be set up. In primary schools, because most curriculum areas are taught in this one space, the teacher will need to take different subjects into account when planning how to set up the room. There is also a tendency for primary teaching in some subjects to be more discovery based, and to involve less sitting at a desk to work.

Of course, for many secondary school teachers, a room of their own is an unfulfilled dream. The difficulties caused by teaching in a number of different classrooms can have a huge impact on your stress levels as you move between rooms, lugging a heavy box of books or equipment. Sadly, in a school with accommodation issues there is little teachers can do to rectify the situation.

How should I set up my room?

One of the most important decisions for secondary, and indeed primary, teachers to make is whether to put the desks in groups or rows. There are a number of factors that might influence your decision.

- *The attitudes and behaviour of the children:* Highly motivated and well behaved children will generally find it easier to cope with desks placed in groups than their less well behaved counterparts. A difficult or poorly motivated class may do better if the desks are set out in the more formal arrangement of rows facing the teacher.
- *The learning needs of the children:* If you teach a class or classes where the children have special needs (for instance problems with literacy), it is very important that they are able to see the board clearly, and this may have an influence on your preferred set up. It is also important for children with hearing problems to be able to see the teacher's face clearly when he or she is talking to the class.
- *Your preferred teaching styles:* A teacher who tends to use whole class activities that involve a lot of board work will find desks placed in rows a more suitable arrangement. Similarly, if much of the learning is based around group work, clearly the tables should be arranged accordingly.
- *The subject(s) you teach:* In the primary classroom, the whole range of subjects will be taught, and it may be that the desks need to be changed between rows and groups to suit the area of the curriculum. In the secondary classroom, there will be subjects such as Science which may use specific furniture (i.e. lab tables) that can only be set up in one way.
- *The space available:* Generally speaking, grouping desks takes up less room in the class than putting them in rows. If your room is small, you will need to think carefully about how you can maximize the space available for your students.

What's in the primary classroom?

Having worked with both the youngest primary school children and the oldest at secondary school, I'm well aware of just how different primary and secondary classrooms are. For many secondary teachers, there is little in the room beyond desks, chairs, a whiteboard and some shelving (of course this depends on the subject being taught). The primary classroom is generally a much more interesting and personalized space within which to work and learn.

When you are deciding how to lay out the different furniture, etc., in your room, it may prove helpful to make yourself a paper plan to experiment with. That way you can move the different elements around easily, to see what works best without having to physically lug furniture around until you're sure where you want everything to go.

If there are heavy items to be moved, do enlist the help of the caretaker (if possible) or another teacher. Here is a list of some of the things that might be included in the primary classroom space, particularly at the lower end of the age ranges (i.e. Nursery, Reception and Year One children).

- A carpet or mat for the children to sit on, for instance when taking the register or listening to stories.
- Small desks and chairs where the children can do written work.
- A flipchart or whiteboard.
- A book box containing a range of different reading books.
- A cloakroom area for the children to store their coats and lunch boxes.
- A carpeted play area where children work on activities such as Lego and model making.
- A listening area with tape recorders, headphones and musical instruments.
- A Drama area where the children can set up a shop, dress in different costumes, and so on.
- An Art area with paint, brushes, and a sink.
- A place for sand and water, and other messy work.
- Labelled drawers for each child's work and equipment.

Setting up the primary classroom

When you're looking at how you might set up a primary school classroom, there are a number of considerations to take into account.

- Matching the room layout to the age of the children and consequently the type of curriculum activities they will be undertaking.
- How you are planning to organize any ability or other groupings.
- What should be done for any children with particular special educational needs.
- How the children will access the resources.
- Keeping the children's movement through the space as unimpeded as possible.
- Health and safety issues that may arise when the children move around.
- Keeping messy activities near the sink or the playground.
- Ensuring that all children can see the board, or using a flipchart that can be moved around from place to place.
- The noise levels that will be caused by different activities.

This diagram shows one possible layout of a primary classroom for Reception year children.

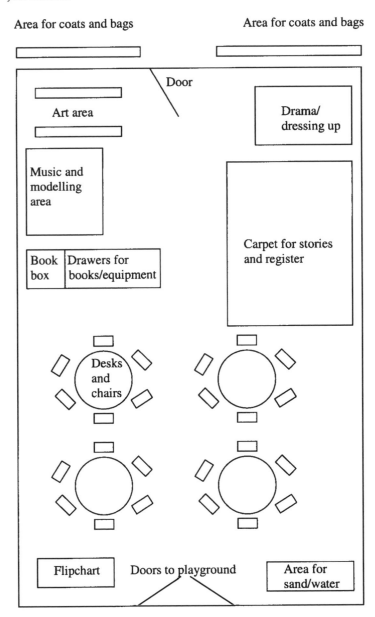

Area for coats and bags

Area for coats and bags

Door

Art area

Drama/
dressing up

Music and
modelling
area

Carpet for stories
and register

Book box	Drawers for books/equipment

Desks and chairs

Flipchart

Doors to playground

Area for
sand/water

155

8 Classroom teaching

Classroom management

The term 'classroom management' covers the whole spectrum of management issues that a teacher has to deal with in his or her classroom. There's actually a surprising amount to consider, and the way that you manage all these different aspects of the classroom will have a powerful influence on how effectively your children learn and also on how well they behave. The experienced teacher gets into a pattern of setting up the classroom in the way that best facilitates learning, so that he or she instinctively manages the classroom environment and routines without too much thinking (or stress). If you are new to teaching, the checklist questions below will help you to consider some of the different areas involved in managing your own classroom.

Checklist: The classroom environment
- How do I manage the way that the class enters and leaves the room?
- How do I control the way that the children use the space?
- How do I set up the furniture and equipment within the room?
- What happens when the children need to access equipment?
- What sort of displays do I have, and how do these contribute to learning?
- How do I make the environment as comfortable as possible?
- How do I manage external factors, such as the noise of other classes?

Checklist: Teaching and learning
- How do I manage the delivery of the curriculum?
- How do I ensure that all curriculum areas are covered?
- In what order do I teach each subject or topic?
- How do I engage my students in their learning?
- What different styles of teaching and learning do I use?
- What resources will I use, and how will these be organized?
- How do I manage the child who is not learning successfully?
- How do I manage differentiating for children with different abilities?
- How do I organize the timing of my lesson?

Checklist: Behaviour management
- How do I manage the setting of rules and boundaries?
- What teaching strategies do I use to manage behaviour?
- How do I manage my own behaviour, and its influence on the way my children behave?
- How and when do I apply sanctions and rewards?
- How do I manage low level disruption?
- What do I do if a serious incident occurs?
- How do I manage the aftermath of a serious incident?
- How do I manage the stress that poor behaviour causes me?

Behaviour management

Managing behaviour is a hugely complex subject. Some teachers find that they are instinctively rather good at managing the behaviour of their students, while for other teachers this is an area of real concern. Most of us do find behaviour management to be an issue right at the start of our teaching careers, while we are still learning the ropes. After all, being asked to stand in front of a large group of children or teenagers and get them to listen to you is never going to be straightforward! You can find some useful ideas and advice about managing behaviour in the sections that follow. You'll also find more information in Chapter 3 under the heading 'Getting your class to behave'. If you want to learn more about behaviour management, and get a practical and realistic overview of the subject, try my book *Getting the Buggers to Behave* (published by Continuum).

What makes a good manager of behaviour?

Even if you feel that maintaining discipline is not something that comes naturally to you, it is certainly possible to learn how to be a good manager of behaviour. The diagram shown here gives you a mini guide to successful behaviour management. You can find some more detailed ideas in the section below on 'Strategies for behaviour management'.

ATTITUDE

confidence
certainty
high expectations
+

AWARENESS

of boundaries
of sanctions/rewards
of how the children are behaving
+

APPROACH

enthusiastic
assertive but not defensive
positive
sense of humour
sense of perspective
flexibility and humanity
=

SUCCESSFUL BEHAVIOUR MANAGEMENT

Whole school behaviour policies

A whole school behaviour policy is a document that sets out the school's approach to behaviour. The policy might begin by listing the school's expectations of its students, staff and parents. This could take the form of a list of school rules, or alternatively perhaps a charter that sets out what the school views as the appropriate approach to learning and discipline. Many policies focus on the way that everyone should behave and work together to ensure success. The policy will also give details of what will happen to students who behave and work well, and to those students who choose to misbehave rather than conform to what the school requires of them.

What makes a good behaviour policy?

There is a huge difference for the teacher between simply having a whole school behaviour policy on paper, and having one that actually works well in practice. Here are some factors that go towards making a policy really work for the classroom teacher.

- The policy is not just a paper exercise, but is used effectively on a daily basis, and across the whole school.
- When first devised, this was done in consultation with teachers, rather than without hearing their views and feelings.
- The policy is constantly being reviewed and updated, to ensure that any parts which do not work are altered. The policy is able to adapt as the children, the teachers and the school change over time.

- The contents and application of the policy are made 100 per cent clear to students, parents (and staff). Everyone knows where they stand.
- The policy sets out exactly what the school expects from its students (and teachers) in terms of attitude, effort, behaviour and work.
- The policy is a clear and effective part of the whole school ethos.
- It puts the emphasis on positive aspects, such as rewarding good work and behaviour, rather than on constant punishment.
- The policy puts the teachers in a position where they know exactly what to do, and who to turn to, if students do misbehave.
- When sanctions do have to be given, there are methods of ensuring that these are enforced and followed through every time (right up to the most senior level).
- It asks the students to make an informed choice about the way that they behave, and puts the decision making in the child's hands, rather than the teacher's.
- The policy is seen to support the teacher as a professional, and to trust in his or her judgement.
- It encourages consistency, but also allows for individual approaches to discipline.
- The students view the policy as fair and reasonable, and as being fairly and consistently applied by all staff.

Rewards and behaviour

A positive and enthusiastic approach, in which good work is expected and rewarded, can pay huge dividends in terms of behaviour. An ethos where hard work is the norm, and misbehaviour is dealt with consistently and effectively, is far more useful than a school where punishment for failing to comply replaces rewards for successful cooperation. As far as possible, try to see rewards as your first line of defence, for instance greeting a class by asking 'Let's see who wants to earn a merit mark today!' Some other ideas for rewarding your students are shown here. Top of the list is a smile, one of the most powerful weapons in your armoury of rewards.

Some different types of reward

a smile!
verbal praise
written praise
merits and commendations
certificates
positive referrals to tutor
phone calls home
letters home
school awards

Strategies for behaviour management

As I noted above, it is far better to encourage good behaviour (and work), rather than having to deal with poor behaviour as it arises. I do fully understand how difficult it is with some children and at some schools for the teacher to get good behaviour, but even in the worst case scenario it is worth trying some of my ideas to see what happens.

The following ten strategies are designed to help you encourage your children to behave well, so that you can hopefully avoid having to deal with misbehaviour. See the next part of this section for what to do if they don't behave as you wish.

**Top 10 strategies
for
encouraging good behaviour**

1. Wait for silence
2. Expect the best
3. Tell them what you want
4. Give them 'the choice'
5. Use the 'deadly stare'
6. Control your voice
7. Praise one, encourage all
8. Set the boundaries
9. Set them targets
10. Learn to laugh!

- *Wait for silence:* I repeat this strategy in every book that I write, and for a very good reason: because it is the single most effective thing that a teacher can do to get his or her classes to behave and learn properly. Whatever it takes (and however long you have to struggle), *never ever* address a class until they are sitting in silence, looking at you and ready to listen to what you say. I promise you, it's crucial. Depending on the children you teach, to achieve silence from your class, you might try:
  - Simply waiting for them
  - Giving a 'silence command', such as 'I want everyone looking at me and listening please'
  - Using sanctions for chatty individuals or whole classes
  - Giving them a shock, for example pretending to bang your head on the desk, or storming out of the room theatrically.

Note: For more ideas about how to actually get silence from your children, see my books *Getting the Buggers to Behave* and *Sue Cowley's Teaching Clinic.*

- *Expect the best:* Children will generally live up, or down, to what you expect of them, both in behaviour and in work. Always expect them to behave impeccably, and express surprise (rather than anger) when they don't.

- *Tell them what you want:* Our students need to know where they stand, so tell them exactly what it is you want. One good way of doing this is to use 'I expect' statements right from the word go. Let them know that 'I expect you to listen in silence when I'm talking' and 'I expect you to stay in your seats unless you have permission to get up'.

- *Give them 'the choice':* Pass the responsibility for behaving appropriately over to your students. This is your classroom: you are in charge of ensuring that learning can take place. Essentially, the children have a choice — between doing as you ask, or accepting the consequences of their non-compliance.

- *Use the 'deadly stare':* Non-verbal messages are a very powerful tool in getting good behaviour. Learn to perfect the deadly stare, so that a single look from you will silence your students immediately.

- *Control your voice:* Our voices give away our inner state of mind, and can also influence the way that our students behave. Learn to use your voice calmly and quietly, and this will help you control your class.

- *Praise one, encourage all:* A quick word of praise to a student who is doing what you want, rather than a snap of annoyance at those messing around, will encourage the rest of the class to behave in the appropriate way.

- *Set the boundaries:* When you first meet your class or classes, let them know where your boundaries are — what you will and will not accept. A good way to visualize boundaries is to think of them as a box within which your students must stay.

- *Set them targets:* We all like to have something to aim for. Set targets for how your children should behave, as well as how they should work. A quick target of 'I want everyone to work silently for ten minutes, starting from now' can prove very effective.

- *Learn to laugh!:* Using humour in the classroom will show your students that you are human, and consequently encourage them to respect you. Being able to laugh at yourself when you make a mistake offers a good counterbalance to the moments when you must be strict, and so helps lighten the atmosphere in the classroom.

Many (perhaps most) teachers are, of course, faced with misbehaviour on a daily basis. The key to avoiding, or at least lessening, the stress that this misbehaviour causes is to have a number of strategies for dealing with the problem. In addition to helping you cope with stress, these strategies will also make it less likely that the misbehaviour reoccurs in the future. When the children see you dealing fairly and rationally with their actions, they quickly come to realize that you are a teacher who cannot be messed with!

**Top 10 strategies
for
dealing with misbehaviour**

1 Use 'I want' statements
2 Stay calm
3 Remove the audience
4 Defuse, don't escalate
5 Don't rise to the bait
6 Build a 'wall'
7 Make them decide
8 Sanction the behaviour
9 Follow it through
10 Make the sanction count

- *Use 'I want' statements:* The effective teacher tells the child exactly what he or she wants. Rather than asking little Sammy 'Would you mind stopping that chatter now?', use the more assertive statement or command 'I want you to stop talking right now and listen to me, please'.
- *Stay calm:* However natural it is to get wound up by poor behaviour, this will only ever add to your problems. A calm teacher will deal more effectively with the problem, and will also encourage the child to stay calm too.
- *Remove the audience:* When a child is confronted about his or her poor behaviour in front of the whole class (the classic 'would you like to explain why you did that to the rest of us?') it becomes far more likely that they will create a scene. Instead, take the child to one side, or even out of the room, before you chat with them.
- *Defuse, don't escalate:* It is only natural, when faced with rudeness or confrontation, to react in a similar vein and start a 'tit for tat' battle with the child concerned. However, a relentlessly calm and polite approach will demonstrate appropriate behaviour to the child, and will also give them nothing to feed off. Do everything you can to defuse the situation. This includes bringing your voice and tone right down, until you are speaking with an almost hypnotic calm.
- *Don't rise to the bait:* Much misbehaviour is designed to get a rise out of the teacher. If you refuse to rise to the bait of a child whose aim is to wind you up, the tactic becomes meaningless and a waste of time.
- *Build a 'wall':* A very good way to avoid rising to the bait is to build a 'wall' between you and the behaviour. Imagine that a wall stands between you and the child, and that however badly he or she misbehaves, you are completely impervious to its effects. That way you are in a far better position to deal calmly and rationally with the situation.

- *Make them decide:* When you do have to use sanctions, keep reminding the child that they have a choice at every stage. They can accept the current level of sanctions, or repeat the misbehaviour and earn a higher level of punishment.
- *Sanction the behaviour:* If a child feels that the punishment is a personal attack, this is far more likely to create confrontation. Make it clear that it's the behaviour, and not the child, that is being sanctioned. In addition, keep the whole situation as depersonalized as possible. You can do this by blaming the school rules for the fact that you have to impose a sanction.
- *Follow it through:* Every time you apply a sanction, you *must* follow it through, for example chasing children to serve a detention, if they do not turn up. Otherwise, the sanction is meaningless and not worth imposing in the first place.
- *Make the sanction count:* If you set a detention, spend time during that detention actually talking to the child about his or her misbehaviour. Often, children don't actually understand why they are being punished, and need things set out clearly for them. Hopefully, this discussion will prevent a reoccurrence of the behaviour that earned the sanction.

Applying sanctions

Although rewards and other strategies are very important, this is not to say that sanctions are unnecessary, rather that they should be viewed as a last resort. A classroom in which sanctions are constantly in use has the potential to become a very negative and confrontational place. The teacher who intervenes quickly when misbehaviour occurs, and who then applies sanctions consistently and fairly, will generally have to use them far less than a teacher who does not really understand how they work. Shown here is a quick guide on how you might intervene with misbehaviour and then apply sanctions in an effective way.

Quick guide to applying sanctions

Misbehaviour

Intervention One: The 'deadly stare'
Teacher gives 'deadly' look in direction of child
Unspoken message *'Are you sure you want to mess with me!?'*

Misbehaviour repeated   or ... child decides to behave

Intervention Two: The 'choice' is made clear
Teacher beckons child to side of room
Teacher explains choice
'You decide. Behave as I expect or accept the consequences. If you do that again, you will force me to use sanction 'x'.'

Misbehaviour repeated   or ... child decides to behave

Sanction Level One: e.g. written warning
Teacher explains child's 'decision'
'You decided to continue the misbehaviour. That misbehaviour earns this sanction.'

Misbehaviour repeated   or ... child decides to behave

Sanction Level Two: e.g. short detention
Teacher repeats explanation of child's 'decision'

Misbehaviour repeated   or ... child decides to behave

Sanction Level Three: e.g. long detention
Teacher repeats explanation of child's 'decision'

Misbehaviour repeated   or ... child decides to behave

Sanction Level Four: e.g. child sent out
Teacher explains why child has received the 'ultimate' punishment

Types of sanction

Sanctions vary widely from school to school. In some schools, the sanctions to be used will be a prescriptive part of a whole school behaviour policy. In other schools, much will be left to the discretion of the teacher. In fact, the clearer the policy is about exactly what sanctions should be used, and when they should be applied, the easier life will be for the teacher. Here are some of the sanctions that you might have at your disposal.

Some different types of sanction

verbal warnings

written warnings

red and yellow cards

detentions

referrals to manager

phone calls home

letters home

being put 'On Report'

Detentions

The detention is perhaps the most commonly used type of sanction. In some schools detentions work very well as a deterrent, while in others they do not work at all. Much depends on factors such as the school ethos, and the way that the children view detentions as a sanction. When a detention is given, it must be followed through if it is going to work in the future, and this can prove exhaustingly time consuming. Here are some general points about detentions.

- Detentions might be imposed on an individual or on the whole class. Be careful about using whole class detentions, which can be seen (correctly) as unfair.
- The short 'same day' detention is often served during break time, lunchtime or after school, and is usually taken by the class teacher who imposed the punishment.
- Same day detentions are (legally) allowed to be no longer than 15 minutes.
- If a longer detention is to be served, 24 hours' notice must be given to the child's parents or guardians.
- As well as short, same day detentions, longer departmental or faculty detentions might take place in the secondary school, perhaps once a week. These could be used for the child who has failed to serve a short detention.
- Some schools also offer senior management or school detentions, and indeed some will make a repeat offender serve detentions on Saturdays!

Behaviour and written evidence

Although it would clearly be impossible to keep written evidence of every incident of misbehaviour, it is important for you to keep a note of any serious incidents which occur. The Education Act (1996) says that such a report should be made in every case where force is used by the teacher. I would also advise you to keep a record of any serious incidents in which you did not have to intervene physically.

This written evidence can be crucial, both for the teacher's sake (should any complications arise, such as an accusation that you mishandled the situation) and for the child (in dealing with the problem at its root cause). Try to write your report as soon as possible after the event, while it is still fresh in your mind. Your school may have an incident book in which you can make a note of what happened. Do ensure that you keep a copy when you write in the incident book, or pass on a written report to somebody else. There are a number of very good reasons why this written record is important, especially in the case of serious incidents such as those described in the sections below.

- An accumulation of written evidence will allow a child with serious behavioural issues to receive the proper help that he or she needs.
- Although it is increasingly difficult for schools to exclude very poorly behaved

students, this type of written evidence is essential in creating a case for such a child to receive specialist help.

- If there is any comeback from the incident on you as a teacher, it is vital to have written evidence of what actually happened.
- It is very easy for the memory to distort an incident after the fact. It is also relatively easy for a child to bend the truth to get a teacher into trouble.
- Writing a report about the misbehaviour that occurred is all part of acting as a professional.
- The written report can be copied and passed on to the relevant people, for instance the head of year or other manager responsible for behaviour issues.
- Writing down the details of an incident can be cathartic – a good way of dealing with the stress that the incident might have caused for you as a teacher.

What should be included in the report?

It is a good idea to include the details listed here in your written report of the incident.

Written report of serious behaviour incident

Your name

The child's name

Other children who were involved
(for example, victims or witnesses)

The date that the incident occurred

Where the incident took place

Details of exactly what happened

What you did to try to de-escalate the situation

How the incident was dealt with at the time

How the incident was followed through afterwards

Who else helped to deal with the problem

Any injuries that occurred, to children or staff

Any other damage that occurred

If force did have to be used,
What this was and why it was necessary

'Serious incident'

What is a 'serious incident'?

Although (thankfully) still reasonably rare, you should be aware that serious incidents of misbehaviour can and do occur in schools. For the most part, the teacher will avoid extreme behaviour by the way that he or she handles the children within the classroom. However, there will be times when (often for reasons outside your control) a student 'goes off on one' and completely loses control over his or her behaviour. At this point, if it is appropriate you are entitled to make a physical intervention. See the sections below for more detail about what 'reasonable force' is, and when it might be used.

Examples of a serious incident could include a physical attack by one student on another, a fight between two students in your classroom, or a physical attack on you as a teacher. Other serious offences include catching a student with a weapon (such as a knife), with drugs, or in the process of committing a crime. As well as experiencing serious incidents within your classroom, you may also be faced with a serious incident happening in the corridor or the playground.

Dealing with the serious incident

In any serious situation, your first priority is ensuring the safety of the children (both those involved and others in the vicinity) and of course of yourself. With some incidents, the situation may actually require you to use physical intervention, but always view this as a last resort. In all instances, if you feel that physical intervention is going to put you at risk of injury (for instance from a student who is bigger than you), then do not intervene yourself but call for help instead. The guidance from the Education Act states that teachers are allowed to use reasonable force in a 'wide variety of situations'. These situations fall into three main categories.

- Where a student might injure him or herself or others.
- Where a student is causing damage to property (including his or her own).
- Where the child is behaving in a way that prevents 'good order and discipline' from being maintained (both inside the classroom and in the school as a whole).

As soon as a serious incident begins, take the following steps

Dealing with the serious incident

Send a reputable child to fetch help, preferably from a senior manager

As far as possible, remove other children from the immediate vicinity

If possible, use behaviour management strategies to calm and de-escalate the situation

If this is not working, try shouting loudly at the students to stop what they are doing immediately

If this does not work think, as calmly as possible, how (and whether) you are going to intervene
**DO NOT INTERVENE IF YOU HAVE
ANY DOUBTS OR IF YOU ARE
LIKELY TO GET YOURSELF INJURED**

If all else fails, and the situation warrants it, use reasonable force to stop the incident, or to prevent injury from occurring

What is reasonable force?

The Education Act guidance helpfully states that 'there is no legal definition' of this term, and that it must depend on the individual circumstances of each case. The advice is to use reasonable force only when the situation really warrants it, and also when all other avenues of resolution have been tried. (Of course, when two students are at each other's throats, the natural reaction is to try and prevent them from hurting each other.) If it is required, the reasonable force that you use would normally take some form of physical intervention.

What is 'physical intervention'?

The government's guidance suggests that you might use some of the following strategies to intervene.

- Putting yourself physically between the students.
- Standing in front of the child to block his or her way.
- Holding the child.
- Pushing or pulling the child.
- Leading the student by the hand or arm.
- Moving the child using a hand on his or her back.
- Using a more 'restrictive hold' (but only in extreme circumstances).

At all times you should ensure that your physical intervention doesn't actually hurt the child, and that it cannot be 'considered indecent'. Although the temptation will always be to dive in when two children look like they are going to hurt each other, the best advice is to put the safety of your class, yourself (and your career) at the top of the agenda. You can find more information about all the legal issues concerned with teachers and the use of physical intervention from the DfES, at www.dfes.gov.uk/publications/guidanceonthelaw/guidance.cfm.

Behaviour management programmes

In recent years, behaviour management has become an increasingly important subject, due to an actual or perceived increase in the number of problems with behaviour that teachers face. There are a number of different programmes available to assist schools when creating their behaviour policies. You may find your school participating in one specific programme, or extracting elements from various different types of approach. An outline of one programme is given below: the 'assertive discipline' approach, which has been used widely in recent years.

'Assertive discipline'

Author: Lee Canter

What's it about?
- Teaching students to make choices about their behaviour.
- Students understanding the consequences of the way that they behave.
- The teacher taking an assertive and positive role in dealing with behaviour.

What's involved?
- A set of rules and directions about appropriate behaviour.

- Using positive responses when students follow the rules.
- A hierarchy of consequences (or sanctions) when they disobey.

What are the benefits?
- It's made very clear what will happen if the student does misbehave.
- The school can develop a consistent approach to misbehaviour.
- Teachers and students are aware of the consequences of their actions.

What problems are there?
- The system can be too prescriptive to allow teachers to deal with different individuals and a variety of situations.
- Some students get into trouble constantly.
- Some students may actually choose to misbehave in order to get excluded.

Differentiation

Differentiation is all about meeting the needs of the different students in your class or classes. It could be that you have some children with specific and severe learning needs, or simply that you teach a wide ability range within one group or class. In an ideal world, the work that we set would be matched exactly to each individual child. In this ideal world, we would of course be teaching classes of only 10 or 15 children, and we would be given plenty of time each day to plan for their differing needs and abilities. In the real world, differentiation tends to be a little more haphazard. There are a number of ways in which schools and teachers differentiate for their students.

- *By setting:* Organizing the children into different sets gives the teacher a better chance of matching the work to the students' needs, because the majority of the class are working at the same or a similar level. Setting may take place in some subjects at primary level, by mixing children across the year groups (see page 230 of Tracey Nightingale's interview for an example of how this can work). In the secondary school, children may be set from Year Seven (perhaps in the core subjects), at GCSE level, or not at all.
- *By activity:* Teachers may differentiate the work that they set by giving a range of activities to their class. These activities would offer differing levels of difficulty, and the children would be asked to complete the activity appropriate to their own level of ability.
- *By presentation:* Even when the activities are the same, it could be that some children need a different form of presentation in order to understand the work. For instance, children with literacy problems may need a simplified version of the class worksheet.
- *By amount completed:* Children will naturally differentiate their work because they will finish different amounts of work within the same timescale.

In this case, the activity is much harder for some children than for others, and consequently the amount completed is far less. (This type of differentiation may lead to frustration and disaffection for the less able.)

- *By outcome:* Just as with differentiation by amount completed, this relies on a natural process of differentiation. With every piece of work, the end result or outcome produced will differ according to the abilities of the child completing it.

Marking

Marking, like teaching, is a balancing act. Unless you are planning to work every available hour of the day and night, it really is not possible to mark every single piece of work in detail. At some point, you will need to make difficult decisions about exactly how you are going to do your marking. The temptation is to mark everything very quickly, using the 'tick and flick' method described below, because this gives the impression of completeness. However, your choice of marking style should obviously be informed by the impact it will have on your children's learning. The benefits and drawbacks of some different marking styles are described below.

'Tick and flick'

Description: The teacher puts a big tick or cross on each paragraph or question, then flicks to the next page. At the end of the work a brief comment such as 'good work' or 'could do better' is written, and a grade or result is given.

Benefits:

- The work looks marked: both children and parents tend to appreciate this.
- The teacher gets an overall sense of how well the child is doing, and where his or her strengths and weaknesses lie.
- The resulting grade can be recorded in the teacher's mark book.
- This method is the fastest of all.

Drawbacks:

- The student gets little or no sense of why he or she is making mistakes, and how to put them right.
- Consequently, there is little real educational value in terms of improving the student's learning.
- For weak students, a series of crosses on a piece of work can be demotivating.

'Close' marking

Description: With 'close' marking the teacher corrects every error and makes detailed comments about what the student is doing right/wrong and gives targets for improvement.

Benefits:

- The student is given detailed information about the strengths and weakness of his or her work.
- The child also sees what the errors are, and what the correct piece of work would look like.
- This method offers good value in terms of improving work and developing the learning.

Drawbacks:

- This marking method is very time consuming, especially where a large number of mistakes have been made.
- The weaker student will end up with a piece of work covered in the teacher's pen, and this is potentially very offputting.
- Unless the child actually takes the time to read through the work carefully, and to understand his or her errors, this detailed marking is effectively wasted time.

Marking for specific errors

Description: With this marking style, the teacher highlights a particular area for which he or she will be marking with a specific piece of work. The focus or target might be set with the class as a whole, or with each individual. For instance, the teacher might decide to look closely at the use of punctuation, or at the content of the work, rather than the spelling or grammar.

Benefits:

- The children (and teacher) work together to focus on a specific area of their learning and work.
- The teacher can focus on the different strengths and weaknesses of each child. For instance, asking the weak speller to focus on his or her spelling, while the child with poor punctuation skills focuses on using full stops and commas correctly.
- This method offers a compromise between the speed of 'tick and flick' and the slowness of 'close' marking.

Drawbacks:

- Not all the errors in every piece of work will be corrected. This can sometimes lead to complaints from parents (e.g. that the teacher is not correcting the spelling).
- The method does require the teacher to take time to set targets and to focus carefully on the chosen area.

You can find some samples of different types of marked work in Chapter 14 of the Toolkit (pages 275–276).

Marking: some time-saving tips

There are a number of ways that the enterprising teacher can save time with his or her marking. Many of the tips given below also offer benefits in terms of your children's learning.

- *Do it yourself:* Asking the child to review and mark his or her own work before it is handed in is a very effective way of encouraging your students to reflect on what they have done. This self review also gives the teacher a starting point for his or her own marking. For instance, you might ask the child to write comments at the end of a piece on different areas of the work, such as spelling, punctuation, content, and so on.
- *Swop and mark:* This method is useful for tests with factual answers, for instance a maths or spelling test. The children swop their work with a partner and the teacher (or indeed a child) reads out the answers as the students mark each other's work.
- *Marking during lessons:* It is possible, just sometimes, to find a lesson in which you can actually do some marking. This might be a period of silent reading (perhaps last thing on a Friday when the class is too tired to misbehave).
- *Marking non-written work:* There can be a tendency to focus on the marking and assessment of what our children write. Oral and practical work also needs to be marked, and these assessments are usually best done when the work is actually taking place, thus saving the teacher time. For instance, a group of children might give a talk to the class, and you could mark their contributions as they do this.
- *Give non-written homeworks:* Similarly, not all homeworks need to be written ones. Other useful (non-marking intensive) tasks include memorizing passages or facts, researching a topic, planning for written classwork, and so on.

Assessment

The effective teacher carries out a process of more or less continuous assessment of his or her students, whether this is on a formal or informal basis. There are a number of very good reasons why teachers assess their students, and also some not so good reasons for assessment.

- So that you know where the children are at a certain point in their learning, in terms of skills, understanding, and so on.
- To inform the work that you give the class in the future, both the content, and the level of difficulty involved.

- So that you can check how far the children have progressed in their learning.
- In order to see the differing levels of ability and understanding within the class.
- To find out what the class do and do not know about a particular subject or topic.
- To encourage the children to learn more about a topic, or to memorize specific details (for instance in the spelling or times tables test).
- To check whether the students have understood or learnt the work set (for a test or in class).
- To check for special educational needs or other individual learning requirements.
- To help you differentiate the work for children who have different learning needs.
- To prove what the teacher or school is adding in terms of 'value'.
- To prove the 'high' standards that a child, class or school has achieved.

Informal assessment

Much of the assessment that we do as teachers is actually subconscious, or performed in an informal way. For instance, during a class discussion you might be forming opinions about how well each individual within the class contributes, and consequently making an informal assessment of their oral work. Similarly, when a child shows you a piece of work, you will immediately judge or assess whether or not it is up to the standard which you know that child can achieve. When you mark a child's exercise book, you may not give or record a score or grade for each individual piece of work. However, you will be assimilating the standard achieved into your overall understanding of the student's ability and the amount of progress he or she is making.

Formal assessment

Formal assessments will generally involve the recording of a grade or mark, and perhaps a comparison of how each child has fared across a class or year group. Formal assessments include class tests, baseline assessments, examinations such as SATs and GCSEs, and so on. Some teachers might use a weekly spelling test, to check their children's progress and to ensure that they are memorizing a number of words each week.

Formal assessments in the shape of exams can have their benefits for the classroom teacher, beyond the actual information that they provide on how well each child has fared. For instance, many teachers will notice how forthcoming SAT exams encourage a greater focus and motivation from many of their students. Formal ('baseline') assessments at the beginning of primary or secondary school can be a useful diagnostic tool in discovering what point the children have reached, and who might need additional help with specific subject areas.

Assessment is often described as being either 'summative' or 'formative'. Summative assessment provides a summary of the point that the individual child has reached at the end of a topic, Year or Key Stage, for instance a final grade in the GCSE exams. Formative assessment is used on a day-to-day basis. It is designed to inform the teacher about the child's current level of progress, and show where the teacher and student need to go next, for instance informing the work that the teacher plans for the next lesson.

The downsides of assessment

It is easy to imagine that assessment is always a helpful and informative tool within the classroom. However, this is not always the case, and it is important for the teacher to be aware of the downsides of assessment for his or her students. The main two problems are the potential for demotivation, and the stress that formal assessments can cause.

- *Demotivation:* For the weakest students in a class or year group, it can be very demoralizing and demotivating to undergo formal assessments. This is particularly true for those assessments that make comparisons between children of the same age. It cannot ever be particularly pleasant to know that you are way behind your peers in the work that you do.
- *Stress:* There have been reports recently on the high levels of stress which children are feeling, from an increasingly early age. An awareness that an exam or assessment is very important, and a sense that you are going to 'pass' or 'fail', is potentially very stressful for the young person. This is perhaps especially so for those children whose parents are extremely keen for them to do well, and also for children who do not tend to do well in exams.

There are a number of ways in which teachers can help their children cope with assessment, both in the classroom and in the more formal setting of exams.

- *Keep the results private:* Although it might save you time, don't read out the results of a test in front of the whole class. If you wish to do this, offer individual children a choice of whether or not you read their results out loud.
- *Teach them revision techniques:* The effective teacher lets his or her children know how to revise, how to memorize facts or organize their time, and so on.
- *Teach them 'how to pass' exams:* Children also need to know the best way of approaching an exam: for instance using their time wisely, how marks are awarded, how to plan their essays effectively, etc.
- *Talk to them after the assessment:* It really is worth sparing the time to talk through results of an assessment, especially with any children who are particularly anxious, or who have underachieved. Explain to the children why they got the results they did (whether this was poor technique or lack of effort), and how they can improve next time.

■ *Let them know you still care:* As teachers, our primary concern is not about getting the top results, but about getting the best that we can out of each child, and helping them to grow and develop as people. We need to show them that the marks they achieve do not affect our opinion of them – they are all still important individuals to us, irrespective of their exam grades.

Self-evaluation

Being able to evaluate yourself as a teacher is part and parcel of continuing to develop as a professional. When we are first starting out in teaching, as a student or an NQT, we are actively encouraged to evaluate ourselves and our teaching on a regular basis. We are also subjected to regular observations and evaluations from our tutors and our colleagues.

However, as you become more experienced (and busy), you may find yourself evaluating the work you do in a far less conscious way, or perhaps not at all. With all the other pressures of the job, all the issues to worry about outside of our teaching, the tendency is for us just to get on with it in the classroom. And when we do have a bad lesson, or a bad day, it is very tempting to just say 'forget about it' and try to put it behind us without too much deep consideration.

In my opinion, this lack of continuing reflection is (although perfectly understandable) a real shame. In my forthcoming book *How to Become an Outrageously Good Teacher*, I suggest that self-evaluation and reflection is a crucial part of being a professional, and of continuing to develop your teaching skills. On the other hand, no teacher needs or wants to be continually evaluating him or herself. Stick, perhaps, to the times when something has gone particularly well or particularly badly wrong.

Why should I evaluate myself?

Why, then, is it so crucial to evaluate yourself, and to reflect on what happens in your classroom? Below is a list of some of the reasons. Bear in mind that evaluation is not just about looking at and analysing yourself and the way that you work, it is also about looking at how a certain situation might have led to problems in your classroom, and understanding why this was.

■ *Identifying weak spots:* Even for the best teachers, sometimes something does go wrong in a lesson, whether with the work that you've set, or the behaviour that you received. When this happens, it's important to work out what it was that went wrong, and think about how it might be fixed so that it doesn't happen again.
■ *Dealing with emotional fallout:* In the situation where you are suddenly faced with serious misbehaviour, there will inevitably be an emotional factor for you as a teacher, and as a human being. If a child turns on you and

throws a stream of abuse, you need to consider why this happened. When you evaluate the situation, it could be that the behaviour had nothing at all to do with you as a teacher, but simply that the child was having a particularly difficult day. Alternatively, it could be that you made a contribution, that you somehow 'set them off'. By analysing the situation in detail, you will gain a better understanding of what occurred, and help yourself deal with the emotions involved.

- *Identifying strengths:* As well as looking at the negative side of your classroom practice, evaluating yourself also allows you to understand what your strengths are. Perhaps you conceived and delivered a lesson that worked particularly well. If this is the case, try to understand *why* it was so good, so that you can create similar lessons in the future. Maybe you dealt with a difficult incident of behaviour in a way that defused and resolved the situation instantly. As well as the importance of understanding how and why these things work, it is also a wonderful idea to share your successes (and the strategies behind them) with your colleagues.

- *Giving yourself a pat on the back:* Taking the time to consider that 'super lesson' allows you the opportunity to congratulate yourself, to revel in your own abilities as a teacher. Although everyone tells us that rewards and praise are crucial in our work with our children, it's not all that often that we are praised as teachers, so we need to learn to do it for ourselves!

How do I evaluate myself?

The following tips and advice give you some ideas about how you might undertake a self-evaluation, and the areas of your work that you could consider. As well as looking back on a lesson that has gone well (or badly), you might also select a specific lesson to evaluate, before it takes place.

- *Narrow the focus:* Rather than trying to evaluate everything you do in a particular lesson, try instead to focus on one area of your practice. This might be behaviour management, lesson planning, or timing and organization.

- *Consider yourself as a teacher:* As well as thinking about the external aspects of your work, such as lesson planning, look too at your own skills as a teacher. Consider particularly the verbal and non-verbal signals that you use with your children, how effective (or not) these are, and why they do or do not work.

- *Put yourself in their shoes:* Although it is difficult, do try to see yourself as the children see you. Often, we will focus on what we see as our students' bad behaviour, rather than thinking about what we might have done to provoke the situation. For instance, is the work we have set too easy or difficult, leading to boredom or frustration?

- *Use a video or tape:* If you can bear to, videoing or taping yourself is an invaluable way of seeing your teaching as the children see it. Be warned, though, it is never pretty looking at yourself in action!

- *Get some feedback:* Your students are the 'consumers' of the educational product that you offer, so why not ask them for some feedback on what you do, and don't, do well? It can be tough hearing the criticisms of your students, but you can be sure that they will pick up on those tiny faults and mannerisms of which you are totally unaware. (You may also find that they give you some lovely positive feedback.)
- *Look at incidents from start to finish:* If you are evaluating the way in which you dealt with a problematic incident, think about the time leading up to the event, and what happened afterwards, as well as the actual incident itself. Often, there are clues here as to why the problem occurred.

9 Beyond the classroom

Admin

Paperwork is truly the enemy of the teacher, because it causes us stress, and it gets in the way of the real job, which is helping children to learn. Because they are individuals, teachers come into the job with widely varying levels of organizational ability. Some people are naturally tidy, and take to all the paperwork like a duck to water. Others are destined to face a huge pile of papers on their desk throughout their teaching careers. Here are some top tips for dealing with admin effectively, without allowing it to become an issue.

- *Empty your pigeon-hole regularly:* When you first start teaching, it can make you feel rather special having a slot with your very own name on it. However, before long, the pigeon-hole becomes a source of much misery and heartache. The problem is that both highly important and completely meaningless bits of paper will get shoved into your pigeon-hole and if you fail to empty it for a few days, it will be stuffed full of forms to fill, urgent memos, etc.
- *Deal with it immediately:* As far as is humanly possible, deal with every piece of paper you receive straight away, especially those which can be passed on (or back) to somebody else. If you're given a form to fill out, don't put it in your 'to do' pile (where it may languish for far longer than originally intended). It's far, far better to fill it in right away and then get rid of it.
- *Be ruthless:* Never hang onto a piece of paper just because you 'might need it again'. There is far too much paper in the teaching profession: only by being completely ruthless will you ensure that you can actually find those bits of paper that you really do need.
- *Keep vital info in one place:* There are actually some really important bits of paper, such as class lists, which you will need to keep close to hand, particularly at the start of the year. Keep as much of this vital paper in one place as possible, for instance in a cardboard folder.
- *Have a yearly chuck out:* If you can find the time, go through all your bits of paper once a year and throw out anything that is no longer required.

Quick guide to paperwork

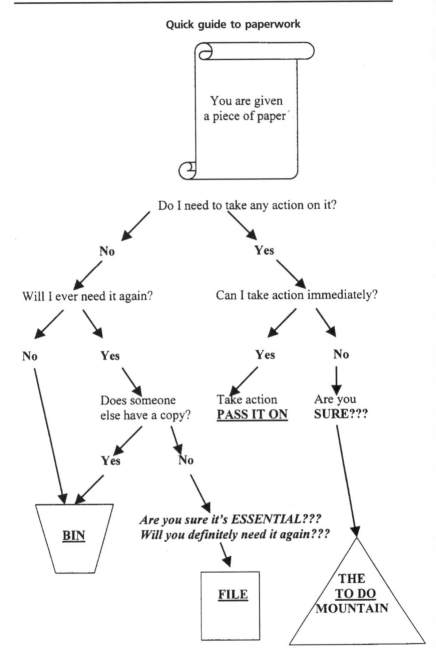

Recording and reporting

The areas of recording and reporting are closely linked to your assessment of your students, which was dealt with in the previous chapter. The teacher's mark book is a vital part of his or her teaching materials. The mark book allows you to keep a record of all marks that your students have achieved. These records will help inform your planning, report writing, overall assessment grades, and so on. You can find a sample page from a mark book in Chapter 14 (page 278).

Top Tip

It can be difficult for secondary teachers to check when a student claims that he or she was absent from class on a day that homework was set.

Avoid this problem by keeping your class register (i.e. absent/present) together with the marks for the class.

When you set a homework, leave a blank line for the marks alongside the class register for that lesson.
(See the mark book sample for an example of how this works.)

Reports come in many shapes and sizes. The handwritten reports that were the norm until relatively recently are increasingly being replaced by typed or even computerized formats, such as SIMs (see below). Reports offer the teacher an excellent opportunity to communicate with the home, and as such it is important that they are written well. You can find a number of different tips below for writing good reports.

SIMs report format

The SIMs reporting format is very similar to the SIMs registers, with which you may be familiar. The registers are sheets on which the teacher marks a student present or absent by filling in a lozenge-shaped mark. The register is then read by a computer software program. SIMs reports work in a similar way – the teacher places a series of marks on the sheet to indicate which comments will be included in each student's report. The computer then selects the relevant comments from a 'bank' created by the teacher or department, and puts them together into each individual report. The main downside to SIMs reports is that they can seem very impersonal and samey (which, of course, they are!).

Tips for report writing

Below you will find some general tips for report writing, as well as some examples of how to write, and not write, a report. You can find some additional advice in the checklists in Chapter 16 (page 288).

- Start each report with a general comment which summarizes the child's progress and overall achievement in your class.
- Frame your comments in a positive, rather than a negative, way as far as possible. The examples below show the difference between the two approaches.
    - Negative: 'Charlie just can't keep quiet. He's always chatting with his friends when he should be doing his work.'
    - Positive: 'Charlie finds it difficult to work in silence. He needs to concentrate on his own learning at all times.'
- Give comments on a range of areas: this would include the child's learning in the subject or subjects, and his or her current levels of achievement, the child's attitude to the work, behaviour in class, and so on.
- Even for your most difficult students, do try to comment on at least one or two things that the child does well. For instance, even for a child who is underachieving, you could include a positive comment about his or her potential (see the 'good example' below).
- Don't let your own emotions about a child shine through in a report. Whilst it may be tempting to let off steam about a kid who's been winding you up all year, your professional duty is to report accurately, effectively and dispassionately on each individual student.
- Bear in mind the potential parental reaction to the reports that you write. With the very difficult child, a negative report may have the opposite effect to that which you intend. Instead of encouraging the child to do better, with the support of his or her parents, a negative report may simply exacerbate a difficult home situation. (Alternatively, the child may decide that it is safer to 'lose' the report on the way home, and it might never even be seen by the parents.)
- Set clear targets for further improvement. These can be referred to in class with the student, and in subsequent meetings and contacts with the parents or guardians.

Report writing

The two examples below show how a secondary English report might be written. The general principles of report writing that are shown here can easily be adapted to different subject areas and to primary aged children.

A 'good example'

Charlie is an able and creative student who has the potential to do very well in this subject. He has an imaginative approach to the tasks set, and his oral work is always confident and clearly expressed. At the moment, Charlie finds it difficult when he is asked to work in silence. He needs to concentrate on his own learning at all times, rather than allowing others to distract him.

Charlie's written work would benefit from much more attention to detail, particularly when checking for spelling errors. He needs to write at greater length, especially when preparing coursework assignments. Charlie is a fluent reader, and he has shown a particular talent for working with the Shakespeare texts we have studied this term. He should now aim to develop his concentration in class so that he can succeed to the best of his ability.

A 'bad example'

Charlie is a weak student who has a poor approach to this subject. He just can't seem to keep quiet and is always chatting with his friends when he should be doing his work. His writing is always full of mistakes, and his spelling is very bad. He doesn't put enough time or effort into writing his coursework assignments, and this means that his grades are not going to be good. Charlie does like to read out loud in class, it's a shame he doesn't put the same amount of effort into his written work.

Examinations

A series of statutory examinations now punctuate the child's school career. Alongside these externally assessed exams, many schools will run annual school exams of their own. These are normally held during the summer term. Secondary schools will also run 'mocks' for their GCSE and 'A' level students in the run up to the real examinations. A brief run down of the timings of formal, externally assessed exams is given here.

Exam type	Usually taken in	Subject areas
SATs	Year Two	English, Maths
	Year Six	English, Maths, Science
	Year Nine	English, Maths, Science
GCSEs	Year Eleven	A wide range
NVQs	Varies, post-16	Vocational subjects
AS levels	Year Twelve	A wide range
A levels	Year Thirteen	A wide range

Preparing for exams

To help your students succeed in their exams, it really is well worth putting in some time helping them to prepare. The tips below give you a range of ideas about how you might do this. For lots more ideas on preparing your students for their exams, see the chapter on assessment in my book *Getting the Buggers to Write* (published by Continuum).

- Let them know what to expect. If children go into an exam without any idea of what is going to face them, they are bound to suffer from nerves. Talk them through the whole process: how long the exam will be, where it will take place, what equipment they might need to have with them, and so on.
- Give your children plenty of practice with old papers, looking carefully at the format of the paper, the way the questions are worded, how the marks are allocated, etc.
- Talk with your students about how and why marks are awarded. Some children find it hard to understand the relationship between the marks available for a question, the amount of time which they should spend on it, and the level of detail that they should include.
- Teach your children 'exam technique', looking at the importance of timing, deciding which questions to answer, how to ensure that they answer the question, and so on.

Pastoral work

The pastoral side of a teacher's job can be extremely rewarding, and it can also be time consuming and emotionally draining. As teachers, we have a special role to play in the care of the whole child. Although our principal responsibility is for educating our students, the teacher is often the main (or only) adult outside the home who will have contact with a child in a professional context.

Some of the children with whom you work will be under the care of a social worker or other specialist outside the school, but the majority will not. Some of the problems that your children bring to you may be connected solely to the school environment, whilst for others the teacher offers a dependable adult with whom to share their fears and concerns about life outside the school gates. An important part of our role, then, is to care for the social well-being of our charges, as well as for their educational welfare.

Depending on how well you relate to your students, you could find yourself acting as an 'agony aunt' or 'uncle' to large numbers of children or young people. This is perhaps especially so at the difficult transition times: the first move into mainstream schooling, the transfer from primary to secondary school, and the change from childhood into adolescence. The list below gives you an idea of the type of concerns you may have to deal with, and is followed by some tips on how to resolve the issues.

- *Bullying:* This may take the form of verbal or physical abuse. Bullying should be taken seriously, both by the teacher and by the school: make sure you find out whether your school has an anti-bullying policy, and what this involves.
- *Friendship issues:* Some children find it hard to socialize and make friends, while others will have traumatic rifts with a particular friendship group.
- *Problems at home:* Students may approach you to talk about a situation at home that is worrying them, for instance a problem with a sibling.
- *Serious issues:* When a problem raised by a child involves child protection issues, it is very important that you know what steps to take. See the sections below on child protection and serious issues for more information.

When your students do approach you with problems that they want to discuss, follow these tips to help resolve the issue in a professional manner.

- *Let them talk:* Sometimes a child will simply need a shoulder to cry on. Try to find the time to let them talk out the issue with you, however trivial you might feel it to be. If necessary, suggest that the child books a time with you after school.
- *Don't get overly involved:* There is something rather pleasing about a child choosing to confide in you, and the temptation can be to see yourself as a bit of an agony aunt or uncle. However, unless you are a professionally trained counsellor, you will not have the proper experience to undertake this role. Do try to keep your emotions out of any pastoral discussions. Getting overly involved with a child can make your day-to-day teaching job difficult.
- *Never promise confidentiality:* Often students will try to make you promise that you won't tell anyone before they reveal their problems. The teacher should never promise confidentiality, because if the issue turns out to be serious (see below) your first duty will be to inform the CPO of the conversation.
- *Make a record:* It is important to keep a record of any discussions which you feel are of a sufficiently serious nature. Make a note of the child's name, when they came to see you, what their problem was, and so on. If necessary, pass a copy of this information to a senior colleague (see below).
- *Pass on your concerns:* In the secondary school, the child's form tutor should be informed about pastoral issues which concern their tutees. In the primary school, if the child is not in your class, you should inform the classroom teacher of what has been said. Depending on the seriousness of the issue, you might also inform the head of year, your line manager, or in serious cases the CPO. These people will take the responsibility for informing the parents as necessary. In some schools a trained counsellor is also available to talk with troubled children.
- *Take them seriously:* Don't try to shrug off a problem which a child chooses to share with you, even when you see it as trivial. You will get children who regularly bend your ear, but this in itself could be a symptom of something more serious.

In the primary school, the pastoral care of a particular group falls mainly to the class teacher, who works with one class for the majority (or all) of the time. In the secondary school, the form tutor takes on responsibility for the pastoral care of one particular group of students. He or she may or may not actually teach this tutor group. See below for more information about the role of the form tutor.

The form tutor

In the primary school, the class teacher is able to develop a close relationship with the children, because he or she sees them all day every day. In addition, many parents or guardians drop their children off and collect them from school, and it is possible for them to maintain relatively close contact with the class teacher on a day-to-day basis. Parents know who their child's class teacher is, and it is not overly difficult to make arrangements for a quick chat about progress, or to air a particular concern.

On the other hand, in the secondary school a child will be only one of perhaps hundreds which the subject teacher sees in the course of the week. Because of this, the form tutor takes responsibility for the pastoral care of the children in a form or tutor group. In Chapter 6, 'Anatomy of a school', you can find a detailed description of the role of the tutor, and hear more about the job from a working teacher/tutor (pages 119–124).

Child protection

Depending on the type of person you are, and the relationship that you have with your students, you may find that a number of children approach you seeking help. Often, these children will be raising less serious concerns with you, such as those to do with friendship, worries about their work, and so on. Of course, these concerns should be dealt with sympathetically, and taken seriously.

However, from time to time you may find that students bring serious pastoral issues to you, and it's vital that you know what should be done in these circumstances. It may be the case that you have serious concerns about the welfare of a particular child in your form or class, even though the child has not spoken to you about his or her problem. Again it is your professional (and indeed personal) responsibility to ensure that these are dealt with in the proper manner. Just a few of the serious issues that you may encounter are listed below.

- Unexplained injuries that suggest physical abuse, for instance frequent bruising.
- A student fears that his friend is becoming addicted to drugs.
- A child tells you that her parents beat her when she does badly in a test.
- A teenage student is worried that she may be pregnant.

What should I do about a serious issue?

Schools must have a designated person responsible for dealing with child protection issues (often called the 'CPO' or Child Protection Officer). It is to this person that you should pass on your concerns. As soon as possible after the child has approached you, document your discussion in full detail, including the child's name, the date, what the child said, and so on. You should then go in person to see the CPO, giving him or her a copy of your notes, and keeping one for yourself. The CPO will then take over responsibility for the problem, and liaise with other agencies as necessary.

The parents' evening

Note: The term 'parents' is used below to indicate the child's guardians. For some children this may be brothers or sisters, foster carers, and so on.

Parents' evenings can be stressful and tiring occasions. However, the majority of teachers also find them a very valuable and important event. In the primary school, teachers may have regular contact with parents or guardians, for instance if they drop younger children off at school. For the secondary school teacher, the parents' evening is often the only form of contact with their students' guardians during the year. Sadly, it is often the case that the parents you most need or want to see at the evening will not attend.

In the run up to the parents' evening, you will probably be given an appointments sheet so that you can book individual time slots for each child. If you are a secondary school teacher with a large number of students, it may be that you need to double book the children within each time slot. If this is the case, you should ensure that you keep each discussion very short and focused (see the section below for ideas about how to do this). There are a number of very positive aspects about the parents' evening.

- The evening provides a way of creating an initial contact with the home, particularly if the student is experiencing problems.
- Teachers are able to pass on information about the student's strengths and weaknesses.
- The teacher is able to highlight any particular concerns, for instance about weak literacy skills or problematic behaviour.
- Many parents are very happy to support the work that their children do in the classroom, but are unsure about how to do this. The parents' evening allows us to explain more about the role they can play.
- If the child attends with his or her parents, the teacher can extract promises about future effort, work, behaviour, and so on.
- The teacher can check with the parents whether they are happy to be contacted directly in the event of any problems occurring.

You can find lots of ideas for surviving the parents' evening in Chapter 16 (page 289).

What should be in the discussion?

If you only have to see a limited number of parents, you can spend quite a substantial amount of time over each discussion. However, if you do have a large number of parents to see, you will need to be concise and very focused in order to fit everybody in. Here are some ideas about the format that your discussion might take.

- A summary of where the child is now, in terms of work, progression, behaviour, attitude and so on.
- Details of the individual child's strengths and weaknesses within the subject (secondary) or the curriculum (primary).
- Information about any specific concerns, or areas of weakness that need further work.
- Targets on which the child should work.
- Ways in which the parents can help you as a teacher.
- Details of forthcoming assessments, for instance SATs, GCSEs, and how the parents can help the child prepare.
- Any questions that the parents may need answered.

Extracurricular activities

Extracurricular activities are those which take place outside of the normal timetable and curriculum. These activities might be run before school, at lunchtimes, after school, or even on the weekends. Teachers can get involved in a huge range of different activities, depending on their own personal expertise in a subject or area, or simply on what they enjoy doing. Teachers may become involved in actually running and supervising an activity, or they may offer their assistance in a more peripheral way, for instance organizing the props or costumes for a school play.

For some secondary teachers, the subject that they teach involves extracurricular work almost as a matter of course. This includes teachers of Music/Drama (the school production) and teachers of PE (the school sports teams). Those teachers who do run these large-scale after school activities are generally all too happy for their colleagues to help them out. There are a huge range of activities with which you might like to get involved, from the computer club to the sports team, the school production to the Duke of Edinburgh award.

Unless you are teaching Drama or PE, running extracurricular activities would not generally be part of your job description as a classroom teacher. For posts in some independent schools, great emphasis is placed on a willingness to contribute to this aspect of school life. In any case, although participating in extracurricular activities is obviously hard work and time consuming, there are a number of valuable reasons for getting involved.

- These activities offer a great way of developing relationships with students outside the classroom environment.
- Your students get the chance to see you as a real person, and consequently build their respect for you.
- You can get to meet children who you don't actually teach. If you do teach these children in the future, they will already have developed a good relationship with you.
- You can help children develop skills outside the normal curriculum.
- The teacher can also develop his or her skills beyond the day-to-day job.
- Active participation in these activities looks great on your CV.

Trips

A school trip can be a very positive experience, both for the students participating, and for the teachers involved. For many children a trip is a rare opportunity for a day out of school, doing something completely different, or seeing somewhere new. Teachers are, however, perhaps becoming more wary about the implications of taking children on a trip. We certainly need to be fully aware of the extent of our responsibilities, and about the 'duty of care' which we owe to our students both on and off site.

A school trip might take place during the school day, for instance a visit to a museum. Alternatively, it could be an evening event, such as going to the theatre. Some trips are longer, for instance the popular 'residential' which is sometimes held in the early years of secondary school. In some cases, a school trip will be to an overseas destination, and this would include the skiing trip and MFL visit or exchange.

There are a wide range of health and safety considerations involved in setting up a trip. Before the event, a detailed risk assessment should be done, by a person trained in what to do. Parental consent must also be given. If you are an inexperienced teacher who wishes to arrange a trip, do make sure that you get help from a senior and experienced member of staff who is aware of all the legal niceties.

10 Pay, promotion and career development

Teachers' pay

Salaries vary widely in teaching according to where you teach, the type of post you hold, and the school you work in. In addition, teachers' salaries are reviewed and raised on a yearly basis. Changes to teachers' salaries reflect a number of factors, including the difficulty of recruiting and retaining staff, how highly teachers are valued by the society in which they work, union negotiations, and so on. The following comments are designed to give a generalized overview of how teachers' pay works.

- There are different pay spines or scales, e.g. for leadership, ASTs, qualified and unqualified teachers. In Scotland there are different scales for main grade, chartered and principal teachers.
- Head teachers will be paid according to the size and type of school in which they work.
- Teachers are paid their salary according to the number of points they have on a particular spine.
- Classroom teachers move up one point on the spine for each year's experience, until they reach the top of the main payscale.
- At this stage, they may (or may not) move onto the next spine, for instance passing the threshold.
- Additional allowances or points are given for
  - management responsibilities, e.g. heads of department
  - number of years' experience
  - recruitment and retention
  - SEN responsibilities
  - London weighting (additional money given to teachers living in and around London, to take account of the higher cost of living in the capital).

For more specific details about teachers' salaries and the pay scales/spine points, see www.teachernet.gov.uk/pay.

Working conditions

Scotland

Teachers in Scotland were guaranteed a 35 hour working week from 1 August 2001. They were also promised the introduction of a maximum contact time, in the classroom, of 22.5 hours per week.

England and Wales

The 'School Teachers' Pay and Working Conditions Document' explains your conditions of employment, i.e. your pay and professional duties. The points below summarize details about the amount of time that you are actually required to work under your contract.

- Teachers working full-time have to be available to work 195 days in the school year. Of this time, 190 days are those on which you have to actually teach students. The remaining five days would normally be used for whole school and INSET activities. (*Note*: These conditions do not apply to heads, deputies, ASTs or part-time staff.)
- You are required to work 1265 hours during the school year.
- You cannot be made to supervise at lunchtimes, and you must be given a break 'of reasonable length' between school sessions or at lunchtime (i.e. between noon and 2 p.m.).
- You are also required to work extra hours so that you can fulfil your professional duties, which includes marking work, writing reports, preparing lessons and so on. This time is not specified, and is not included within the 1265 hours.

Promotion

After a year or more as a teacher, you may well be looking for your first promoted post. Sometimes, in the larger secondary schools, the post will actually come looking for you! For instance, a vacancy could arise and you may find yourself in the enviable position where one of your managers asks you to apply. In smaller schools, and in the primary environment, it could be that you need to move on to another school in order to find a promotion opportunity. If you are interested in promotion, and in managerial posts, do take a look at the interviews with managers in Chapter 6, 'Anatomy of a school'. These will give you a good idea of both the ups and downs of promoted posts.

If you do take a promotion within your current school, bear in mind that it can be quite difficult to change the relationship you have with your colleagues. Once you become their manager instead of just a fellow member of staff, this will alter the nature of the way that you work with them. On the other hand, taking a promotion can be hard work, and it is doubtless easier to adapt to a new job in a school where you already know all about the way things are run.

Moving schools

Some teachers are happy to spend a long period of time in one school, whilst others are keen to move on every few years. Much will depend on you as an individual, and also on the type of career path you hope to take. Below is a list of points 'for' and 'against' moving schools for you to consider if you are thinking of taking this step.

'For'

- Gaining a greater breadth of experience, which could be useful for your future career path, and which will certainly help you develop your teaching skills.
- Facing new challenges in a new environment to help you avoid becoming stale or bored.
- Working with a different group of students, perhaps moving from the 'easy' to the 'challenging', and consequently developing new classroom management skills.
- Shaking up your world a little. Teaching can become very easy and safe if you work at one school for a long time.
- Finding out how your students (and the staff) really feel about you when you listen to the farewell speeches and read the cards.
- Hopefully getting lots of presents!
- A chance to make a complete change to your image as a teacher. For instance, a relaxed teacher can choose to come across as strict at a new school.

'Against'

- Having to learn the ropes all over again, which can prove stressful for the first term or so.
- Working with different policies, rules, and so on, and getting used to new systems.
- Having to find your way around a completely new environment.
- Getting to know large numbers of new names and people, both staff and students.
- Potentially, students 'trying you out' and misbehaving to test a new member of staff.

Passing the threshold

The threshold was introduced to give a financial reward and incentive to good classroom teachers who prefer to stay in the classroom, rather than move into management. Teachers are assessed against eight 'national threshold standards of effective teaching'. If they pass the threshold, teachers move onto a new, higher pay scale. Once on this higher scale, progression upwards is not automatic each year, but depends on the teacher's performance within the school.

In order to apply to pass the threshold, teachers fill out an application form and pass this to their head teacher. The head then writes his or her comments on the form, before it is passed to an assessor. Teachers who pass the threshold are sent a 'threshold letter of confirmation'. For more information on threshold, see the DfES website, www.teachernet.gov.uk.

INSET

The training that you undergo while working as a teacher is known as INSET, or in-service training. INSET generally falls into two different categories: school based training, which is usually provided for a number of staff at one time (often the whole staff), and training for which you are given a day out of school to attend a course, perhaps at a hotel or other training venue. Schools will generally have one or more INSET days at the start of term, when the teachers and other staff gather together to be trained. (In reality, these days are often used for whole school meetings, departmental time in a secondary school, and other focused activities, in addition to actual training.)

School based INSET

The school based training that is done during the academic year will be linked to aspects of the school development plan. For instance, the head teacher might feel that a focus is needed on one specific issue (such as behaviour), and he or she might spend a large part of the training budget for the year on that particular topic.

As mentioned above, many schools have one or more INSET days at the start of the school year. There are a total of five statutory INSET days within the academic year when the students are not at school, and the teachers gather for training. In-school training may also be called 'twilight', which is training done after the students have gone home for the day. Some of the more common subjects for INSET are listed below.

- Behaviour management – creating and developing school policies, strategies for managing behaviour, focusing on specific students and what can be done to help them.
- SEN – developing policies, differentiation, inclusion.
- Curriculum based work – training for a new syllabus, developing schemes of work, moderation.
- OFSTED inspections – preparing for an OFSTED visit, feedback and whole school review after the event.
- New initiatives – national literacy and numeracy strategies, and so on.

Training outside the school

In addition to school based training, teachers should also get the chance to take training courses at other venues (often during school time). For instance, a newly promoted subject coordinator or head of department might undertake training to help prepare them for this new role; an NQT might be given INSET on classroom and behaviour management. Some out of school training days are actually moderation meetings (where teachers of a subject get together to cross-check their grades against those given by their colleagues).

It is the teachers who can be bothered to book their places and fill out the relevant forms who get the chance to go on INSET outside of school. It really is worthwhile taking up every opportunity for training that comes your way. There are a number of reasons why this is so.

- The training is (often) useful and valuable.
- You will be adding to your own 'continuing professional development'.
- You can get new ideas and find out about new ways of approaching a subject or area.
- You get the chance to mix with teachers from other schools, and to make a useful network of contacts.
- Attending INSET days looks good on your CV, or on a job application form.
- You get the chance for a day out of school. (If possible, book a course for a time when you know you are going to be tired and in need of a break, for instance the middle of the second term.)

In addition to general INSET, some schools offer finance or other forms of support for teachers who wish to take a further qualification, such as an MA, MEd or MBA. Again, if you are offered this opportunity, do consider taking it, although bear in mind the time commitment and additional workload involved.

Teaching and other careers

The skills that you develop as a teacher, and the experiences which you undergo, naturally lend themselves to a number of other related fields. Some teachers, after a few years in the profession, find themselves increasingly interested in a particular area of education, such as child psychology or special educational needs. Alternatively, some teachers will simply find themselves exhausted by the job, and unwilling to continue working as a full-time teacher. Below are some ideas about careers into which the teacher might move.

- Educational psychology
- LEA advisory and inspection services
- Counselling and mentoring work
- Educational consultancy and training
- Writing curriculum materials and books for teachers.

In addition to these areas closely related to teaching, think also about the type of skills you have that might be applicable out in the wider world. It is worth doing a brief 'skills audit' of the skills that you have developed, so that you can emphasize these when applying for other posts. For instance, the classroom teacher will have developed a huge range of abilities, including the following:

- managing large groups of people
- organizing paperwork and work time
- forward planning

- assessing and recording performance and progression
- target setting.

Educational shows

Educational shows offer teachers a chance to view new resources and curriculum materials; to attend seminars, INSET sessions and talks by leading educationalists; and also to try out new products, such as educational software. There are three large shows during the academic year.

- BETT, Olympia, London
- The Education Show, NEC, Birmingham
- SETT, SECC, Glasgow

For more details see the BETT website www.bettshow.com.

Private tutoring

Working as a private tutor can offer the teacher a useful source of additional income. Teachers may take on tutoring work via an agency, or may organize their own work, perhaps via small ads in local shops and papers. You may also find that parents at your school ask you to tutor their children. Generally speaking, it is best not to tutor children in your own class. The problem is that the divide between teacher/student is harder to maintain, and you may find parents expect you to treat their child differently, because they are paying you to tutor him or her. It is also inadvisable to set up tutor sessions on your own school premises, because of insurance and legal issues.

Teaching overseas

Teaching is a very mobile career, and for those who want to, there are plenty of opportunities to work overseas. Working in a foreign school offers teachers a wonderful way of seeing the world, of experiencing different cultures, and also a way of adding to the range and quality of their teaching skills. However, there are also pitfalls in teaching overseas for the unwary (see the interview below with a British teacher working overseas to get some idea of what can go wrong).

Many schools in Europe and beyond will teach a different syllabus to that which is common in UK schools. This may be IGCSEs (international GCSEs), or it could be the International Baccalaureate (IB) syllabus. You can find full details of the IB programme at the IBO's website: www.ibo.org. In brief, the IB programme is divided into three sections – primary years (PYP), middle years (MYP) and diploma. These correspond in age groups to Key Stages One and Two (PYP), Key Stages Three and Four (MYP) and 'A' levels (diploma). The IB programme is, generally speaking, much broader in scope than the system followed in the UK. There is an emphasis on a fully rounded education, and the programme is far less orientated towards formal, statutory assessments.

British teacher working overseas

Name withheld

Q. Did you do another job before going into teaching?

A. I never had a career before teaching. I did originally spend four years studying to be a textile technologist. That's what I'm qualified as. But I couldn't get a job so I ended up working the summer in the States at a camp. I tried to stay there, getting work where I could and then moving on. I worked at the state fair in Phoenix, Arizona for a couple of weeks, sleeping under the table of the dime pit I was working at. I made a surprising amount of money considering all people were doing was throwing dimes onto a table.

Q. What made you decide to become a teacher then?

A. I worked on a summer camp on Skaneateles Lake, upstate New York for four summers. After the third summer someone (a fellow Brit teacher) said to me 'What are you doing with your life? You'd make a really good teacher.' I thought about it and got myself onto a BEd Physics course when I got back from my travels in the USA.

Q. What was the BEd course like?

A. It was a two-year course with about 15 other people all over 21 years old. It was a course for people who were moving careers. Many were ex-steelworkers and industry based people.

Q. Did you teach in the UK before going abroad?

A. Yeah, I taught in Birmingham, at an inner city type school with a multiethnic intake. I was there for two years. I taught Physics and Science. In my second year I was promoted to outdoor education officer. The school had a very good support system for the teachers so they did quite well. It could have been so much worse, but I was glad to leave.

Q. Why did you decide to go and teach abroad?

A. My partner has always wanted to work abroad and happened to see one suitable job advertised in the *TES*. We applied about two weeks before the Easter break and heard nothing. We didn't tell anyone we'd applied. Then during the second week of the Easter holidays we got back home at 1 a.m. after a week's skiing. We had to go up to Liverpool the following morning for the interview. The day before we went back to school we were offered the job and accepted. I had a feeling that everyone was surprised at our move back at school — maybe it was just the suddenness of it?

Q. Tell me about that first job, then. Where was it, and what was it really like?

A. It was a British boarding school in Africa. I taught Physics there and was in charge of the expedition section of the Duke of Edinburgh Award scheme that we ran up to Silver level.

Q. And did it live up to your expectations?

A. In some ways yes — the school told you what life was like — how tough things could be. But the job itself was great … small classes … money spent well … big IT budget … great lifestyle …

Q. And then what?

A. And then we made a mistake … we moved schools.

Q. Why was it a mistake?

A. There were a lot of problems with the way the school was run, a lot of the staff had problems with the Principal. Anyway, the upshot was that we had to leave mid contract — we couldn't even do the honest thing and resign! We were advised by many — including the head of section — to just go. We had to forego our August salary, but at least we were out of there.

Q. So I guess you were much more careful when you applied for your next job?

A. Yeah, we were very careful to ask all the right questions about our next job. For instance, we asked whether our salary was dollar linked? 'Yes' was the answer. Was there tax? 'Yes at 30 per cent'. What was our accommodation like? 'A house with a garden off campus.' All this from a convincing head who was very good up front.

Q. And then?

A. And then we arrived . . . we got put in a second storey flat, with neighbours downstairs who had 10 free range (but mostly up our stairs) turkeys, three dogs that roamed free (we wanted a dog hence wanting a garden), 100 chickens in the garage and they really stank. They butchered them after six weeks and processed them at the bottom of the stairs. They were lovely people just trying to make a living . . . what can you say? The building had no fence round it and was next to a main road . . . in fact paths led all through the property. This meant we had numerous security alerts.

Q. It sounds terrible . . .

A. Yeah, I've never been so badly lied to in my life. The day after we arrived we complained, but nothing happened. Then we found out the tax rate was 35 per cent, and the salary was only 50 per cent dollar linked. This is important, because in the first two months the currency devalued by 35 per cent! Hence we asked at interview. Well, after a fruitless meeting in which the head claimed he never said such things, we resigned at the beginning of the second week in September.

It put us in an awful position because it looked poor on the CV to have left two jobs. However, we weren't prepared to waste our time at places that were unprofessional . . . what's more damaging is the question? These sort of schools have an incredibly high turnover of staff. Sorry I went on about that one. I guess I feel I want to tell the world to be careful about getting jobs in some countries! I feel better now.

Q. So that's the downside of working abroad. What are the benefits of teaching overseas? Are there any!?

A. Yeah, of course there are. The lifestyle – it's great! The culture – seeing things you don't see when teaching in the UK.

Q. Any specific moments that stick in your mind?

A. There any many . . . seeing Vic Falls and travelling in Zimbabwe was great . . . I really liked it there. Camping on beaches, going night swimming and having barbies. We made many Aussie friends who we miss but will be able to visit in Oz some time. The food in Africa was fantastic.

On a sad note, I can't get over the number of people dying because of Aids. Our cleaner was a grandfather. He had buried three nieces, two nephews and his eldest son. The reason he had to bury the nieces and nephews is because their parents were already dead. It's ridiculous. The mid range generation of people is just disappearing. They will have labour and skill shortages in a generation's time!

Teacher in Thailand

Korrutai Yujaroen

Q. Why did you decide to become a teacher?

Korrutai – Because I like to be a teacher. In Thailand teachers are very respected and honourable. Therefore it is a great and important occupation. Everywhere in the world has and needs teachers.

Q. How did you qualify to become a teacher?

Korrutai – I got a teacher certification in Thailand. I took my BA in Linguistics and MEd in Psychology and Guidance at Chiang Mai University.

Q. Tell me about your first teaching job.

Korrutai – I have been teaching in international schools for four years. I started my first full-time job two years ago at an international American boarding school, founded on the mountain in Chiang Mai. I worked as a Thai language instructor. I also taught chess, Thai cooking, and worked as a tour guide and with swimming activities. I helped the students in the girls' dorm. I taught Seventh grade to Tenth grade. I learnt a lot from that experience, working with foreigners, such as language, working style, relationships and behaviour.

Q. What did you do next?

Korrutai – Then I passed the screening test to study my master's, and I moved to work at a day school in Chiang Mai, a Christian school set up over 40 years ago. I taught, helped in kindergarten, worked in the library, substituted for elementary classroom teachers and helped with the reading club. I taught kindergarten to Eighth grade. Out of school time I work as a tutor, teaching English to Thai students preparing for their University Entrance Examination. I have been appointed as Head of Thai Studies at an International School in Rayong (Eastern Seaboard) for the next academic year.

Q. What is it really like working as a teacher? Is there anything special about being a teacher in Thailand?

Korrutai – If you want to be a teacher you have to prepare yourself as a parent in a way. I mean you are not only a teacher, you are building future adults and raising children. You also have to be like babysitter and ruler at the same time. In

Thai, teachers are called '*Kruu*'. It means hard or heavy. For me, I think teaching is not hard but classroom management is the hardest part. However being a teacher is great. You see your students grow. You finish your work and get results year by year. You are proud of yourself for doing that. And you look forward to seeing your students with smiling faces at school and saying good morning to you.

Q. Does poor student behaviour cause you any problems?

Korrutai – I want to say that both poor and rich students misbehave but they cause different problems. Some penalties that I use are, separate a kid to sit by himself and think of what he has done, why he did that, why it is wrong, etc. Or give them extra homework with a letter to the parents for signature. Or tell the problem kid to work extra after school or at recess with you. If it's a big problem, I send them to the principal.

Q. What's the best thing about being a teacher?

Korrutai – You are learning about yourself and confronting new experiences at the same time. A teacher has to be alert to everything that happens in the world both previous or current times, has to observe and experiment everything, has to be creative, has to be curious all the time. You also have holiday that human deserves. If someone say teaching is a boring job and it's a job for lazybones, I will definitely say that's wrong!

Q. What's the hardest thing about being a teacher?

Korrutai – The worst things about teaching career are dealing with old conservative bosses and grading the end of school. Moreover the salary that international schools give to Thai teachers and to foreign teachers are very different.

Q. What changes have there been in Thai education recently?

Korrutai – I work in the international schools, which have a different style and system from Thai schools. Recently in Thailand they have been evaluating the curriculum and instructing teachers to train children how to think, learn and solve problems by themselves (be independent). Now there is a law that every teacher has to have teacher certification. The theory sounds great but in practice it will take time, because old conservative Thai teachers or head masters or directors still don't accept the changes, which are happening in every school in Thailand.

Q. Tell me about your new job. How do you feel about being promoted?

Korrutai – I took the position as Head of Thai Studies after thinking hard about whether I can do it and I should take it and whether I should quit my previous job. Finally I say yes, they offer me this job, it shows that they believe in my abilities. I love adventure and challenges. You cannot know what will happen in the future but you can choose what to do each day.

Q. Would you recommend a teaching career to others?

Korrutai – Yes! I always recommend a teaching career for my friends, neighbours and people I know. But I have to tell them not to expect high compensation.

Q. Would you like to work overseas if you had the opportunity?

Korrutai – Yes. I would like to work in Europe or America.

Q. Any final thoughts?

Korrutai – Yes, being a teacher is marvellous. You deal with innovatory humans (not robots or machines). It is an important job because teachers are helping the future of the world. Nevertheless, teachers get underpaid. Even in the future, when kids can learn from computers at home, I still prefer sending kids to see teachers and friends at school.

11 Other issues

Supply teaching

There are a number of times in a teacher's career when he or she might turn to supply teaching. It could be that you are having trouble finding a permanent job, or in finding the right job or school for you. It might be that, like me, you want to continue teaching, but that you need to combine part-time supply teaching with other work or family commitments. It could be that you simply enjoy the flexibility and experience of working at a range of different schools. Before you consider full- or part-time work as a supply teacher, think carefully about all the potential benefits and drawbacks. You'll find some points below that you might like to consider.

The benefits

- Supply teaching is relatively well paid.
- Supply teachers have less paperwork to deal with than permanent teachers.
- Although you may be involved in doing some planning and marking, this will certainly be less than for a permanent teacher.
- You won't be required to attend after school meetings or parents' evenings.
- You won't have to run extracurricular activities.
- You get to see a whole range of different schools, and learn more about how they work.
- You get to teach a huge variety of children.
- If you really don't enjoy working at a particular school, you're not stuck there for longer than one day at a time.

Do note, though, that many of these benefits do not apply to a situation where a supply teacher takes a long-term contract. In these cases, you would certainly be expected to do the planning/marking and attend the relevant meetings.

The drawbacks

- Students do tend to try and take advantage when they have a supply teacher (it's only natural, after all).
- It can be a lot harder to discipline children who don't know you, but who do know that you're a supply teacher.
- You will be moving around from school to school, and for some people this lack of continuity is unsettling.
- You may have to travel a fair distance to some assignments.

- Some people (other teachers included) have a negative image or experience of supply teachers.
- You are not guaranteed work.
- Some times of the year are busy, while other times are relatively quiet.
- You won't get paid if you're sick, or during your holidays (although some agencies do offer sickness and holiday benefits).
- You don't get to develop long-lasting or in depth relationships with the children, or with the other teachers at a school.

Again, do note that many of these drawbacks do not apply to supply teachers working on a long-term contract.

Supply agencies

In the Directory at the back of this book, you'll find details of a number of different agencies. These agencies differ a great deal. Some are national chains, which cover the whole of the UK. Others are local, small-scale operations, perhaps set up by a teacher or group of teachers to serve their local area. When choosing an agency (or agencies) for which to work, there are a number of issues to take into account.

- Whether the interview process seems professionally organized and handled.
- The type of benefits and support they offer.
- Whether they provide training, illness and holiday pay, pensions advice, and so on.
- How well you get on with the consultant for whom you would work.
- Whether the agency takes account of your preferences about schools and areas in which you would like to work.
- If you're an NQT, how clued up they seem about the induction process.

The following interview gives you an overview about what applying to and working for a supply agency is like.

Anne Good

Candidate Development Manager

Recruit Education Services (now Celsian)

Q. How does a teacher go about applying for supply work with Celsian?

Anne – A teacher can apply to us through several different routes. They can apply via our website by completing a short application form and one of our consultants will contact the teacher within 24 hours to discuss their application further. Alternatively, they can contact us via email on enquiries@celsiangroup.co.uk. Teachers can also phone their local branch number on 0845 606 0676 or go along to their local branch where there is a dedicated team of consultants ready to speak with them directly.

Q. What happens once a teacher has applied for supply work?

Anne – An experienced education consultant will speak with the teacher and ask them a number of questions to ensure that they meet our criteria for work. This will involve a conversation about their qualifications, recent and relevant experience, the type of work they require, the location in which they would like to work and their availability. They will then be invited into the branch for a face-to-face interview. We will require them to bring with them their original qualification, names and addresses of professional referees covering the last five years, their DfES and GTC numbers, identification (passport or birth certificate), and up-to-date CV, their National Insurance number, bank details, police clearance status, medical history, passport photographs, P45/P46 tax forms and if they are an overseas teacher we will need to see their visa. The interview process takes an hour.

During the interview the consultant will ask questions to enable them to understand the teacher's needs, skills, abilities and types of work they are looking for. The consultant will also discuss Celsian's philosophy and our core values such as professionalism and quality. This will enable the teacher to get a clear picture of the company they will be working for. The teacher will also be given information on how they will be contacted for assignments, how they will be paid and the support they can expect from their Celsian consultant.

The interview process will help us to identify the teacher's strengths and weaknesses so that we can find them the assignments that will best suit them. We will then complete the references and checks and contact the teacher as soon as they are cleared for work. We issue our teachers with a Celsian handbook, which explains all of this information in detail.

Q. What makes a good supply teacher?

Anne – Obviously a teacher needs to be well qualified in their chosen subject. They also need a professional approach, and to be adaptable and resilient. They need to be flexible and interested in the pupils' education and welfare.

Q. What advice would you give to a first time supply teacher?

Anne – First and foremost a supply teacher needs to be well prepared with lessons pre-planned. The teacher will also need to take some back-up materials so that they can adapt flexibly as circumstances demand. They also need to take their own resources in case there are none or only limited resources available. All this information and other helpful hints are available in our supply tips sheet, which we issue to our teachers and discuss at interview. Their personal consultant encourages them to call them if they have any problems or concerns about their assignments. Their consultant will keep in regular contact with them too, so support is always on hand. So our advice is always, to keep in contact and to keep a dialogue going. And of course, the Celsian handbook, which we give all our teachers at interview, will provide advice on how to prepare for their assignments.

We also run regular training seminars, such as Behavioural Management and Inclusion, which we encourage all our teachers to attend. We would also recommend that teachers affiliate themselves to a professional body and that they make use of the many government helplines and websites available to them.

Q. What would you say are the most important things for a supply teacher to do and remember when on an assignment?

Anne – Some schools have an orientation pack to help supply teachers settle into school. I would strongly recommend that supply teachers ask if the school has such a pack. If one is not available the teacher should always remember to ask a member of the school team for help and guidance. They should also find out who is the health and safety representative and Child Protection Officer at the school. It's vital that they read the school's discipline policy. Teachers should also familiarize themselves with the school's rewards and sanctions policy in order to provide a consistent learning environment for the pupils. They should also ask if there are any other school policies of which they should be aware.

On a personal level, they should check on lesson and break times and ask if any pupils in their class have any special requirements. When available they should use any work set by the school. They should also mark the pupils' work if required, and leave a report for the class teacher about how the lesson or lessons went and any discipline issues. We provide a pro forma handover report in Celsian handbooks for this purpose.

Q. What sort of benefits do you offer your supply teachers?

Anne – We provide access to a stakeholder pension scheme through Legal and General. We also have 'exclusives', our unique benefits package, which offers discounted products and services. These include holidays, sick pay insurance, mobile phones, leisure club membership, hair and beauty treatments, electrical goods, CDs and DVDs. We also offer an extensive training programme and the opportunity for them to work in a flexible environment. Plus, of course, ongoing support and guidance from our personal consultants.

Q. Could you tell me a bit about the training you provide?

Anne – We offer free training to all of our teachers. There is an extensive menu of seminars on offer and more are being developed all the time. We listen to what our teachers tell us they need and develop a seminar for them. Each branch organizes at least two of these seminars per term. A team of highly experienced education training professionals deliver the seminars. They are generally held after school or on a Saturday and they are great social events too.

We have also developed a unique package for our NQTs called CareerStart℠. This supports them through their induction process by offering them guidance with their action planning and Career Entry Profiles as well as support throughout their assignments. There are three free seminars for them too; all focused around the induction standards. These are Education and the Law, Classroom Management and Continuous Professional Development.

Q. What sort of reasons do teachers have for coming to do supply work with you?

Anne – There are a number of different reasons. Some want to experience many different schools to find out which they prefer before taking on a permanent job. Many of our supply teachers are returners to work. Some are NQTs looking for their first post. Also teachers who have taken early retirement like the flexible benefits of working on a supply basis. International teachers also have a preference of working on supply to match their lifestyle needs.

Supply work via an LEA

In Scotland, the standard route for working as a supply teacher is via the LEA. Elsewhere, there are opportunities to work for your LEA, but the efficiency of the arrangement will depend a great deal on where you live, and how well your local authority is run. If you are interested in working via the LEA, you should contact your local authority or RSM (recruitment strategy manager) direct.

Tips for supply teachers

It can be tough being a supply teacher – I know because I do it myself. But it can also be great fun, so long as you follow some basic rules. The tips that I give below will be particularly useful to those teachers doing supply for the very first time. They should help you to impress the schools that you visit, enjoy the assignments that you take, and survive even when the kids do decide to put you through hell!

- *Never arrive late:* Always, yes *always*, arrive on time for assignments, even if this means leaving home earlier than you think is necessary. When you get to the school, do report to reception – most schools have some form of security nowadays, and will require you to sign in and perhaps get a pass.

- *Get the information you need:* Many schools will give you a 'supply teacher's pack' when you arrive, which should include the information listed below. If you are not given this before the school day starts, do make sure that you get hold of:
  - a map showing the school layout;
  - a copy of the school's behaviour policy, or at the very least some information about the sanctions that you can use;
  - information about the rewards system at the school;
  - the timings of tutor time, lesson times and breaks;
  - the name of someone to refer badly behaved students to if things do go wrong.
- *Make contacts:* If possible, introduce yourself to the head of department (in a secondary school) or to a management figure (such as a deputy head) in a primary school. These people will often prove very useful points of reference if you do experience problems.
- *Come equipped:* Take your own tea or coffee, mug and milk. Although some schools provide these free of charge, you will often find that there are no refreshment facilities, even for guests.
- *Find out about routines:* Before the day starts, try to find out what the usual routine is for the subject or class you are teaching. For instance, what are the children used to doing when they arrive at the lesson? Do they normally line up outside? Is the register taken at the start of the session? In a practical subject, what arrangements are made for changing?
- *First impressions are crucial:* Start your lessons hard, especially if you are unsure what type of children you are going to be teaching. With a nice class a teacher who gives a tough impression to begin with will do no harm to his or her reputation, and with a difficult class it can make the difference between a nightmare lesson or day, and a good one.
- *Start as you mean to go on:* The first three minutes are crucial in setting the tone and letting the children know what you expect. Often, just the knowledge that they have a supply teacher will be enough to persuade them to try it on. So, aim to be in the classroom when the class arrive, and focus on the basics first. This includes commands such as 'coats off', 'ties on', 'go straight to your seats', 'books out', and so on (all leavened with the word 'please' of course!). If it seems appropriate for the situation and the location, ask the class to line up outside the room before you allow them in. This helps give the impression that you are a teacher not to be messed with.
- *Lay down the basics:* Set down some ground rules and expectations right at the start of the lesson. For instance, I like to give my classes two choices. They can either behave appropriately and do as I say (and see the 'nice' side of me), or they can mess me around, try it on (and consequently see the 'nasty' side).
- *Be positive:* Try to stay positive and friendly. Use comments such as 'you're already making a really good impression on me' if the class enter the room in an appropriate manner. That way, you will set up the expectation of a positive and fun lesson or day.

- *Be hard to fool:* Don't believe everything that the children tell you! For instance, if they try to persuade you that 'we normally wear our coats in class', you can be 99.9 per cent certain that they are trying it on. Often, a class will inform you that 'we've already done this work'. If they do try to use this excuse, simply tell them that they'll be able to do it extra well second time around.
- *Do your admin:* Make sure you get your timesheets signed and in to your agency if you want to get paid. If you are working at the same school all week, you might find that the school are willing to fax a copy of your timesheet to your agency on the Friday, to ensure that it arrives on time.

Getting the best out of your supply teacher

How well a supply teacher gets on depends a great deal on how the school or department treats him or her. If you are in a position where you use supply teachers, and you want them to be as successful as possible, here are some tips that you might find useful.

- *Good planning is still vital:* Don't leave work that the children will find boring, or that they will finish before the end of the lesson (*please*). It can be very tempting to rush off a few photocopied worksheets (I know, I've done it myself), but if the lesson does not suit the class, you are not giving the supply teacher the opportunity to work successfully with them.
- *Give them the info they need:* Take the time to explain the basic patterns and routines to the supply teacher, as these can differ widely from school to school. For instance, does the class normally line up outside the room before the lesson starts? Is the register taken at the start of the lesson, or at the end? Are the children expected to work in silence?
- *Keep changes to a minimum:* Try to minimize disruption to the class, for instance do not combine a room change with a visit from a supply teacher. Children often react badly to unexpected changes in routine, and not having their normal teacher is already an unusual situation.
- *Offer your support:* A brief visit by the head of department or other manager at the start of the lesson can really settle down the class and allow the supply teacher a chance to succeed. A comment that you will be returning to check up on the class later, and ensuring that the teacher has not had any problems, will really help out.

OFSTED

OFSTED is designed to give an independent overview of the school being inspected. An inspection will take place at least once every six years. The organization looks at the standards a school is achieving, and also at their progress (or lack of it) since the last inspection. After an inspection has taken place, OFSTED gives a written report on what the school is doing well, and also where its weaknesses are. These reports can be a useful source of information for parents (and for teachers looking to move to a new school).

However, OFSTED can only really provide a snapshot of the true situation in a school, because inspections take place in what is essentially an artificial environment. It is of course inevitable that staff try their best to impress when OFSTED appear. Teachers will plan in great detail (perhaps far more than they usually do); displays will be beautifully presented; graffiti will be scrubbed from the walls. There are even stories (hopefully anecdotal) of some schools suspending their 'worst' students for the OFSTED week.

An impending OFSTED inspection can be a source of great stress for teachers. It is natural to worry about whether your lesson planning will be viewed as up to scratch, and how your students will behave when the inspectors are around. You may find that your children behave perfectly when an inspector is in the room; alternatively you may find they turn into little horrors to show you up. Much will depend on the relationship you have with each class.

If you've not yet been through an inspection, you will probably have heard many horror stories about what the inspection will involve, of teachers failing and schools being closed. In the run up to the inspection you will certainly have an additional workload: writing detailed lesson plans, getting books marked up to date, and so on. Many thanks to my fellow teacher Kirsty for her wonderful description of OFSTED as the 'Office for Stress, Tension and Endless Distress'. I think this sums up many teachers' feelings about the whole process!

You can find a bank of OFSTED reports at the organization's website: www.ofsted.gov.uk. It is well worth taking a look at these, because they give you a very good idea about the type of areas that OFSTED will be inspecting. You can find some ideas about surviving OFSTED in the 'checklists' (Chapter 16, page 291).

What is OFSTED looking for?

Around two thirds of the inspectors' time will be used to observe what actually goes on in the classroom. The inspectors evaluate each lesson that they see and give grades from one (poor) to seven (excellent). While they are observing your work, the inspectors are looking for a whole range of different things.

- The type and quality of planning you do.
- How good your teaching is.
- What you're actually teaching.
- How well your students are learning.
- The type and quality of evaluation you do.
- How well the students apply themselves to the lesson.
- The attitude and behaviour shown by your students.

What should I do to prepare for OFSTED?

Essentially, preparations for OFSTED are simply the things that a good teacher would normally try to do in the course of his or her working life (if we weren't always so busy!). If you spend a little bit of time ensuring that you have covered all bases, then you can give the best impression possible and show what you are really capable of as a teacher. As I have mentioned, OFSTED can only provide a snapshot of how a school really works on a day-to-day basis, but it is worth making at least some effort to play the game. The list below gives you some factors to consider in the weeks leading up to inspection.

Planning

- Plan your lessons carefully, and in sufficient detail. You may find that your school has a standard format that fulfils OFSTED criteria, which they ask you to use during the inspection. Take advantage of this if it is offered.
- Take special needs into account. Show that you know which children have specific learning needs and what these are. Demonstrate that you are planning for these needs.
- Differentiate the work carefully.
- Think about equal opportunities, cross-curricular possibilities, and multicultural issues.
- If you can find the time, talk these plans through with a colleague. This might be your head of department in a secondary school, or a teacher experienced in working with your year group in a primary school.
- Have a copy of your lesson plan available to hand to an inspector if she or he does arrive at your room.

Teaching

- Write the learning objectives on the board before each lesson begins, and refer to these in your teaching and review work.
- Make sure you use a variety of tasks and activities within each lesson. Employ different teaching and learning styles: whole class teaching, class discussions, individual, paired and group work, and so on.
- Give your lessons pace, energy and enthusiasm.
- Set work that will engage the students, especially if the children in your school have low motivation.

Classroom management

- Think about how your class enters the room, and how quickly and well they settle to work.
- Ensure that any resources required are easily accessible, and consider how the children are going to access these.

- Use calm and purposeful strategies to deal with any behavioural issues that do arise.
- Consider how well the end of your lesson is managed. Give plenty of time to finish off the lesson and to get the children sensibly and safely out of the room.

General issues

- Make sure that the children's exercise books are marked up to date.
- Check that your displays are neat, interesting and linked to the children's work.
- Think about potential health and safety issues in the classroom: for instance where the children put their school bags and whether there are any hazards around, such as trailing wires.
- Know what the school policies are, and put them into use in your classroom, for instance the whole school behaviour policy.

What other evidence do OFSTED use?

As well as observing lessons, the inspectors will also look at the paperwork that the school, its teachers and departments use. This will include school policies, schemes of work and lesson plans, departmental or curriculum handbooks and so on. The inspectors will also talk to the students and their parents. A questionnaire will be sent out to the parents, and a meeting held at which their views can be expressed.

Pensions

England and Wales

Teaching pensions are administered by 'Teachers' Pensions'. If you work full-time in a state school, or independent school that is part of the scheme (and you have not opted out) you will automatically be covered. Pensions and financial arrangements are complex issues, but the overall view is generally that the teachers' pension offers a very good deal compared to other pension providers. Below is some general information about the scheme. Further details can be found at www.teacherspensions.co.uk.

- On retirement, the scheme pays you an annual pension and also a tax free lump sum.
- The normal retirement age is 60 (for both men and women).
- The TP is a 'final salary' scheme, which means that it is based on your final salary, not on your contributions while working.

- If you are working part-time, or as a supply teacher, you need to complete a form and apply to have your work recognized as pensionable.
- You can opt to pay additional voluntary contributions (AVCs) into the scheme.

Pensions

Scotland and Northern Ireland

You can find more details about teachers' pensions in Scotland from the Teachers' Benefits Section of the Scottish Public Pensions Agency (see the Directory for details). Teachers in Northern Ireland should contact the Teachers' Pensions Branch of the Department of Education (see Directory for contact details).

Support systems

With all its varied demands, teaching is a stressful job, and at times all teachers need to turn to others for support. This is especially true at the beginning of your teaching career, but it also holds true throughout the years you spend in the job. There are a wide variety of support systems that you as a teacher can use.

- Your family and friends can offer a shoulder to cry on when times are tough. Do be aware, though, that those who are not teachers themselves may find it hard to fully understand the strains of the job.
- Your teaching colleagues will often be the most wonderful source of support that you can find. In my experience, this is especially so in the tougher schools where I have worked. Perhaps the sense of a shared, difficult experience makes us feel more like a team, and consequently more inclined to help each other out.
- Your managers, and induction tutor (if you're an NQT), have a responsibility to help ensure your welfare. A good line manager or head of department can make the difference between feeling properly supported and feeling completely alone.
- Government helplines for teachers may offer an additional source of support, and one which is confidential if you do have particular issues. 'Teacherline' is one such phone support line, which was set up by charity and government (see the Directory for contact details).
- The unions have support services that can help you at times of need. They also offer an invaluable source of legal advice and assistance. (See the next section for more information about the teaching unions.)

The teaching unions

There are a number of teaching unions. You can find contact details for each of these unions in the Directory section at the back of this book. The unions are, in alphabetical order:

Association of Teachers and Lecturers (ATL)
National Association of Head Teachers (NAHT)
National Association of Schoolmasters, Union of Women Teachers (NASUWT)
National Association of Teachers in Further and Higher Education (NATFHE)
National Union of Teachers (NUT)
Professional Association of Teachers (PAT)
Scottish Secondary Teachers' Association (SSTA)
Secondary Heads' Association (SHA)

Which union you choose depends entirely on your own personal preference. It could be that you find one particular union more responsive and efficient in dealing with your initial enquiries; it might be that you have a particular stance on an issue connected to teaching (such as whether strike action is or is not acceptable), and you feel that one of the unions best represents your own philosophy; it could be that you want to join either a big or a small organization; alternatively, it might just be that you get on well with the union rep of a particular union in your own school.

There is absolutely no obligation for teachers to join a union. However, there are a number of reasons why you might consider union membership:

- *Legal advice:* The legal representation that the unions offer is becoming increasingly important for teachers, with the threat of legal action ever present.
- *Support:* The unions offer a useful support service and many have helplines that members can call with any questions that they have.
- *Getting your voice heard:* Membership of a union gives you a chance to have your say in debates about the teaching profession.
- *Campaigning for teachers:* The unions do important campaigning work to try to make conditions better for teachers.
- *Discounts:* There are many discounted services on offer, such as cheaper car and travel insurance.

The unions are very keen to get you to join them while you are a student: perhaps the feeling is that once you've joined a particular union, you will tend to stay with them in the long term. As a teaching student, you will be offered free union membership, and often a reduced rate during your NQT year and perhaps your second year in teaching.

You can see sample interviews below with two of the teaching unions: the NASUWT, one of the largest unions, and the PAT, one of the more recently formed, smaller organizations.

213

> NASUWT
>
> National Association of Schoolmasters
> Union of Women Teachers
>
> Website: www.teachersunion.org.uk

Q. How many members does the NASUWT have?

A. Almost 200,000 teaching membership.

Q. How much do new teachers have to pay to join the union?

A. For NQTs membership is free for the Autumn term and 50 per cent for the next two years.

Q. How was the NASUWT formed and how has it changed over the years?

A. The NAS was formed in 1919 and the UWT in 1965. Their merger in 1975 meant 20 per cent female membership. There is currently 64 per cent female membership.

Q. What makes the NASUWT special?

A. Although the NASUWT is an educational organization, making representations to government and others on education issues, conducting original research, responding to government Green Papers, etc., it considers its main role as an advocate for teachers. Hence its slogan of 'Putting Teachers First'.

Q. What does the NASUWT feel is the main role of a teaching union?

A. The main role of the Association is to enhance teaching as a career and provide protection and support for the individual teacher facing problems.

Q. How does the Union fulfil this role?

A. The Association does this by seeking to make teaching more financially rewarding; protect teachers (and pupils) from violent and disruptive pupils; reduce workload, especially bureaucracy; provide professional advice to members on current initiatives, and give prompt legal and professional support.

Q. How is the NASUWT structured, and how can members get more involved and influence the union's decision making?

A. Members are grouped in schools, each with an elected school representative. Both members and representatives are sent regular communications. All members are invited to local association meetings. There is at least one local association within each local education authority. In large authorities there may be several, each covering a part of the area. The views of the meetings are sent to the National Executive or submitted as a motion to Annual Conference.

44 Executive Members are elected by all members in each of 33 regional districts. The National Officers of the Association are elected by a ballot of all members. Annual Conference is made up of representatives from 360 local associations.

Q. What publications does the NASUWT offer its members?

A. All NASUWT publications are listed on the website. The publications are free to members (unless stated otherwise). Members receive a monthly newspaper (during term time) and a termly magazine.

Q. What benefits could a teacher expect on joining the union?

A. Policies to make teaching more financially rewarding; protection from violent and disruptive pupils; the campaign to reduce workload, especially bureaucracy, both nationally and in the individual school; professional advice on current initiatives; legal representation and trade union support when assaulted by a pupil or parent, injured in an accident, accused of misconduct, or having a grievance with the employer. Also, a wide range of concessionary services.

Q. Are there any special forms of help or support that the NASUWT offers to student teachers?

A. The NASUWT has linked up with the NUS to provide a unique service to *ALL* education students offering general advice and information on all issues relating to student teachers; problems with mentors in schools, tutors in colleges; financial concerns including government incentives and student loans; change of course, deferment or withdrawal; representation in academic appeals, and legal actions arising from school placements.

Q. Finally, which issues in education does the NASUWT feel are of most importance to the profession, and how does the NASUWT go about dealing with these issues?

A. As far as the NASUWT and its members are concerned the main issues are disruptive pupils, teachers' workload, and teachers' pay. The Association campaigns on these issues and has successfully defended its right to protect members from violent pupils in both the High Court and Court of Appeal.

PAT

Professional Association of Teachers

Website: www.pat.org.uk

Q. When was the PAT set up and why?

A. In 1970 by a group of teachers who having seen the effects of teachers' strike action on pupils wished to commit themselves to the principle of not striking.

Q. How is the PAT looking to raise its profile as a teachers' union?

A. By increased media coverage, through advertising, exhibitions and seminars, and on the internet.

Q. What makes the PAT special?

A. Its no-industrial action rule – putting children and students first; independence from the TUC; UK-wide representation; commitment to representing the whole team from nursery to tertiary – teachers, heads and support staff, as well as lecturers, nursery nurses, nannies and other child carers in the public and private sectors, and a more personal approach due to smaller size.

Q. What does the PAT feel is the main role of a teaching union, and how does it fulfil this role?

A. Looking after the interests of its members and helping and advising them individually as well as representing them nationally. It fulfils this role through its network of local officials and head office staff in Derby and Edinburgh.

Q. What is the organizational structure of the PAT and how can members get more involved in their union?

A. PAT is run by an elected General Secretary, National Council and Committees, section committees, and local Federations and Branches. Members can go to local meetings and stand in elections for local and national posts. There is more information on the 'About the Association' page on the PAT website.

Q. What benefits could a teacher expect on joining the union?

A. These are wide-ranging. You can see full details at the Membership Benefits page of the website.

Q. What forms of ongoing support does the PAT offer to its members?

A. Help and advice on practice, pay and conditions nationally and locally, plus information in journals, advice publications and on the website.

Q. Which educational issues does the PAT feel are of most importance to the profession?

A. PAT's 'Election Manifesto' sets out a number of key priorities the union would like to see implemented. The main points of the Manifesto are a national register of childcarers; a universal entitlement to funding for nursery education for three year olds; commitment to improved working conditions for all in childcare and education; a rationalization of salaries for the 'Whole Team' in education (teachers, head teachers, teaching assistants and other support staff); guaranteed non-contact time for classroom teachers (time out of the classroom for training, marking, etc.); funding to be provided to maintain staff and pupil ratios, the use of mentors, continued staff development and links with training agencies; national funding for a National Curriculum; and consideration of the effects of assessments on pupils.

General teaching councils

There are separate GTCs for Scotland, Wales, England and Northern Ireland. These councils are responsible for promoting the profession, and for ensuring high professional standards. The GTCs also hold a register of people who are qualified to work as teachers. You can find out a lot more about the role of the GTC in England in the interview below with Carol Adams.

```
Chief Executive

General Teaching Council for England

Carol Adams
```

Q. Could you tell me about your first few years in teaching?

Carol – I went into teaching because I loved my subject, History. I'd have spent all my time out at historic sites and castles if I could! The more History you can do for real, on site, the better. I taught History in inner London comprehensives for six years – these were large, very challenging schools. I taught the whole range from Year Seven to 'A' level, and I taught large numbers of children who were failing. I found inner London children fantastic, I loved the challenge of teaching children who didn't want to be there. There was a very strong bond between people who taught together in those days. This was in the early 1970s.

Q. How was the job of a teacher different at that time?

Carol – The expectations of the children were lower in general, which meant that poor behaviour was more likely to be tolerated. Individual teachers had to organize their own discipline within a school structure that fundamentally didn't set sufficient boundaries. Also, we decided what to teach. It was pre National Curriculum and you taught based on your enthusiasms, on the material available in the stock cupboard, and on your team of colleagues.

Q. Do you think it's a shame that the curriculum is much more prescriptive now than it was when you started teaching?

Carol – I do in a way. I think we've got the balance wrong, that you need to have the flexibility to teach what enthuses you. With a lot of teaching, it doesn't actually matter what the content is, so long as you can enthuse children and they gain in skills and confidence. I think that having that choice enabled us to be very creative and it inspired us to work phenomenally hard outside of school because we wanted to.

Q. And will we ever return to a situation where there's less prescription about what teachers have to do?

Carol – There are signs of it, and we have to be hopeful. It's part of a huge debate about accountability, which is of course fundamental to working in the public service. Accountability has gone in a direction where it's linked to external controls and checklists. If you go down that route, it's very hard not to get into total prescription. If you don't trust professionals, then you've got to prescribe everything they do. We've got to return to a better balance, in which you trust professionals' judgements more, and make sure they've got the systems to do the very best job. We're in danger of going down a path where all the emphasis is on people being seen to do the right thing, rather than asking what the right thing is.

Q. What path did your career in education take after your time as a teacher?

Carol – I worked for four years as an education officer in the Tower of London. It was marvellous: we had a load of artefacts, we did lectures, trails, study visits, dramas, all sorts. It was living history. The children loved it – the visits gave them a shift in their understanding about history. After that I managed the ILEA History and Social Sciences Teacher Centre. We ran professional development for teachers and produced teaching materials. Then I became an ILEA Inspector for Equal Opportunities Gender. I published a book called *The Gender Trap* with a colleague and I was also involved with teacher colleagues in a series of books called 'Women in History'. After that I was the Assistant Chief Education Officer in Haringey for two years. Then I worked in Wolverhampton and Shropshire as a Chief Education Officer. In 1999 I came to work at the GTC. They've all been fantastic jobs, every single one of them.

Q. What do you think makes a good teacher?

Carol – A combination of knowledge and commitment to your students. You need to be honest, to have total integrity in what you're doing. A good teacher has enthusiasm, passion and creativity, and with that goes humour and so on. It's also about really recognizing the students as human beings, having great respect for them. That means caring about them in a unsentimental sense.

Q. And how can we recruit more good teachers, and retain those we already have in the profession?

Carol – In essence, it's about enabling teachers to feel they are doing a really good job, to giving them maximum job satisfaction. They need the feeling that they've succeeded and that their pupils have too. At the heart of what gets to teachers and reduces morale is feeling that they can't do a good job. In my experience, teachers actually like teaching, but many of them no longer love the job of being a teacher. Teaching can be the most satisfying, rewarding, wonderful job. I think we're very hypocritical as a society when we say that, but then we don't actually enable teachers to enjoy the job.

Q. What sort of things prevent teachers from getting job satisfaction?

Carol – It's partly to do with over-accountability, where the focus is on filling in detailed lesson plans, assessments, and so on, spending more time *proving* what you're doing than actually doing it. For instance, inspection is perceived by teachers as all about people being *seen* to do something, rather than looking at what they're actually doing. There are some bright people in the system who do their best to subvert that, but you need outstanding leadership to enable the whole school to stay focused on the right thing.

There's undoubtedly been too much initiative and change. Politics has come before education and governments have been badly advised about the capacity of human beings to absorb and implement change. People can only take on so much at once. If you throw too much at people, they feel like they're failing, they feel that they're not doing a good job if they haven't actually managed to execute 10 initiatives that day.

The workload's got bigger. I don't think it's so much the volume of the work, but the nature of the work. People being told to do things they don't want to do. I don't think teachers have ever had any problem working long hours. When you first become a teacher you recognize that you're either going to go insane and work 24 hours a day, seven days a week, or you're going to strike a balance. Potentially, every lesson could be a dynamic multi media show, but you can't do that. So, you're sensible, you work hard on the things that you find creative and satisfying. But what is getting to teachers is that they're spending long hours doing things they don't particularly value. Doing someone else's task, not the one you've set yourself.

The less you trust people, the less they feel trusted, the less willing they're going to be to invest in their own judgement, their own professionalism. They're going to say, 'fine, I'll tick the box!'.

Q. Could you explain the role of the GTC?

Carol – First of all it's to be a professional body that can speak up for teachers on professional issues. We represent teachers' views to government and the world at large. Our job is to connect with teachers. What is it they need to do their job properly: what kind of development, support, education systems, resources? What constitutes good teaching and learning? What will retain them in the profession? How do we recruit them? What should we do about their professional development? It's not about negotiating pay and conditions: that's the job of the trade unions.

The other part of our role is as the standards body for the profession: being responsible for high standards, and demonstrating the high standards of the profession. We have a role in hearing the cases of a tiny number of teachers who are dismissed for misconduct or lack of professional competence. The Council decides (and the majority of them are teachers) whether that person is fit to go on being a teacher. It's not like a trial, it's more like a tribunal. Tied in with that we've written a Professional Code about the values of being a teacher. We got responses from about 30,000 teachers to help us write this. We also award qualified teacher status, and we're responsible for the induction appeals.

Q. How does the GTC have an influence? How can you actually help to change teachers' working lives for the better?

Carol – All our advice is developed as policy, which the whole Council has to approve. We start by going out and talking to teachers at teacher meetings. The committees work up policy advice, and then we go and meet the Secretary of State and present it formally. For example we've presented policies on teacher retention, professional development and workload. We've also given advice on the White Paper on the future of teaching. Meanwhile we're also working at a staff to staff level, liasing with the DfES and other agencies. What you don't get is government turning round one day and saying 'right, the whole of the GTC's demands are going to be met'. Just as they bargain with the unions, so they'll take on board only some of what we ask. Bits filter through, but it has to be argued subtly and effectively. It's not just 'get rid of OFSTED or league tables', it's finding a sensible framework for accountability.

Q. Do you feel that you're actually starting to have an impact on what happens, and if so, in what way?

Carol – The government is starting to take teacher retention much more seriously. We're running a retention forum with all the bodies and parties meeting together to give advice to the minister. We argued very strongly, along with the unions, for professional time. We've always said that the one thing teachers needed was guaranteed professional time to do the full, complex job of being a teacher. In two years we've had quite an influence, actually, but for the teacher in the classroom it's not going to change the world overnight.

Q. Could you give a specific example of an area where the GTC has had an influence on policy?

Carol – We've worked closely with government on the strategy for professional development, and we've secured a scheme for professional development in the early years of a teacher's career. Teachers in the two years after induction get a specific entitlement to professional development. This is currently a pilot going on in a number of LEAs, and we're pushing for it to be evaluated and extended throughout the whole country. We've persuaded the government that it's a funding priority to extend this to all teachers in their second and third years. We've focused on teachers in the early years of their careers because we think that you've got to do something to stop people leaving the profession. We are also responsible for the sabbatical scheme and we are working on a framework to describe and support professional learning.

Q. How does the GTC find out what teachers really think, and how does this influence your work?

Carol – We do that through endless interaction: a constant process of trying to build up a strong evidence base. GTC staff and members go out to head teachers' conferences, schools and LEAs. We also hold teacher meetings. We write directly to every school in the area explaining that they'll get a half day's cover and encouraging a diverse range of teachers to attend. At the meeting there's an introduction from me, then groups of teachers discuss specific questions, working with a facilitator and a note-taker.

Our Code of Professional Values and Practice was devised in that way. We asked teachers if they wanted a code, what use it might be put to, what should be in it? It's a quite new approach, asking teachers what they think about professional issues, recording it and demonstrating to them that their advice gets fed back into our policies. Teachers have found that quite unique. One very interesting finding to emerge is that the professional experience of being a teacher is incredibly different depending on the school that you're in. Some teachers feel supported up to the hilt, with professional development coming out of their ears, others feel bullied, lacking in morale, over-worked and completely over-stretched.

Q. What will the GTC do for teachers in the longer term?

Carol – If we're successful, we'll contribute to teachers being better understood by the public, being better regarded, and having better support and resources to do the job. We've also got an important role in mapping out the future, because education's going to change and our job is to make sure that teachers have a say in the future of education. The GTC is a long-term, 10-year project, if we're going to bring about recognizable improvement across the whole system. I don't believe in quick fixes: change has got to be sustainable in the long term.

Q. What about the relationship between the GTC and the unions?

Carol – We work very well with them in many ways. They do our training for members on regulatory work. The sensitivities around the unions have been on policy areas, and increasingly we're succeeding in working with them and we've got to work together for the sake of teachers. For example, the NUT is very active in teachers' professional development and so we are already beginning to work in partnership with them in a number of projects.

Q. Could we talk about the thorny issue of fees? That's caused a lot of resentment right at the start, hasn't it?

Carol – I understand teachers' resentment, but we are working incredibly hard to sort it out, with the unions and the employers. The ground was never laid to prepare teachers for an independent professional body, supported and funded by the profession. The fee is the price of independence and it came as a shock to many teachers. We've had to persuade government that it needed sorting out, because we do understand how teachers felt about the issue. Teachers have now been given a special allowance of £33, which is £10 more than the fee. It's being paid as an additional allowance in their salaries, so that it can be paid to part-time teachers as well.

Q. And what about supply teachers?

Carol – Those employed by LEAs will also get the full amount as an allowance on their pay. The only teachers who won't get it are those who work for agencies, but we hope that the agencies will pay it. Employers are responsible for making sure that everyone they employ is registered, and it's also the responsibility of teachers as professionals.

Q. What would you say to teachers who feel that the GTC is just another imposition from above?

Carol – There was far too little debate about the GTC before it started work. When I was appointed there was nine months to set the whole thing up, and the elections were already underway. There should have been a higher profile and well managed debate from the beginning. It's been a really tough beginning, but hopefully we can make up for it now.

Q. And finally, anything else that you'd like to add?

Carol – Teachers do a fantastic job – they're committed, highly professional, they work long hours. That needs to be said without qualification or equivocation. Sometimes you have to stop and think: at this moment there are 25,000 schools in which children are being taught in an orderly fashion. It's astonishing really that teachers do that so well.

Teaching is suffering from a lack of other professional support for problems in the communities they serve. There isn't the multi-disciplinary support that is needed, and teachers are dealing with problems that need the intervention of other agencies. I don't support the view that teachers shouldn't be social workers – every teacher is involved in social issues, and it does teaching a disservice to say that shouldn't be their job. But there's so little back up now, services have been cut, and that causes difficulties for teachers. It's not a comfortable message.

I'm more interested in what happens to the profession, than with the success of the GTC. The GTC's just a vehicle, it's not about building our power, it's 'can we contribute along with teachers', can we help to galvanize change, to make teaching a better job, more creative and rewarding and to continue to raise standards? That's the challenge.

Disciplinary procedures

The governing body of your school is responsible for deciding on disciplinary rules and procedures, and making it clear to all the staff what is and is not acceptable behaviour. Teachers may be disciplined for 'misconduct', and in order for this to lead to dismissal it has to be very serious, or repeated on a number of occasions. For instance, this might include being late on repeated occasions, being absent from school without authorization, or not meeting the standards of work that are required. Teachers may also be charged with 'gross misconduct', and this can lead to instant dismissal. These sort of charges would be for serious contractual breaches, such as theft, physical violence or incapacity due to drink or drugs.

If a teacher is charged with 'gross misconduct', they will be suspended on full pay while an investigation is undertaken. With any disciplinary charges, you are entitled to receive full details of the offence, and to have a colleague or union rep with you at any meetings. You also have a right of appeal once a decision has been made.

Disciplinary procedures would normally have a number of stages: at each stage it should be made completely clear what the offence is, and why the warning has been given. A first, oral warning would be given for a less serious offence, followed by a written warning for further offences, or for more serious misconduct. After this, the teacher should then receive a final written warning that they will be dismissed if they do not comply/improve.

A record of written warnings is kept by the school, and these should be completely confidential. ACAS recommends that these warnings are disregarded after a certain amount of time has gone by (six months for minor offences, a year for a final warning).

Section 2

Case Studies

12 Planning in the primary school

In this chapter you will find a full case study of the planning that a primary school teacher undertakes. The case study gives you a chance to find out about the different considerations that the primary teacher must take into account when planning, and also to see some examples of real documents that are used in a primary school. You can read a further interview with Tracey Nightingale, the teacher featured, in Chapter 5 where she talks about her experiences as an NQT.

Although the detail and format of the planning will vary from school to school and from teacher to teacher, hearing Tracey's story should give you a good idea about what is involved in this area of your job. Planning at primary level means working with each of the National Curriculum subjects, as well as taking into account the Literacy and Numeracy strategies. As you can see from Tracey's case study, this means that the teacher must be very well organized, with a clear overview of both the children's and the curriculum requirements.

> Year Three Class Teacher
>
> Bentinck Primary School, Nottingham
>
> Tracey Nightingale

Q. What planning does your school ask you to produce?

Tracey – At Bentinck we're asked for a long-term plan, medium-term plans for each curriculum subject and weekly literacy and numeracy plans. How detailed these plans are seems to be a matter of personal and professional judgement, and the emphasis on this has changed recently. I think it also depends on the senior management and the head teacher's priorities. In a previous school, they never looked at my medium-term plans (I was on long-term supply), but always wanted a copy of my weekly numeracy and literacy plans in a file to be looked at by the subject coordinators, etc. When I moved to Bentinck our acting head teacher asked for the medium- and long-term planning. When John, our permanent head teacher, came back, having never worked with him before, I wasn't sure what he'd expect so I had all my planning done for the start of term. [You can see Tracey's head teacher's comments on planning at Bentinck below.]

On a personal level, I don't feel as confident trying to teach without having planned the lesson first. I don't stand there with the plan in front of me, but have it on the wall so I can have a quick glance at it before the lesson starts and make sure I've got all the resources, etc., prepared.

> **Tracey's head teacher's comments** – *I do, of course, understand the importance of planning, but in the end what matters are outcomes. Planning is a tool for the teacher to help them do the job. If excessive planning leads to a poor work–life balance then the quality of a teacher's work may deteriorate. As a head, I would only want to start monitoring the detail of a teacher's planning if I had concerns about the quality of outcomes. Teachers are professionals and need to make their own decisions about the level of planning detail they need to do a good job. This may vary. I don't expect teachers to hand in planning for me to 'mark'. I think that is professionally demeaning.*
>
> *However, some planning (long- and medium-term) must be available to subject coordinators to allow them to monitor coverage and progression. This is collated centrally in a file for this purpose. I also request that weekly outline plans for literacy and numeracy are displayed in the classroom to allow any substitute teacher to pick up learning objectives, etc., if a teacher is absent.*

Q. How do you go about your overall planning?

Tracey – I start by looking at the QCA scheme of work documents and decide how many and which ones I'm going to cover. Then I split them into the three terms, making sure I've rotated those subjects that we don't have enough time to do all year round. That forms the basic format of my long-term plan. Then I look at each term and count how many weeks we have. I do a medium-term plan for each subject with one lesson per week. So I end up with medium-term plans for nine subjects (usually two medium-term plans per subject, per term). For literacy and numeracy I look at the scheme of work and do weekly plans. So in a year I'll have done one long-term plan, approximately 36 medium-term plans, and about 78 weekly plans. Phew!

Q. And when do you do the majority of your planning?

Tracey – I do the majority of my planning in the holidays or at weekends. In fact, I do very little of it actually at work. I get the long-term plan, and the first term's medium-term plans done during the summer holidays. I also try to get as many of the literacy and numeracy weekly plans for that term done as possible. During the Christmas break I do the second term's medium-term plans plus literacy and numeracy plans. Then I do the same for the third term during the Easter holidays. Any numeracy or literacy plans I don't get done during the main holidays I do at weekends.

Q. Roughly how much time would you say you spend on planning?

Tracey – It's quite difficult to say as I've never sat down and actually thought about it, I just do what I need to do to get the work done. During term time I spend about two or three hours each weekend doing planning for the following week. During the holidays it varies. During the summer break I try to have a complete break for a couple of weeks. Towards the end of these holidays I spend the majority of my time doing planning. It's really hard to think exactly how much I really do but I'd guess about 80 hours (a very rough estimate). During the Easter and Christmas breaks I'd estimate about the same. During half terms I try to do as little as possible, just a few hours here and there.

Q. How do you set about planning your teaching within the different curriculum areas?

Tracey – I plan topics within each curriculum area, for example Science topics, History topics, etc. [You can see samples of History and Science plans at the end of this interview.] ICT is usually related to another curriculum area, as this gives the children a sense of purpose. I divide work into curriculum areas, each subject having a slot in the timetable. Some subjects are taught in rotation with others throughout the year because of time constraints, for instance Design and Technology is rotated with Art and Geography is rotated with History.

Q. How do you timetable different subjects into the day?

Tracey – The mornings are a set timetable of literacy and numeracy. In the afternoons it's a personal decision when each subject is taught. Logistical issues such as hall & ICT suite usage have to be taken into consideration but it's more or less a free choice after that. I try to split my afternoons into two sessions so there are usually four lessons in each day. We don't have an afternoon play so giving the children a change of subject and pace seems to keep the momentum going longer. The exact timing of lessons depends on what subject it is. [You can see a copy of Tracey's timetable at the end of this interview.]

Q. And how do you decide how long to spend on each subject?

Tracey – The school follows government guidelines on the amount of time given to literacy and numeracy. With other subjects I see how much time I have left in the afternoons after I've taken into account when I have PE, Music, singing, etc. When I know how much time I have left I share this out between the other subjects. I try to give Science a little more time then the other subjects, because it's a core subject. The length of time given to other subjects really is a matter of having the time available and personal judgement on how long is needed. For example, Art or D&T take longer because they are practical (and messy) subjects. PSHE involves mainly discussion which children find difficult to sustain for long periods so this is a shorter lesson.

Q. How do you incorporate the Literacy and Numeracy strategies into the day?

Tracey – From Mondays to Thursdays we have a literacy lesson for the first hour of the day (either before or after assembly), and then an hour of numeracy after playtime. On Fridays we have 'Good Book' first thing, followed by a half hour session of mental maths practice, then literacy work after playtime. Of course, some elements of these subjects cross over into other areas, such as correcting spellings, etc. On Friday afternoons I have a spelling and handwriting session with about half of my class (the other half are taken by another teacher for more differentiated work). [You can see samples of blank literacy and numeracy planning sheets at the end of this interview.]

Q. Could you tell me a bit more about what 'Good Book' is?

Tracey – Good Book is an extended assembly we have on a Friday morning (it lasts about 45 minutes instead of 15 minutes). Each teacher nominates a few children from their class who have done something particularly good during the week. It might be a piece of good work, trying really hard at something, making improvements in attitude, perseverance, etc., or improved attendance. We have a large display in the hall. Each class has a rocket with a smoke trail. Teachers write the child's name and reason for being in Good Book on a star and on a certificate. In Good Book, the nominated children go up to the front, a class at a time, and are praised for their achievements. Their work is shown to the school, stars are stuck on the display and they take the certificate home. Parents are also invited.

Q. Is there a regular daily and weekly pattern to your teaching?

Tracey – I tend to do the same subjects on the same days each week. I think this gives the children a sense of routine and it helps my organization too. I have a learning support assistant working with me on Monday and Tuesday afternoons, so I tend to do Science and Art or Design/Technology on those days because of the organizational issues. Other subjects, where I need the hall, the playground, and the ICT suite, are timetabled as a whole staff to ensure we all have access.

Q. How do you deal with the need for differentiation?

Tracey – It really depends on the subject. For literacy and numeracy we 'stream' the children. My class (Year Three) and the Year Four are divided into three groups according to ability so the children have work that is more suited to their capabilities. The same thing also happens for Years Five and Six. Each teacher then differentiates within their groups. We've found it's a lot easier to differentiate this way as each group has a smaller spread of ability. The scheme of work I use for literacy and numeracy has differentiation suggestions so I mainly use these. For other subjects I either differentiate my outcome, have LSA support for help or alter the task slightly.

Q. What sort of teaching and learning styles do you use within your lessons?

Tracey – I tend to start my lessons with whole class discussion/explanation for the first 10 or 15 minutes, then I'll send the children off to do the task I've set them. Sometimes this is an individual task, other times it's a task I'll ask them to do in pairs or small groups. This sometimes depends on the nature of the task, for example discussion, problem solving or sharing resources in groups, or if I'm trying to assess each individual child's knowledge and understanding. I try to use a mixture where I can so that the children get a chance to express their own ideas, as well as share them with other children and develop their interpersonal skills.

Q. And how do you organize resources within the classroom?

Tracey – Resources that children use every day (pencil, rubbers, sharpeners, rulers, crayons, felt pens, numeracy and literacy writing books) are kept on the children's tables. They are all colour coded so they know which table they belong to. Other books are kept in baskets on the side in the classroom. Any additional equipment is divided between the tables when needed. Children are responsible for looking after the equipment and making sure it is tidied away into the correct places. We try to discourage children from bringing their own equipment into school.

Classroom resources, for example Maths equipment, reading books, etc., are kept in designated areas of the classroom so all the same subject equipment is together. Anything the children are not allowed free access to is kept in my store cupboard.

Q. Do you make your own resources, or use what the school already has?

Tracey – A mixture, depending on what is already there. If I need a resource and we don't already have it in school then I'll try to make my own or find a way around it. We're quite a well resourced school and we don't mind sharing things with other staff so we can usually find what we need.

Q. At Bentinck, do teachers of different age groups work together on planning?

Tracey – We're a single form entry school so there is only one class per year. We all tend to do our planning individually but we share our ideas with the other teachers. The Year Four teacher and I try to develop some continuity in routines,

231

etc. We share our long-term plans so that we can plan trips which will be useful to both classes. For example, last year I did a Science topic on the teeth and eating, she did one on the body, and then we went to the body zone at Eureka. Some of the QCA units are designed to be taught in either age group so we both did the same unit on Henry VIII's wives and went on a Tudor Christmas trip together.

Q. And what role do subject coordinators play in planning?

Tracey – We have a subject coordinator for every subject. They tend to focus more on ensuring the necessary resources are available. Because we follow QCA or other schemes of work for the majority of subjects, most basic planning is already done.

Q. Do you ever feel that planning takes up too much of your time, or is this time well spent?

Tracey – Personally I think it's time well spent as I do what I need to feel confident when I'm teaching. Because I've only just completed my first year with my own class, I've only just started being able to reuse planning I've done before. I expect (and hope) this to mean that the amount of time I spend planning for the next year will be a lot less.

Q. And finally, what about the planning you did when you were a student? What are your feelings about that?

Tracey – I found planning quite difficult when I was a student, mainly because you're trying to do it according to how each school wants you to do it, as well as satisfy the course criteria. It's a lot easier now schools use QCA and other schemes of work. There are more ideas of how to teach different concepts around, and with more experience, I now have my own stock of ideas too.

I think a lot of the planning I was asked to do as a student teacher was a waste of time in hindsight. We'd have to do a long-term plan, a medium-term plan, a weekly plan and a daily plan, plus evaluations of each lesson. This did decrease slightly towards the end of the course but not a great deal. I think when you're learning to teach, the most important thing is the actual teaching. Too much emphasis was placed on making sure you'd written every little detail down. I know this was supposed to help us think our lessons through, but overall I felt it was time consuming, often frustrating and I never really looked at them again once I'd done them.

I try to reuse ideas and plans where I can, if it's appropriate. This was difficult before I got my own class as I was teaching different Year groups. Now I have this class I am able to use last year's planning, adapting it where necessary.

Weekly Timetable

	9.00–10.30		10.45–12.00		1.15–2.30	2.30–3.15
Monday	Literacy	**PLAYTIME**	Numeracy	**DINNERTIME**	Science	RE/Music
Tuesday	9.00–10.10 Literacy / Assembly (HT)		10.45–12.00 Numeracy		1.15–2.15 D&T/Art	2.15–3.15 Geography/History
Wednesday	Assembly (KS2) / 9.30–10.30 Literacy		10.45–12.00 Numeracy		1.15–1.45 PSHE	1.45–3.15 Swimming (Followed by reading)
Thursday	9.00–10.10 Literacy / Assembly (DHT)		10.45–12.00 Numeracy		1.15–2.00 Singing	2.00–3.15 ICT
Friday	GOOD BOOK / 10.00–10.30 Numeracy (Mental Maths)		10.45–12.00 Literacy (Reading)		1.15–2.15 Handwriting & Spellings (Mrs B's group out)	2.15–3.15 PE (Mrs B + target groups)

233

Literacy Hour Planning

Week beginning:

Unit title:

Objective:
Range =
Word Level =
Sentence Level =
Text Level =

	Whole class Shared reading and writing	Whole class phonics, spelling, vocabulary, grammar	Independent groups task	Plenary
Monday				
Tuesday				
Wednesday				
Thursday				
Friday				

Numeracy Planning

Week beginning: Class/Group: Three   Term: Summer   Teacher: T. Nightingale

Learning Objectives:
Mental

Main

Key Vocabulary:

	Oral / Mental Activity	Main Activity Activity - Differentiation - Resources	Plenary Key Questions - Homework
Monday	Activity: Resources:	Intro: Activity: Differentiation: Resources:	
Tuesday	Activity: Resources:	Intro: Activity: Differentiation: Resources:	
Wednesday	Activity: Resources:	Intro: Activity: Differentiation: Resources:	
Thursday	Activity: Resources:	Intro: Activity: Differentiation: Resources:	
Friday	Activity: Resources:	Intro: Activity: Differentiation: Resources:	

© Bentinck Primary and Nursery School

Unit title: 3B Helping plants grow well. Class: 3 Term: Summer Teacher: Miss T. Nightingale

Learning Objectives	Main Activity Differentiation – EMTAG – Assessment			Resources	Vocabulary
	Introduction	Main & Group Activity	Plenary		
Science Sc1 2h ▪ To ascertain the children's level of understanding of the needs of plants from their work in KS One	Tell children that we are going to be learning about and growing plants. Ask them to think about what they already know. Brainstorm words & phrases they can remember.	Task 1 – concept map of plants. Task 2 – complete page 55. Read through with class then they are to complete unaided. Task 3 – Plant seeds.	Discuss tasks, highlight some of the concepts children have remembered,	Copies of page 155	(children's own vocabulary being assessed)

Lesson One

236

Lesson 2					
Science Sc1 2f, 2h, 2j. Sc2 3c ■ To know that the roots take up water and anchor the plant to the ground. ■ To use systematic observations and measurements.	Ask children to imagine a hot, sunny day and what they feel like. Encourage thinking they'd be hot in need of refreshment. Show wilted plant - what does it need? Why has it wilted? Draw analogy between humans and plants needing water. Discuss how water is taken in differently though.	Pass around weeds and copies of page 63. Ask children to look carefully at plant and discuss how water moved up the roots and stems to the leaves and about the functions of the roots, stems and leaves. Task 1 – draw a labelled diagram of their plant on page 63. Pair up name of part with description of function. Task 2 – set up experiment as page 64.	Bring class together, make prediction on what might happen. * Ensure water levels are checked everyday. Buy and prepare celery for next lesson.	Copies of pages 63 and 64, washed weeds with roots in shallow trays, washed weeds (complete with roots, water, plastic beakers, and elastic bands, cling film.	Anchor, roots, water.

						Fair test
Lesson 3	Science Sc1 2h, 2j, Sc2 3c ■ To know that water travels in tiny 'pipes' through plants. ■ To know that information from previous experiments can be used in planning new experiments.	Make observations of results from roots experiment in Lesson 2. Draw conclusions. Take cut flowers and put into vase of water. Discuss why we put cut flowers into water. Talk about tiny pipes through which plants carry water. Look at end, of flower, suggest that this is difficult so will use celery.	Explain that previously put celery in coloured water. Examine celery. Children draw and write about how water is carried.	Discuss the investigation and the colour of the celery. Reinforce concept of water travelling up the stems of the celery.	Celery (with ends cut a few days prior), containers, food colouring.	
Lesson 4	Science Sc1 1a, 2d, 2h, 2j, Sc2 3a ■ To know that plants need water, but not an unlimited amount, for healthy growth.	Discuss how to set up an experiment to prove statement that plants need water, but not unlimited amount, for healthy growth.	Set up experiment. Record how experiment is to be carried out, how it is fair, etc.	*Plants to be taken home over half term by teacher and watered according to instructions of experiment.	Seeds, planted in Lesson 1	Fair test

© Bentinck Primary and Nursery School

Note: Lessons 1-3 of an 8 lesson scheme are shown

Unit title: **Why did Henry VIII marry six times?**   Class:3   Term: **Autumn**   Teacher: T. **Nightingale**

Learning Objectives	Main Activity Differentiation - EMTAG - Assessment			Resources	Vocabulary
	Introduction	Main Activity	Plenary		
Lesson 1					
• To think about what makes a good king or queen. • To be able to identify features and characteristics of portraits and pictures. • Learn information about Henry VIII's character and facts about his reign.	Discuss what makes a good king or queen and how they keep control. List qualities.	• Explain type of person Henry VIII was and sort of king. Discuss qualities children would like in a monarch. • Look at portraits and pictures. What do they think of his appearance? Do the qualities listed match his pictures? Does he look strong, brave, etc.? • Discuss job description (what and how used). Children to write job description for position of King Henry VIII. • Differentiation = ↑ decorate poster in appropriate style. ↓ Support with ideas and writing.	Share job descriptions. Assessment = Can they draw up realistic job description? Can they explain what qualities Henry had that made him a good king?	Description of Henry VIII, information books, portraits and pictures of Henry VIII, copies of 'Job Description for a King'.	Monarch, king, queen, reign, portraits, character, characteristics, job description.

Lesson 2	• To know about power and the importance of a king. • To be able to identify what a monarch did and did not do.	Discuss hobbies and duties. What hobbies do they have? What duties? Who did they do them for? What if they don't do them? Make list of things they know Henry liked to do.	• Makes list: things Henry would do, and things he would not do. Develop understanding of time period (e.g. he would not have a Playstation!) • Children make own lists of things Henry would and would not do. Think about rewards and punishments for not doing them. • Compile class list. Discuss if his life was easy or difficult. • Take list of things he did do – transfer into 'hobbies' and 'duties.' Compare lists as class. Differentiation = ↑ Illustrate lists. ↓ Prepared list of possible activities.	Discuss any discrepancies and clarify concept of hobbies and duties. Assessment = Do they understand the difference between hobbies and duties? Can they categorise what Henry would have done and not done?	Descriptions of Henry, pictures of Henry, copies of 'the life of Henry VIII.	Hobbies, duties, rewards, punishments, consequences.
Lesson 3	• To identify the problems of the Tudor King. • To understand why Henry wanted a male heir. • To know about the reasons for his divorce from Catherine of Aragon.	Discuss why Henry wanted male heir. List reasons and put in order of importance. Discuss what would influence his choice of wife.	• Show picture of Catherine of Aragon. Do they think she would make a good wife for Henry? Why? • Tell story of their marriage. Focus on what Catherine was like and why Henry chose her. • Work with partner to write letter to a friend as if Henry explaining reasons why marriage didn't work. Differentiation = ↑ Research other wives using information books. ↓ Match with partner to do writing.	Read letters out. Compare reasons for marriage failure. Assessment = Can they explain why Henry wanted a male heir? Can they explain the reasons for him wanting to divorce Catherine?	Story of Henry's marriage to Catherine of Aragon, pictures of Henry and Catherine of Aragon	Heir, king, divorce,

13 Planning in the secondary school

In the secondary school, the planning format used varies from department to department. Depending on the management requirements and philosophies at your school, your planning may be heavily proscribed, or you may simply be given a topic area to focus on, and left to your own devices to decide which lessons to deliver. Below is a further interview with Carl Smith, the teacher featured in Chapter 1 (page 14).

The case study that follows shows the planning that Carl Smith and his department use. As you will see from Carl's comments, as an experienced teacher he finds that delivering the content of the lessons becomes second nature after a while. The chance to repeat lessons that you have taught before is very helpful in developing a more confident teaching style, and in allowing you to become more responsive to your students' needs.

> Secondary School Science Teacher
>
> Second in Department, Key Stage Three Coordinator
>
> Turves Green Girls' School and Technology College, Birmingham
>
> Carl Smith

Q. What planning documents does your school ask your department to produce?

Carl – We have a department development plan which details the long-term aims of the department. This covers things like ICT, staff development, and the introduction of new schemes of work. This year we've had new Key Stage Three and Key Stage Four syllabuses to introduce. We also have schemes of work, so that what we deliver is 'bespoke' to our department and the staff and resources it contains.

In addition to that, we have a plan for the recording of results and assessments. We're lucky in having a member of staff who is an absolute whiz at designing excel spreadsheets, so we can type scores straight into a class list and then the software will aggregate, average and level for us.

Q. And how do you go about day-to-day planning as an individual and a department?

Carl – I'm not the best planner. I rarely use a written plan (unless OFSTED are in). At Key Stage Three the department utilizes a written scheme that we bought in. An in-house scheme written alongside matches our expertise/resources with the original. Our in-house schemes are usually written on a lesson by lesson format. We also use a similar in-house scheme for Key Stage Four, which is adapted to the exam syllabus. So my planning would just be 'Year Nine, topic four, lesson three'. The scheme would then detail activities, resources, homework, alternative activities and health and safety. The latest bought in scheme at Key Stage Three also includes numeracy and literacy information. We're going to adapt the in-house one to include this, and the Key Stage Four one is in the process of being rewritten.

Q. How does the department organize its planning on a longer-term basis?

Carl – We produce a plan of the delivery of all the topics for each year group, so that the entire syllabus is delivered to a timetable. Planning for this keeps teachers on track and tries to eliminate any clashes for resources which can happen with some topics. With Key Stage Four the topics have to be taught to finish on the dates set by the exam board for the module tests. We have a little more freedom at Key Stage Three with the dates but we all have to finish in the time available.

The six modules in each of Years Ten and Eleven are delivered roughly two per term. The classes have four Science lessons a week. One teacher has them for two doing one module, and another teacher has them for the other two doing a second module. Year 11 modules are a little shorter to fit them in before the pupils leave in May. Each individual set will have its own route through the topics. Teachers swap every term so that fresh teachers teach fresh topics with each class. Thus specialists can deliver the same modules to each group in turn rather than having to teach all modules. We also plan coursework days. There is one of these for Year Ten in July and one for Year Eleven in November.

Q. How does the department work together on planning?

Carl – Usually different people take responsibility for certain areas. As Key Stage Three coordinator I produced all the Key Stage Three schemes to match the bought in scheme. At Key Stage Four we each wrote particular modules according to our specialisms or according to who taught what first. For instance, I was the first to deliver the single Science so I wrote the scheme as I went along.

We produced our schemes to a format that we all agreed on so that everyone followed the same route. This meant that we produced a uniform set of schemes which, because they were stored electronically, could be modified by anyone when necessary.

We have just agreed to spend some time towards the end of this (Summer) term to examine the revision classes we are currently doing with Years Nine and Eleven. We are all producing resources and also using some pre-prepared lessons provided by the DfES; the idea being to produce a departmental set of resources that have been proven in class and that can be duplicated and presented properly well in advance of delivery, using our excellent technicians.

Q. How do teachers in your department go about personalizing their lessons?

Carl – We have always regarded the schemes as guides. They detail all that should be delivered and all the resources available. Everyone is free to pick and choose what works best for them and to use additional materials that they might find or produce. All departmental meetings have an agenda item 'Sharing best practice'. This is where we would formally show to each other any improvements or modifications we might have. These would be added to the scheme ASAP after the meeting. In practice we would already have shared this sort of thing informally by passing around worksheets, etc., rather than waiting for a meeting. But the meeting allows the 'sharing' to be recognized and recorded.

Q. Do you ever feel that you are overly prescribed in what you are asked to teach?

Carl – Yes. The modern National Curriculum is very prescriptive in its content. The new QCA Key Stage Three one even more so as it ties down individual topics to particular years rather than anywhere in the whole Key Stage. But we have found that having our own bespoke schemes gives us the freedom to teach to our own styles using familiar resources and ideas.

Q. How do you go about setting up resources for your lessons?

Carl – We have Science technicians who help us, otherwise there wouldn't be time to get it all in!

Q. What sort of balance of practical and theoretical lessons do you have?

Carl – Probably we don't do enough practicals. We try to get a balance but some topics are just not suited to practical work given our level of resources. For example, the 'Waves and Radiation' topic in Year 11 is pretty well all theory. If we had a Sixth form we might have some suitable resources available, but there you go.

Q. What impact have the Literacy and Numeracy strategies had on your planning and teaching?

Carl – Probably outside of Maths we are the most numerate department. We are currently about to have a numeracy day to tell the staff how it can enhance their lessons. This has been planned by a cross-curricular committee with reps from every faculty, so it should match all of our needs. Literacy has been incorporated into schemes but I have to say it probably hasn't had the impact that people thought it might.

Q. How do you go about differentiating the work?

Carl – We teach in ability groups. Also, the schemes of work are differentiated to suit all abilities. The new Key Stage Three scheme has loads of downloadable SEN resources from its website. It already contains a wealth of higher ability resources as well.

Q. Do you find yourself referring to a plan before or during lessons, or is it all second nature by now?

Carl – A bit of both. Sometimes the resources of textbooks are guide enough but sometimes it helps to look back at the schemes to look for alternative activities. Also as new activities come along (we are very hot on kinaesthetic learning at the moment) then these can be added to the schemes for future reference.

Q. As a Science teacher, what health and safety issues do you have to take account of in your planning?

Carl – All activities have to be analysed for potential hazards and ways to reduce or eliminate them. Risk assessments must be recorded. A lot of data can be obtained from outside organizations such as CLEAPPS or CRONERS, then adapted for our use.

Q. What about when you first started teaching? How did you plan then?

Carl – Thinking back to when I began teaching I did follow the format used on TP for the first year or so. However, once you've gone through the cycle a few times the actual content becomes second nature. This is particularly true in a subject like mine, where groups get rotated so you might teach the same topic to three different groups, one after the other. In my previous school, when OFSTED came in we were asked to plan for each class using an exercise book, writing a lesson plan on a single page. At my present school we produced an A5 planning/information sheet, a copy of which was left on the side should an inspector put their nose around the door.

Q. I understand that you're working as a mentor with ITT students. What type of planning do they have to do?

Carl – I have recently begun mentoring students and these days the amount of planning they have to do beggars belief! They have to produce pages of plans (at least four pieces of A4) for each lesson using pro formas with prompts and big spaces for notes. Then we have to fill in huge (12 page!) tick lists covering scores of criteria and that's before we actually give any meaningful feedback to the student.

Q. Could you tell me a bit about the sample documents we have here [see end of this chapter]?

Carl – These are examples of a Key Stage Three and part of a Key Stage Four topic. The former is an adaptation of a bought in scheme matching it to what we have, the latter is written direct from the syllabus. Of course, these schemes are now being superseded by the latest AQA (KS4) and QCA (KS3) orders and so might not match the very latest criteria.

The first one, 'SN.9.6 Reactivity', is a Key Stage Three unit from the scheme that we are currently replacing with the new QCA. It's a Year Nine unit and so will still be in use until the end of Summer 2003 when the new stuff should have superseded it (just in time for the next change!).

The second one, 'NEAB 14 Scheme' is a Key Stage Four scheme written for our Single Science course. [*Note*: This sample shows lessons 1–12 of a 25 lesson scheme.] This course is currently in its final year with the current Year 11. The current Year 10 are following the new AQA syllabus and we are in the process of writing new in-house schemes for these. They will follow a similar format but will include numeracy, literacy and more detailed risk assessments to bring them up to the latest standards.

There is also a sample of a Year Seven teaching roster, which is the plan that we produce to organize delivery of all the topics for each year group. This allows us to avoid any double booking of resources.

Q. And finally, how do you feel about the constant changes that are made to the curriculum?

Carl – We find this very frustrating, and very expensive. The school spent many thousands of pounds buying in the Science Now scheme of work for Key Stage Four around four years ago. Now we are having to spend similar sums replacing all the textbooks and resources to cover the new QCA scheme over the next three years. Couple this with the many hours we will all spend producing a new in-house scheme to go with it and you can see that the constant fiddling is a costly business. The new Key Stage Four syllabus will also have a heavy time penalty on the scheme writers and, if we can find the money, require us to spend on new textbooks, etc.

TGGS Science Dept.

Topic: Reactivity (Unit 6)   Year: Nine

Scheme of Work

Compiled by: C Smith ©

Science Now!

Lesson	Aims (key ideas)	Resources	Possible practical activities	Equipment	Other (risk assessment etc.)	Homework/ additional classwork
One	Burning metals. Some metals react more easily than others.	Textbook pages 82 and 83. Worksheet 6a Core/Help.	Burning copper, magnesium and iron in a bunsen flame.	Mg ribbon, wire wool, copper foil, bunsens, goggles, heatproof mats, tongs.	Magnesium is best done as a demonstration, avoid looking directly at the flare. Wear goggles and tie back long hair when using bunsens.	WDYK page 83. Assignments 6a Review 6a page 98.
Two	Fizzing furiously. Metals can be placed in a reactivity series.	Textbook pages 84 and 85. Worksheet 6b Core/Help/ Resource.	React metals with hot and cold water and dilute acid.	1M HC1, boiling tube, beakers, bunsens, tripods, gauzes, HP mats, tongs, goggles. Mg ribbon, Ca granules, Zn powder, Cu turnings, Fe filings, Pb foil.	Heat acid by placing boiling tubes in a hot water bath. Wear goggles and tie back long hair when using bunsens. DO NOT react calcium with acid!	WDYK page 85. Assignments 6b Review 6b page 98.
Three and Four	Reactivity.	Worksheet. In what order do metals react with vinegar?	AT.1 opportunity.	Dilute HCl or ethanoic acid. Selection of metals. Lab glassware.	Beware when handling acids. Wear goggles.	Write up investigation.

Lesson	Aims (key ideas)	Resources	Possible practical activities	Equipment	Other (risk assessment etc.)	Homework/additional classwork
Five	Who's the bully? A metal will displace another metal that is lower in the activity series. Reactive metals can displace hydrogen from acids. Carbon can displace some less reactive metals from their ores.	Textbook pages 86 and 87. Worksheet 6c Core/Help/Ext.	Displacement reactions.	Solutions of: copper sulphate, iron sulphate, lead nitrate, magnesium sulphate, silver nitrate, zinc sulphate. Solid copper Turnings, iron filings, lead foil, magnesium ribbon, zinc granules.	Wash hands after handling chemicals, particularly lead and its salts.	WDYK page 87. Assignments 6c. Extras 6c page 94. Review 6c page 99.
Six	Breaking up by heating. Compounds of reactive metals are difficult to break up. Compounds of less reactive metals are easily broken up.	Textbook pages 88 and 89. Worksheet 6d Core/Help/Ext.	Heating carbonates to produce oxides and carbon dioxide.	Carbonates of copper, calcium, sodium, iron, zinc plus any others. Pyrex test tubes with delivery tubes angled down at 90 degrees. Lime water, bunsens, HP mats, clampstands.	Wear goggles and tie back long hair. Remove delivery tube from lime water before stopping heating to avoid 'sucking' back.	WDYK page 89. Assignments 6d. Extras 6d page 95.

Lesson	Aims (key ideas)	Resources	Possible practical activities	Equipment	Other (risk assessment etc.)	Homework/ additional classwork
Seven	Discovering metals. Only unreactive metals are found naturally. Most exist only as compounds.	Textbook pages 90 and 91. Video 29g Fire, Earth and metals.	Pupils can heat copper oxide and graphite in test tubes to produce copper. DEMO. Iron oxide can be heated strongly for 15 minutes in a crucible with graphite. A magnet will detect any iron produced. Pupils could use the copper oxide they made in the previous lesson when they decomposed copper carbonate.	VCR. Pyrex test tubes, copper II oxide, graphite, tongs, bunsens, HP mats, tripod, pipeclay triangle, crucible and lid, iron III oxide, magnet.	Beware of trailing leads from VCR. Tie back long hair and wear goggles when heating tubes. Hold tubes at 45 degrees, aiming away from others. Place hot tubes on HP mats.	WDYK page 91. Assignments 6e. Extras 6e page 96. 96.
Eight	Reactivity at work. Iron and steel are strong but will rust unless protected.	Textbook pages 92 and 93. Worksheet 6f Core/Help. Video 55b A Rusty Tale.	Protecting iron nails using metals of different reactivities. May best be done as a DEMO.	Nails, test tubes in rack. Strips of magnesium, copper, aluminium, lead. VCR.	Wash hands after handling lead. Beware of trailing leads from VCR	WDYK page 93. Assignments 6f. Extras 6f page 97. Review 6f page 99. Test yourself unit 6.
Nine	End of unit test	End test unit 6.	Record results from previous lessons experiment.			

NEAB Modular Science (Single Award)
Scheme of Work
Topic 14. Environment, Inheritance and Selection.

Foundation Level

This topic has been written for Foundation level students. Some higher level work has been included where it is felt it aids understanding.

This scheme has been planned around 27 lessons (approximately nine weeks' teaching). This may need to be amended in light of term lengths and other factors that may reduce or extend the time available.

Available Resources:
Science Foundations Biology text book.
Science Foundations Biology Supplementary Materials (Copy attached).
Chemistry Counts by Graham Hill

Additional worksheets (Copy attached)

■ Environment 6	■ Inheritance 6
■ Environment 7	■ Inheritance 7
■ Inheritance 1	■ Inheritance 8
■ Inheritance 2	■ Inheritance 9
■ Inheritance 3	
■ Inheritance 4	
■ Inheritance 5	

Video programmes:

■ 35e Breathing	■ 16b Fossils
■ 58a Greenhouse Effect	■ 58g Evolution
■ 56h Gene Genie	■ 21a Darwin and Evolution
■ 56g Horses for Courses	■ 24e Being Born

Note: Lessons 1–4 of a 9 lesson scheme are shown

GGS Science Dept.

	Scheme of Work			NEAB Modular	
Topic: Environment, Inheritance and Selection (Topic 14)	Year: Eleven (Set 6)		Compiled by: C. Smith ©		
Lesson	**Aims (syllabus details)**	**Resources**	**Possible practical activities**	**Equipment**	**Other (risk assessment, etc.)**	**Homework/ additional classwork**
One and Two	14.1 Survival and habitat	Textbook pages 92, 93, 94 and 95	Set up choice chambers with light/dark chambers and place maggots or woodlice in there. Or carry out a survey of the school grounds to search for woodlice, recording locations and numbers, then discussing the environmental factors that woodlice seem to favour. The Dataloggers could be set up to record light and temperature changes over a 24 hour period.	Choice chambers, black paper, maggots. LogIT boxes with temperature and light probes.	Students should wash hands after handling maggots or carrying out survey around grounds.	WYNTR pages 93 and 95.
Three	14.1 Survival and adaptation	Textbook pages 96, 97, 98 and 99.	Using an accurate balance the rate of water loss from different types of leaves could be determined.	Balance, selection of fresh leaves.		WYNTR page 97 and 99.

Lesson	Aims (syllabus details)	Resources	Possible practical activities	Equipment	Other (risk assessment, etc.)	Homework/ additional classwork
Four	14.1 Adapting to conditions	Textbook pages 100, 101, 102 and 103.	Use quadrats to sample the school field and record populations of daisies, dandelions, etc. The enclosed garden in main block has an interesting distribution of dandelions which may be affected by the shade given by buildings.	Quadrats, tape measures.	Wash hands after working on field.	WYNTR pages 101 and 103.
Five	14.1 Competition.	Textbook pages 104, 105, 106, 107, 108, 109, 110 and 111.	Mainly a theory lesson working from the books.			WYNTR pages 105, 107, 109 and 111.
Six	14.2 Human effects on the environment (Water).	Textbook pages 128 and 129. Chemistry Counts pages 34 and 35.	Discussion about water pollution. Sewage discharge into the sea is a topic that often provokes comment from the class.			WYNTR page 129.

Lesson	Aims (syllabus details)	Resources	Possible practical activities	Equipment	Other (risk assessment, etc.)	Homework/ additional classwork
Seven	14.2 Human effects on the environment (Air).	Textbook pages 130 and 131. Chemistry Counts pages 30 and 31. Video 58a Greenhouse Effect.	Set up about a week before the lesson two large beakers. In both place some wet cotton wool and cress seedlings. In one place a small beaker of sodium metabisulphite solution, in the other place a beaker of tap water. Cover both with cling film. The metabisulphite will give off sulphur dioxide which replicates acid rain. The seeds in the acid beaker will not grow. When uncovering the beakers use damp UI paper to show the acidic environment.	Large glass beakers, cotton wool, cress seeds, small beakers, cling film, sodium metabisulphite solid. VCR.	Although the quantity of sulphur dioxide produced is very small, be aware that it may cause a reaction in some asthmatic pupils if sniffed directly. Beware of trailing leads from VCR.	WYNTR page 131.
Eight	14.2 Human effects on the landscape.	Textbook pages 132 and 133. Worksheet Environment 6.	Use the worksheet to emphasize what governments could do to reduce the environmental damage caused by human activity.			WYNTR page 133.

Lesson	Aims (syllabus details)	Resources	Possible practical activities	Equipment	Other (risk assessment, etc.)	Homework/ additional classwork
Nine	14.2 Human population explosion.	Textbook pages 134 and 135. Worksheet Environment 7.	Cut and stick activity on worksheet.	Scissors, glue and spreaders.		WYNTR page 135.
Ten	14.3 Shared characteristics.	Textbook pages 136 and 137. Video 47c Genetics.	Get the pupils to make a list of characteristics they think they have inherited from their parents or that may run in their families.	VCR.	Beware of trailing leads from VCR.	WYNTR page 137.
Eleven	14.3 Differences in species.	Textbook pages 138 and 139. Worksheet Inheritance 1.	Use the worksheet to carry out a height survey. Other factors such as eye colour, shoe size, etc., may also be recorded and plotted.	Meter rules attached to a door frame.		WYNTR page 139.
Twelve	14.3 Chromosomes.	Textbook pages 140 and 141. Worksheets Inheritance 2 and 3. Video 56h Gene Genie.	Pupils can cut up the worksheets and match pairs of chromosomes.	Scissors, glue, spreaders. VCR.	Beware of trailing leads from VCR.	WYNTR page 141.

Proposed Teaching Roster for Year Seven
September 2001

The department has decided to purchase the 'Exploring Science' scheme published by Longman. This scheme as it stands does not meet exactly the QCA scheme but is reasonably close. Longman have agreed to replace any Year Seven resources that we purchase with the new, revised (and fully matching) resources when they come on stream in February 2002. Until then we shall have to utilize the matching portions of the scheme and deliver the rest when the new resources arrive. To facilitate this I have created a draft roster in which the first two terms (approximately) are taken from the current scheme and the third term is used to 'mop up' the other topics. Planning for two terms will allow us a little leeway should the new schemes be delayed, and some time for checking them before use.

Autumn Term

QCA unit No.	Exploring Science unit No.	Unit Title QCA/Exploring Science	Notes
7L	P2	The Solar System and Beyond/**The Earth and beyond.**	Moving on Up topic. Additional resources available from BASS but may only be suitable for higher abilities.
7A	B2	Cells/**Cells and their functions.**	Good match. Can be taught as written.
7D	B1	Variation and Classification/**Classification and use of keys.**	Will require one or two additional lessons on variation and adaptation to supplement the Exploring Science resources.
7G	C3	Particle Model. Solids, Liquids and Gases/**Particle Theory.**	Changes of state not required in this unit. KS2 covers this topic thoroughly and so delivery may be easier than anticipated.

Section 2 - Case Studies

Spring Term

QCA unit No.	Exploring Science unit No.	Unit Title QCA/Exploring Science	Notes
7H	C1	Solutions/**Solutions and Indicators.**	Do not teach the Acids and Alkalis part of the C1 topic as this is covered later in the year.
7K	P1	Forces/**Forces.**	Good match. Can be taught as written.
7B	B4	Reproduction/**Human Life Cycles.**	Good match. Can be taught as written.
7I	P4	Energy Resources/**Energy Resources.**	Good match. Can be taught as written.

Hopefully the new, improved resources should be available and ready to use. The best match for three of these topics is currently found in Year Eight units from Exploring Science.

I have given them their names as quoted in the textbook but these may change, as may the unit numbers in the reprinted scheme. The topics as presented in the current Year Eight book are a good match to the QCA documents.

QCA unit No.	Exploring Science unit No.	Unit Title QCA/Exploring Science	Notes
7C	B3	Environment and Feeding relationships/**Habitats.**	
7J	P3	Electrical Circuits/**Electric Circuits.**	
7F	C2 or 4	Simple Chemical Reactions/**Reactions.**	
7E	C2 or 4	Acids and Alkalis/**No corresponding topic yet.**	Revision of Exploring Science should result in acids and alkalis being taken from unit C1 and being expanded into a new unit.

Teaching Roster

Autumn Term 2001

Set	Staff	Moving up		Cycle 1	
7M	CS	7L / **P2**	7A / **B2**	7D / **C3**	7G / **P1**
7E	CxS	7L / **P2**	7G / **C3**	7A / **B2**	7D / **P4**
7R	PC	7L / **P2**	7D / **B2**	7G / **C3**	7A / **B1**
7/4	PC	7L / **P2**	7D / **B2**	7G / **C3**	7A / **B1**
7/5	RC	7L / **P2**	7G / **C3**	7A / **B2**	7D / **P4**
7/6	AE	7L / **P2**	7A / **B2**	7D / **C3**	7G / **B4**
7S	CxS/PC	7L / **P2**	7D / **B2**	7G / **C3**	7A / **B1**

Note: All groups begin with the Space topic. Additional resources have been supplied by BASS as part of the Moving on Up/Literacy project. These need to be looked at by individual teachers to assess their suitability for each group. Teachers of set 7S may plan their own route through the year.

Spring Term 2002

Set	Staff	Cycle 2			
7M	CS	7H / **C1**	7K / **B1**	7B / **P4**	7I / **B4**
7E	CxS	7I / **B1**	7H / **C1**	7K / **P1**	7B / **B4**
7R	PC	7B / **P4**	7I / **B4**	7H / **C1**	7K / **P1**
7/4	PC	7B / **P4**	7I / **B4**	7H / **C1**	7K / **P1**
7/5	RC	7K / **C1**	7B / **B4**	7I / **P1**	7H / **B1**
7/6	AE	7H / **C1**	7K / **P1**	7B / **B4**	7I / **P4**
7S	CxS/PC	7B / **B4**	7I / **P4**	7H / **C1**	7K / **P1**

Hopefully the new improved resources should arrive during this term. Unit numbers may alter. New resources can be phased in at any convenient point.

Summer Term 2002

Set	Staff	Cycle 3			
7M	CS	7C / B3	7F / **C2**	7J / **P3**	7E / **C4**
7E	CxS	7F / **C2**	7C / **B3**	7E / **C4**	7J / **P3**
7R	PC	7C / **B3**	7F / **C2**	7J / **P3**	7E / **C4**
7/4	PC	7C / **B3**	7F / **C2**	7J / **P3**	7E / **C4**
7/5	RC	7F / **C2**	7C / **B3**	7E / **C4**	7J / **P3**
7/6	AE	7F / **C2**	7C / **B3**	7E / **C4**	7J / **P3**
7S	CxS/PC	7C / **B3**	7F / **C2**	7J / **P3**	7E / **C4**

Units are paired in the cycle to enable a common exam on 10 units to be set.

There are many worksheets for each topic. It is proposed to copy and file quantities of those sheets that are likely to be used. Teachers will be supplied with a full set of sheets and can copy those others that they may wish to use and file these when finished.

Section 3

Teachers' Toolkit

14 Sample documents

Job hunting

Job application form

The following generic job application form is from the *Times Educational Supplement jobs* website, which you can find at www.jobs.tes.co.uk. It shows the type of form that an LEA will send when you apply for a teaching post, and the information that you will need to have to hand.

Post applied for	
School/College/Service	
Closing date for applications	

1. PERSONAL DETAILS (please use block capitals)

Surname	Preferred title
First name(s)	Date of birth
Address	NI Number
	DfEE Number
	Date of qualification
Postcode	Country of qualification
Telephone (home)	E-mail
Telephone (work)	Fax

2. EDUCATION AND ACADEMIC QUALIFICATIONS

School/College/University	From	To	Subject, Qualifications, Grades, Honours
Secondary (post-16)			
Higher Education			
Further postgraduate qualifications (including PGCE)			

3. PRESENT APPOINTMENT (or most recent)

Post held		
School/College address		
Number on Roll		Age range
Date appointed		
LEA/Employer		
Responsibility Points (if applicable)		
Present or final salary/CPS		
Notice required		
Consent to contact place of employment		

4. PREVIOUS TEACHING APPOINTMENTS (please start with most recent)

Title of post and name of school/college/other employer	Status F/T or P/T	Type of school/college and age range	NOR	Period of Service From To

5. PROFESSIONAL DEVELOPMENT (please give details of courses relevant to this application and indicate any awards earned)

Course title	Provider	Duration	Dates	Awards (if any)

6. OTHER RELEVANT WORK EXPERIENCE (please start with most recent)

Nature of occupation	Employer	Period of service From To

7. INTERESTS (both professional and leisure)

8. IF THIS APPLICATION IS FOR A SCHOOL OF A PARTICULAR RELIGIOUS AFFILIATION PLEASE INDICATE BELOW IF YOU ARE OF THAT AFFILIATION

9. LETTER OF APPLICATION

> In support of your application, you are recommended to attach a statement giving your reasons for applying for this post. Include any information which you consider relevant to this application, addressing the key areas in the person specification.

10(a) DECLARATION BY APPLICANT

> As this post is classified as having substantial access to children, appointment will be subject to a police check of previous criminal convictions. You are required, before appointment, to disclose any conviction, caution or binding over, including 'spent convictions' under the Rehabilitation of Offenders Act 1974 (Exemptions) Order 1975.
>
> Disclosure will only be required following interview if it is considered that you are the most suitable candidate for the post.

10(b)

> *I appreciate that I must declare any close relationship with a member of the school's Governing Body, or with a member or senior official of the local education authority which has responsibility for the school. I understand that failure to disclose such a relationship may result in my disqualification.*

10(c)

> I declare that the information I have given on this form is correct and I understand that failure to complete the form fully and accurately could result in an incorrect assessment of salary, and/or exclusion from shortlisting, or may, in the event of employment, result in disciplinary action or dismissal.
>
> Signature: Date:

11. REFERENCES

N.B. References will only be sought for shortlisted candidates.

May we approach your referees without further reference to you? YES/NO

The first reference should be your present or most recent employer

(i)		(ii)	
Name:		Name:	
Position:		Position:	
Address		Address:	
Telephone No:		Telephone No:	
In what capacity do you know the above?		In what capacity do you know the above?	
If you were known to either of your referees by another name, please give details:			

12. EQUAL OPPORTUNITIES MONITORING

We aim to create the conditions in which all applicants and employees are treated solely on the basis of their merits, abilities and potential regardless of gender, colour, ethnic or national origin, age, socio-economic background, disability, religion, family circumstance, sexual orientation or other irrelevant distinction.

In order to carry out our equal opportunities policy, we must have some means of monitoring our recruitment and selection. Only by such measures will we be able to recognize potential sources of discrimination and take remedial action. The monitoring form will be separated from the application form and securely stored in the strictest confidence. It will be used for statistical monitoring only.

Please tick box as appropriate					
Sex:	Female	☐		Male	☐
Marital status:	Married	☐		Single	☐
Age:	Below 26	☐		26–35	☐
36–45 ☐	46–55	☐		56–65	☐
How would you describe your ethnic origin?					
Black:	Caribbean ☐	African ☐		Other	☐
White:	European ☐	Other ☐			
Asian:	Indian ☐	Pakistani ☐		Bangladeshi	☐
Chinese: ☐					
Other: ☐	Please specify:				
Do you have any disability as described within the terms of the Disability Discrimination Act 1995?	Yes ☐		No	☐	

Letter of application

Below you will find two examples of letters of application. The first is for a student applying for a first teaching post, the second is for an experienced teacher applying for promotion. For each of these examples I have included a fictitious job that is being applied for, to show you how the sample letter meets the job description.

Letter of application – student teacher

Stanley Hill Primary School
Key Stage Two Teacher

Stanley Hill is an inner city school with a multicultural population. We are looking for a dedicated, enthusiastic teacher to teach Year Five. The successful applicant will be somebody who enjoys a challenge. Applications are welcomed from experienced teachers and NQTs. We are hoping to appoint someone with a special interest in ICT.

Letter of Application

Post: Stanley Hill Primary School, Key Stage Two Teacher
Name: Sally Jones

I would describe myself as an enthusiastic, dedicated and caring teacher. I enjoy hard work and I am keen to build on my initial teacher training in an environment that offers a challenge. I feel that these qualities, and the experiences described below, mean I am well suited to the post of Key Stage Two teacher at Stanley Hill School.

My first teaching practice at Aldridge Primary School offered a supportive environment in which to start my training. I worked with a Year Four class, alongside the class teacher. I developed my lesson planning and classroom management skills. In this practice I focused particularly on differentiating for students with different learning needs. I learnt a great deal about catering for a mixed ability class from my supervisory teacher. I also created a series of differentiated worksheets for developing literacy skills, in line with the National Literacy Strategy.

In my second teaching practice at Keygate Primary School, I taught a Year Two class. I very much enjoyed working with this age group. At Keygate, my supervisory teacher was the ICT subject coordinator, and I had the opportunity to learn about planning for ICT teaching across the

265

curriculum. In addition to teaching the whole class, I also worked with individuals and small groups of children on developing their reading and literacy skills.

My third teaching practice was at Findlay Primary and Junior School, where I had full responsibility for a Year One class. At Findlay School I consolidated my training and developed my classroom and behaviour management skills further. There were a number of children with emotional and behavioural difficulties in this class, and I learnt to use a range of teaching and learning strategies to help them access the curriculum.

My previous experience working in an office environment has allowed me to make effective use of computers in my teaching. During my English degree, and whilst training as a teacher, I have taken a particular interest in ICT. I helped to write and produce a new website for the Education Department at the University. For one of my coursework units I developed a database to analyse children's progress in numeracy lessons.

I feel that the experiences outlined above mean that I am well suited to the role of Key Stage Two Teacher at Stanley Hill Primary School. I would welcome the opportunity to demonstrate my aptitude for the post in an interview.

Letter of application – experienced teacher

> ### *Barr Wood Secondary School*
> *Head of Faculty: Performing Arts*
>
> Barr Wood is an over subscribed school with beacon status.
> We are looking for a manager with organizational skills, flair
> and leadership ability to develop the faculty further.
> Barr Wood has a long history of successful school productions,
> and we are looking for a candidate who could further this tradition.

Letter of Application

Post: Head of Faculty: Performing Arts
Name: Ben Sampson

After two years in my present post as second in faculty, I believe I have
the experience needed to make the move into a head of faculty role. I
very much enjoy my current position: I take full responsibility for planning
the delivery of Drama at Key Stages Three and Four, and managing the
work of two other Drama teachers. I am also in charge of producing and
directing the annual school production. I would describe myself as an
enthusiastic, imaginative, hard-working and committed teacher. As
second in faculty I have developed my leadership abilities and have also
made some innovative changes to the curriculum we deliver. I am also an
efficient and well-organized administrator.

My first teaching post at Camley School offered an exciting environment
in which to consolidate and build on my training. I taught in both the
Drama and Music departments, in all years from 7 to 13. I developed the
ability to cater for students with a wide range of learning needs. I also
learnt a great deal about balanced lesson planning from my Head of
Department as we worked together to develop the departmental
schemes of work. I very much enjoyed taking my first GCSE Drama group
through to their examination. The students achieved excellent results and
it gave me great pleasure to see *all* my students learn through the
Performing Arts. While at Camley I was involved with three school
productions. In my NQT year I worked as assistant director on 'West Side
Story'. In the two subsequent years I took full responsibility for directing
'Little Shop of Horrors' and 'Romeo and Juliet'.

In my current teaching post, my work as second in faculty has given me
the opportunity to learn about the management of staff, as well as about

267

developing the Performing Arts curriculum. I teach Drama and Music in Key Stage Three, and Expressive Arts at GCSE and 'A' Level. I also work as an induction tutor for NQTs. I have developed a partnership with the local theatre, Bromwich Arts Centre, creating a 'links' programme between the students at our school and professional actors and singers. I have also maintained the school's tradition of two annual drama productions: one a play, the other a musical. I have worked closely with teachers from the Art, Music and Dance departments at the school to develop strong cross-curricular input.

I do hope that you feel, as I do, that I have the requisite experience and ability for the post of Head of Performing Arts Faculty at Barr Wood School. I would very much welcome the chance to discuss my suitability for the position at interview.

Teaching

Lesson plans

There really is no right or wrong way of going about planning: only you can know what actually works for you. The sample lesson plans below give two possible formats for a teacher to use when planning his or her lessons: one brief, the other detailed. For each example I give a blank format, then show you a sample of how a lesson plan might be written within this format. You can find lots more thoughts and ideas about lesson planning in Chapters 7, 12 and 13.

A teacher with previous experience of working with the topics shown below would probably find sufficient detail to run the lesson in the brief plans. These are the type of plans that you might note down quickly in the teacher's planner (see page 142). The more detailed versions give the less confident teacher, or the student teacher, a great deal of additional information to use in preparing, presenting and assessing how well the lesson worked. These plans would be more appropriate for observed lessons or evaluated lessons, or for an OFSTED inspection.

Brief lesson plan (blank)

Topic/Class	
Objectives	
Activities	1.
	2.
	3.
	4.

Brief lesson plan (sample)

Topic/Class	'Twelfth Night' – Theme of love – Year Nine SATs
Objectives	Learning about themes Focus on specific theme (exam prep.) Develop/assess speaking and listening skills
Activities	1. Brainstorm types of love – discussion work in pairs. (Passion, friendship, male/female, family, self, forbidden.)
	2. Whole class share ideas on board.
	3. Pairs – choose one type of love, find examples and quotes from play. Make notes in exercise books.
	4. Oral presentations to class, others take notes. (Homework: write up notes into full paragraphs as though for essay.)

Detailed lesson plan

Subject	Lesson Topic								
Class	Date								
Objectives	NLS/NNS								
SEN	Differentiation								
Task	Timing/Equipment								
Assessment	Homework/ Extension task								

Detailed lesson plan (sample)

		Lesson Topic	Sinking and Floating
Subject	Science		
Class	Year One, mixed ability	Date	12 October 2002
Objectives	– Learning what sinks/floats and why – Predicting outcome of experiment – Discussing reasoning behind prediction – Testing hypothesis – Developing class discussion skills	NLS/NNS	Key terms – sink/float
SEN	Yellow Group – Jamie, Sam and Candice: weak literacy skills	Differentiation	Differentiated worksheet Tracing activity for Yellow Group
Task		Timing/Resources	
One	Discuss words 'sink' and 'float' – what do they mean? Write on board.	5 mins	Board, marker.
Two	Show range of materials – predict whether they will float or sink and discuss why.	10 mins	Materials: wood, plastic, metal, polystyrene, stone, paper, sponge.
Three	Volunteers to come to tank and try each material. Discuss prediction and results. Were we right? If wrong, why?	15 mins.	Materials, tank filled with water.
Four	Complete differentiated worksheet about experiment. Work individually/in pairs.	20 mins	Differentiated worksheets.
Assessment	Mark worksheet – check understanding of task/activities.	Homework/ Extension task	Find 3 more materials to try (from classroom or at home).

Schemes of work

The medium-term plan below provides a very useful outline for a primary school scheme of work. Many thanks to Bentinck Primary School, Nottingham, for sharing this document. (Please note that the format is copyrighted to the school.) In the secondary school, the content of medium-term plans will depend a great deal on the subject being taught.

Unit title: **Class:**   **Term:**   **Teacher:**

	Learning Objectives	Introduction	Main Activity Differentiation – EMTAG – Assessment Main Activity	Plenary	Resources	Vocabulary
Lesson 1						
Lesson 2						
Lesson 3						
Lesson 4						
Lesson 5						
Lesson 6						

© Bentinck Primary & Nursery School

Marked work

Again, there is no one right or definitive way of marking work. So much will depend on the individual child, class, subject and teacher. The examples below show you how different pieces of writing could be marked. You can find more information about marking, and an explanation of the different marking styles in the section on marking in Chapter 8.

'Close' marking

Jamie whent to the park with his freind Ben they play on the slide and they play in the sand. Ben fell of the slide and hurt his nee Jamie whent to get help. It was geting dark and Jamie was frightend.

Jamie whent to the park with his frieeind Ben. Tthey played on the slide and they played in the sand. Ben fell off the slide and hurt his knee. Jamie whent to get help. It was getting dark and Jamie was frightened.

Well done, you have tried very hard to improve your punctuation. Now take care to stick to the same tense throughout and check your spelling in the dictionary.

Marking for specific errors

Note: In this example the teacher has set the marking focus as layout and punctuation.

What do plants need to grow

in our expriment we looked at what plants need to grow properley we found that they need water and light we did our expriment by puting some seeds on a peace of bloting paper then we gave one lot of seeds no water or light, the next lot just water and the last lot water and light.

What do plants need to grow?

I~~in~~ our expriment we looked at what plants need to grow properley. Ww~~e~~ found that they need water and light.

~~W~~Ww~~e~~ did our expriment by:

1. P~~p~~uting some seeds on a peace of bloting paper.

2. Giving ~~then we gave~~ one lot of seeds no water or light.

3. Giving~~,~~ the next lot just water.

4. Giving _ ~~and~~ the last lot water and light.

You include all the right information, but remember to take care with the way you lay out your work, as we discussed. Experiments should be written as a series of points (see my corrections above).

Teacher's mark book

The following sample mark book page shows how a teacher might use his or her mark book to record a range of information about the students in a class. In the sample shown, the teacher records a number of different pieces of data about the children.

- *Column 1:* Surname.
- *Column 2:* First name.
- *Column 3:* Students who were present '/' or absent 'O' on 9.9.02.
- *Column 4:* A list of textbooks issued, which gives the number noted in each book. In this way, the teacher has a record of which child was given which book, for when they are collected back in. If a book is vandalized, or missing, the teacher can pinpoint which child is responsible.
- *Column 5:* Register of present/absent on 10.9.02.
- *Column 6:* Effort and attainment grades for the homework set on that date. See the Teachers' notes for details of what these effort and attainment grades mean.
  (*Note*: Because the teacher has placed the homework column beside the present/absent column, she knows which students were absent on that day, and consequently who would not have done the homework.)
- *Column 7:* Register of present/absent on 12.9.02.
- *Column 8:* Register of present/absent on 16.9.02.
- *Column 9:* Effort and attainment grades for the homework set on that date.

For more ideas and information about using the mark book, see 'Recording and reporting' in Chapter 9.

ST PATRICKS 2002
MARK BOOK FOR CLASS E10 (Sample page)

SURNAME	FIRST NAME	Register 9.9.02	Texts issued No. in book	Register 10.9.02	HOMEWORK 1 Effort/Attainment	Register 12.9.02	Register 16.9.02	HOMEWORK 2 Effort/Attainment
Baggio	Andrea	/	N1	/	B/5	/	/	B/4
Bayer	Frans	/	N2	O	O	/	/	C/3
Benson	Sally	/	N3	/	C/3	/	/	B/3
Davies	Jennifer	/	N4	/	A/2	/	/	A/2
Du Morier	Nicole	/	N5	/	D/3	O	/	C/3
Gomez	Maria	/	N6	O	O	/	/	A/3
Jones	Owen	/	N7	/	B/4	/	/	B/3
Mckay	Angus	/	N8	/	A/1	/	O	O
Singh	Amjan	/	N9	/	A/2	/	/	A/1
Smith	Bob	/	N10	/	A/3	/	O	O

Teachers' notes

Effort grades:
A – Excellent
B – Good
C – Average
D – Below average
E – Poor

Attainment grades:
1 – High
2 – Above average
3 – Average for class
4 – Below average
5 – Low

15 Terminology

From the minute that you take the first step towards becoming a teacher, you'll be confronted by the jargon, abbreviations and acronyms that seem to be an inevitable part of the job. Here's a dictionary to help you decipher the most commonly used teaching terms.

ADHD – Attention Deficit Hyperactivity Disorder
BA – Bachelor of Arts
BEd – Bachelor of Education
BSc – Bachelor of Science
BT – Beginning Teacher
CACHE – Council for Awards in Children's Care and Education
CEP – Career Entry Profile
DfES – Department for Education and Skills
EBD – Emotional/Behavioural Difficulty
EWO – Educational Welfare Officer
GCSE – General Certificate of Secondary Education
GNVQ – General National Vocational Qualification
GRTP – Graduate and Registered Teacher Programmes
GTC – General Teaching Council
GTCE – General Teaching Council for England
GTCS – General Teaching Council for Scotland
GTP – Graduate Teacher Programme
GTTR – Graduate Teacher Training Registry
HMCI – Her Majesty's Chief Inspector of Schools
HMI – Her Majesty's Inspector of Schools
HOD – Head of Department
ICT – Information and Communications Technology
IEP – Individual Education Plan
ITT – Initial Teacher Training
KS – Key Stage
LEA – Local Education Authority
MFL – Modern Foreign Languages
NLS – National Literacy Strategy
NNS – National Numeracy Strategy
NQT – Newly Qualified Teacher
NVQ – National Vocational Qualification
OFSTED – Office for Standards in Education
PGCE – Post Graduate Certificate in Education
PSHE – Personal, Social and Health Education

QTS – Qualified Teacher Status
RSM – Recruitment Strategy Manager
RTP – Registered Teacher Programme
SAT – Statutory Assessment Tasks
SCITT – School Centred Initial Teacher Training
SEN – Special Educational Needs
SENCO – Special Educational Needs Coordinator
SLT – Senior Leadership Team
SMT – Senior Management Team
SpLD – Specific Learning Difficulty
STRB – School Teachers' Review Body
TES – The Times Educational Supplement
TP – Teaching Practice
TTA – Teacher Training Agency
UCAS – Universities and Colleges Admissions Service

16 Checklists

The '10 tip' checklists in this chapter give you practical, realistic and honest ideas about dealing with some of the trickier aspects of the job. The checklists cover areas such as 'your first year', 'getting on with colleagues' and 'dealing with stress'. They are designed to be brief, hopefully amusing, forays into the world of teaching. Turn to them for some advice when you need it, for inspiration when things are going wrong, or for support when your children simply won't do as they're told!

10 tips for surviving your first year in teaching

1. If you can, find yourself a job at a decent school, where NQTs are well supported and helped to develop. There are some schools out there (thankfully rare), which view NQTs as a 'cheap option'. Ask about support for NQTs at your interview, and make sure your school lives up to its obligations (after all, they're getting extra money to support you!).
2. Don't make an enemy of your induction tutor or mentor. No matter whether you like them or not, they are the one who will be responsible for helping you pass or fail that vital first year in teaching.
3. Know what your rights and responsibilities are as an NQT, particularly as concerns your induction. Read the induction guidelines, or look closely at Chapter 5 of this book.
4. Don't take on too much. No matter how tempting it is to direct the school play, run a football team and sit on three or four different working parties, you are far better off dedicating yourself to becoming the best teacher you can be, and to passing your induction year.
5. Ask for help when you need it. Teachers are, on the whole, superb at supporting each other. We've all been there, through the ups and downs of our own first year in teaching. Turn to your colleagues for advice and support – don't keep your problems to yourself.
6. Take a break when you need it, and don't allow yourself to be consumed by guilt when you do so. For instance, a few sessions in the computer room, or a couple of lessons watching a video, can be educational for the students and restful for you. Taking a break also means making a real effort to get to the staffroom during break and lunchtime.
7. If you're too sick to work properly, don't come into school and spread your germs around. Many people find that they pick up every bug going in their first year of teaching. This is probably due to a combination of tiredness and stress, plus the fact that schools are virile places for germs to breed. Don't feel guilty about taking time off when you're ill!

8. Be careful where you sit in the staffroom. Teachers are notoriously territorial, and you don't want to end up sitting in the chair that has been Mr Smith's for the last 10 years. The same applies to mugs – bring in one or two of your own and never, ever leave someone else's mug unwashed.

9. Strike a balance between your enthusiasm and a realistic workload. Have at least one night a week when you don't take any marking home. Try to take one full day off from working at the weekend.

10. And finally, the 'old chestnut'. Start out as strict as you can – you can always relax with your children later on, but you can never get them back once you've lost them (at least until next year, that is). Some people advise that you don't smile until after the Christmas holidays. I'll leave it up to you as to whether you deem quite such a dour approach necessary!

10 tips for better behaviour

1. Never, ever talk to a class until every child is sitting in silence, focused on you and ready to listen. It's nerve racking at first, but once you've set and achieved this expectation, your life will be 100 per cent easier.

2. Set the boundaries for your children right from the start. Let them know what you expect from them, and what will happen if they don't comply. Your school will probably have a set of official boundaries (i.e. the school rules), but there will also be unofficial boundaries – expectations that you as a teacher have of how your students will behave. If it would be helpful, have a chat to an experienced teacher about some suitable boundaries before you meet your students for the first time.

3. Keep your voice calm and quiet as far as is humanly possible, and try to avoid shouting at all costs. Shouting demonstrates a loss of control to your students, it has a tendency to escalate problems, and can sometimes lead to serious confrontations. Shouting can also be very damaging for your voice.

4. Perfect the deadly stare and other forms of non-verbal communication. These can be wonderfully effective, and are far less stressful and tiring than using your voice to communicate all the time. When you become very skilled at non-verbal communication, you may find that a raised eyebrow is enough to silence a whole class!

5. Find out what sanctions the children want to avoid and use these when necessary. However, don't forget that rewards are usually far more effective than punishments. A positive atmosphere, in which you focus on those children who are behaving, is much more beneficial than a negative focus on constant punishment.

6. Look for what's going right, rather than what's going wrong. For instance, praise a child who's working well, rather than punishing one who's being silly. Along the same lines, focus on what you're doing right in the classroom, rather than beating yourself up about what isn't working yet.

7. Talk to your children as you would to any adult. Try not to use phrases like

'don't be so stupid' or 'shut up'. (Although do accept that you are human and that these things may slip out occasionally.)

8. When a lesson or activity isn't working, and the students are mucking around, put yourself in your children's shoes and think about how they might be feeling. Sometimes school can be boring, no matter how good the teacher is.

9. Ask your colleagues (particularly the SEN staff) for help when dealing with very difficult individuals. They may well have some excellent tips and advice that could save you a lot of heartache.

10. Don't bottle up your feelings. Find a sympathetic shoulder to cry on or a friend to rant at, preferably in the privacy of the staffroom. There's nothing shameful about getting upset or irritated when a child has been abusive towards you, but try not to let your students see you becoming emotional.

10 tips for dealing with marking

1. No matter how tempting it is to have your class sitting in silence for an hour doing a test, don't set too many of them – they take ages to mark!

2. Get your students to help out with marking each other's work whenever possible. They love 'playing teacher', and it can be very educational for them to see the standard that others in the class are achieving.

3. Target your marking – mark for a specific skill, such as good spelling or imaginative ideas, rather than trying to close mark all the time.

4. Don't make promises you can't keep. There's nothing worse than agreeing to mark a set of books or a piece of work, then having to stay up until midnight to finish (or worse still, having to explain to your class that you just couldn't do it in time).

5. Marking expands to fill the time you allow for it. Don't give up every evening of the week to marking – you're entitled to a life outside of school.

6. Do try to avoid spilling coffee on that beautiful set of projects that Year Five have spent weeks completing.

7. Set some pieces of homework that don't involve any marking. For instance, researching a topic, memorizing a passage, learning times tables, and so on.

8. Try to mark exercise books regularly, rather than letting the work build up. Don't forget that parents and OFSTED inspectors will be looking through them and making judgements about you as a teacher.

9. Keep a record of the marks you give – exercise books are easily lost, and this excuse is very convenient for a student with poor grades.

10. Prioritize your marking load – GCSE coursework wins over Year Seven exercise books every time.

10 tips for getting on with your colleagues

1. Gossip is rife in some schools. Try not to gossip about other teachers, but if you do feel the urge, make sure that the person you're talking to will keep their mouth shut afterwards. Ensure, too, that you're not gossiping about somebody to their best friend.
2. If you borrow somebody else's equipment, lesson plans, or room, make sure you return them in their original condition. Do remember to say 'thank you' afterwards, and to offer your own services in return. That way, you can build up a network of support and help.
3. Offer your own resources to others (but keep a copy or a record and make sure that you get them back eventually).
4. Don't photocopy large quantities of worksheets either before school or during break time. The large queue of people forming behind you will not be happy. If someone else is waiting to use the photocopier, offer them the chance to jump in, as long as they only have a few copies to make. This will gain you many brownie points.
5. Never ask pointless questions in meetings. It's a guaranteed way to make the meeting go on longer than necessary, and will not make you popular!
6. Don't plan noisy lessons when:
   - the person next door to you is setting a test
   - you are going to be observed
   - the head is doing his/her rounds
   - you're in the middle of an OFSTED inspection
7. Always, always check the cover list. Not turning up to cover a class or lesson is a fast and efficient way to make enemies and get a bad reputation.
8. Always, always hand in your reports on time. Not doing so causes problems right along the chain of command, especially in a secondary school where a long line of people may have to read and approve them.
9. Don't leave unwashed coffee mugs in the staffroom, then claim that you are conducting an important experiment on growing mould.
10. And finally . . . make a special effort to get on with the non-teaching staff at your school. Remember, the head teacher's secretary is one of the most powerful (and knowledgeable) people in the school! The caretaker, office staff, librarians, catering staff, can all make your life far far easier, or an awful lot harder.

10 tips for getting on with your students

1. Show that you're a human being with a decent sense of humour. Laugh at yourself if you do something stupid – better that they laugh with you than at you.
2. Make at least some of your lessons fun, exciting, imaginative or unusual. This may take a little more time in preparation, but it will help engage

your class or classes and will gain you a reputation for being a good, fun teacher.

3. Be in a good mood for as much of the time as is possible. There's surely nothing worse than having to face a moaning, miserable teacher every day of the week. Always try to focus on the positive, on what the children are doing right, rather than what they are doing wrong.

4. Don't shout unless you really can't help it, or you feel that it's essential. Nobody enjoys being shouted at, and it shows the children that you are a teacher who cannot control his or her emotional responses. Even if a fair few students are misbehaving, remember that the majority are probably not doing anything wrong, and do not deserve to be on the receiving end of your anger.

5. Don't say anything to your students that you would object to them saying to you. For instance, never call a child 'stupid' or 'an idiot'. Remember that many of your difficult students are probably spoken to rudely at home, but that you should be providing them with a different, and better, role model.

6. Despite its stress alleviating results, do try to avoid using sarcasm if at all possible. It really is the lowest form of wit, and many children will take you seriously, rather than understanding what you imagine to be your sparkling sense of humour.

7. Take time to listen to your children as individuals, and show an interest in them as people. Find out what they really enjoy and try to incorporate it occasionally into your lesson planning. Taking time to get involved in extracurricular activities can be very helpful in getting to know your children properly outside the classroom environment.

8. Show your students that you want them to succeed, and that's why you make them work as hard as they can. Have the highest possible expectations of them, and express surprise if they don't achieve what they could.

9. Don't punish a whole class for the sins of one individual, either by giving out a whole class punishment, such as a detention, or by shouting at a whole class of children because one student angers you.

10. Remember what it was like to be young, and bring some of that childlike quality to your teaching, your classroom and your lessons. When your children do muck around try to put yourself in their shoes – school can be boring sometimes, no matter how wonderful the teacher is!

10 tips for dealing with stress

1. Take your breaks, rather than working through the day without a rest. You'll be a much more effective teacher as a result, and it'll give you the chance to blow off steam with other adults.

2. Join in with some extracurricular activities. Although it's a drain on your time, it gives you a chance to have some fun, and to see a different side to

your kids. This applies to school trips too – they can be very enjoyable, and the children will really respect you for showing them another side of you as their teacher. The time spent will usually have a very positive impact in your classroom.

3. Don't take insults or abuse personally. No matter how hard to do, remember that a child who behaves in this way usually needs help. It is most unlikely their anger is directed at you as a person, instead it is a result of their own problems.

4. Try to take part in some form of physical or social activity outside of school to help you unwind. This could be playing in a teachers' football or netball team, or simply heading down the pub with your friends on a Friday evening.

5. Share your worries with other teachers – they are probably experiencing the same fears and stresses as you, or have done so in the past. There's a lot of truth behind the old cliché – a problem shared is a problem halved.

6. Try to avoid talking about work all the time – it's vital that you learn to switch off in the evenings. Remember that your husband/wife/partner/ friends/parents may not be all that interested in how little Johnny misbehaved in your lesson that day. Switching off is probably even more vital if you live with another teacher.

7. If your school environment is conducive to it, stay behind after school has finished to do your marking, planning and paperwork. That way, when you leave school for the day you can leave 'work' behind.

8. When a child or class is stressing you out, try to react from your head and not from your heart. This means respond intellectually, rather than emotionally, and never let a bunch of naughty kids wind you up. They're not worth it – focus on the nice kids instead!

9. Keep a sense of perspective, and learn to laugh at yourself when things do go wrong. As Carl Smith says (see 'Voices of experience' in Chapter 1) , 'even in your worst lesson, nobody died'.

10. If you're really at the end of your tether, go and see a doctor. Stress can be a genuine issue that requires medical treatment.

10 tips for successful lessons

1. Set out your aims or objectives at the start of the lesson. Like a group setting off on an expedition, your children need a map of where they are headed, they need to know what the purpose of their journey is, and what to expect while they are travelling.

2. Make at least some of your lessons exciting – bring in an unusual object to use as a starting point, or take a lateral approach to a boring topic. Remember, the more engaged your students are, the better they'll behave and work.

3. Try to give your children the sense that you are energized by and interested

in the tasks you are asking them to complete. The best teachers convey a sense of their love for the particular subject they are teaching.

4. Use short, focused tasks and reward your children for completing each one. Although this takes more energy from you as a teacher, you'll get a much better quality of work and behaviour from your class as a result.

5. Use a balance of different activities, such as writing, reading, talking and group work. This will help your students retain their interest and focus, as well as developing a range of different skills.

6. Ensure that you have a good opening to your lessons. When you invite your class into the room, give a sense of pace and energy about what is going to happen. Get them settled quickly, and ready to start with the appropriate equipment on their tables.

7. Similarly, make sure that the ends of your lessons are well structured. Take time to look back on what has been achieved, and to praise your children if they have worked well. Standing behind chairs is a wonderfully controlled way to finish a lesson or to end the school day. From this position you can hand out praise and reminders about homework, keep behind any troublemakers, and please the caretaker and cleaners by checking for litter.

8. Don't be afraid to make up the occasional lesson on the spot, for instance throwing out that carefully planned lesson in favour of exploring a topical issue that the children raise. Flexibility is the key to good teaching.

9. Try to offer lessons or activities that are going to stretch the most able, as well as offering the least able a chance to succeed. Set extension activities that give your gifted students a chance to shine.

10. Find out what really interests your children, whether it is a particular subject area, such as IT or Art, or the latest craze. Try to incorporate this into at least some of the work that you ask your classes to do, and you'll gain a reputation as a fun and interesting teacher.

10 tips for dealing with paperwork

1. Try to deal with paperwork the minute you receive it. If a form needs filling out, do it on the spot, rather than adding it to the towering pile on your desk.

2. Don't file a resource unless you're sure you'll use it again. The same applies to meaningless bits of paper that you're unlikely to reuse, such as meeting agendas.

3. When you do file a piece of paper, make sure you know where it is so that you can access it again. Work out a reasonably organized filing system early on in the year, for instance dividing resources into different curriculum or topic areas, or by year groups.

4. Remember, there are centralized copies of a lot of paperwork you receive. If there is copy somewhere, bin the one that you've been given.

5. Have a yearly chuck out session. Otherwise you'll end up with that exam syllabus from years ago that you really, honestly don't need anymore.

6. With paperwork that you need to access daily, keep things in one place as far as possible. The teacher's planner is a wonderful way of organizing your school life (see page 142). If these are not provided at your school, ask if you can order one for yourself (and get your school or department to pay for it).

7. Don't leave copies of confidential material, such as SEN reports, lying around where children might be able to find them. As a professional, you have a responsibility for confidentiality regarding your students.

8. Beware of the pile entitled 'to do'. When exactly are you going to 'do' it?

9. Prioritize your admin. If a piece of paperwork comes from the head teacher, deal with it swiftly.

10. Empty your pigeon-hole on a daily, or at least weekly, basis. Otherwise it's sod's law that a crucial bit of paper will get crushed at the back, only to be discovered on the last day of term, when it simply has to be dealt with immediately!

10 tips for writing reports

1. Computerized reports make life much easier, and even if your school doesn't use a computer system, in most cases you will still be able to prepare and print out your reports via a word processing program.

2. If you are typing your reports, and you have a lot of them to write (i.e. in a secondary school), use a bank of comments for poor, average and good students. You can then cut and paste these comments, adding a more individualized sentence to each one.

3. If you are printing out your reports, check them very carefully for errors first. There is nothing worse than printing out 500 reports, all with a spelling mistake in them.

4. Get your reports in on time. The names of the teachers who are always late with reports will be well known in your school. Don't add your name to the list.

5. Take care over the content and presentation of your reports: reports are one of the main types of formal communication with the home. Make sure that you give parents or guardians a good impression of their child's teacher.

6. Be very wary of children with androgynous names. It's incredibly embarrassing to send out a report in which you call a 'he' a 'she'! If there are any children whose names you're uncertain about, confirm their gender in the weeks leading up to report writing.

7. Avoid negative comments in your reports. Although it's important to give a realistic assessment of a child, phrase your comments so that they give positive ideas for improvement. For instance, instead of saying 'Jimmy never listens in class and doesn't follow my instructions', you could say 'Jimmy has

trouble listening in class, and he needs to concentrate fully when he is being given instructions'.

8. Set some targets in your reports, and use these as a part of your daily teaching. For instance, you might set a target for behaviour. When a child arrives at your class each day, you can then refer to this target and discuss the reward the child will earn for achieving it.

9. The parents' evening is a very good time to refer to reports, especially if they have been sent out recently. Talk through the targets you have set with the parents or guardians (and the child if they come too) and ask for support in ensuring these targets are met.

10. If possible, spend some time discussing the reports with the children after they've been handed out. It's important for reports to be an effective tool in improving learning, rather than simply gathering dust in a drawer somewhere.

10 tips for surviving parents' evening

Note: The term 'parents' is used here to cover guardians of any kind. Be aware that some children will attend parents' evening with a foster carer, older brother or sister, and so on.

1. Try to find time to take a break before the parents' evening starts. After a full day at school, you will not be at your best unless you spend some time refreshing yourself. Have something to eat to sustain you through the evening.

2. Do wear your best suit or outfit. You are a professional and should put forward a professional appearance on such public occasions.

3. Remember that the parents are likely to be as scared as you are, if not more so. Do try to make them feel relaxed and comfortable during your discussion. Despite all the damage that has been done to teachers' images over the years, we are still authority figures of a kind.

4. If the child attends with the parents, focus the discussion on making the child aware of his or her strengths and weaknesses. A good question to ask when starting the discussion is 'How do you think you've been getting on this year?'. Involve the child in setting areas for further improvement, and ask the parents to help the child stick to these targets.

5. Keep the discussion brief and focused, rather than feeling the need to waffle on for a long time. This is especially important if you have a large number of parents to see. Keeping people waiting for ages suggests a lack of professionalism. Plus, you really don't want to end up with a huge queue of parents still waiting to see you at the end of the evening, when everyone else is heading home.

6. Make sure that you set some targets for areas where you want the child to improve, as well as discussing their present levels of attainment. You might

link this to a discussion of the child's latest report (see 'tips for writing reports').

7. It can be a good idea to have some work to show the parents, but don't focus your discussion simply on going through the marks that the student has achieved. It's far better to talk from your own impressions and knowledge of how the child is getting on.

8. If you do get the chance to meet with the parents of a child who is poorly behaved (and be aware that these parents may not turn up.), then do ask if you can contact the parents directly if the student continues to behave badly. This can be a wonderful way of motivating a child to improve their behaviour. Parents can be a powerful force in helping you get better work and behaviour from your students.

9. A good way to end your discussion is to ask 'Do you have any questions?'. This gives the parents a chance to raise any concerns or queries, and if they don't have any questions to ask, brings the discussion to a neat conclusion.

10. If you do encounter any parents who become abusive (and this is, thankfully, relatively rare), then direct them to your line manager rather than trying to deal with them yourself. You could also suggest a meeting at another time to sort out their concerns. Above all, refuse to descend to their level, remaining relentlessly calm, polite and professional.

10 tips for getting and dealing with promotion

1. If are you hoping to find a promoted post, show a willingness to do things that are outside of your actual job description. For instance, you might sit on a working party or take on some responsibility for coordinating a curriculum subject. Make sure, though, that you don't show too much willing – you do want paying for the extra work eventually.

2. Look at what Chris Pickering (head teacher) and Geoff Lloyd (deputy head) say in Chapter 6 'Anatomy of a school' about the type of teachers they would look to employ, and to promote.

3. Before you make that application for a promoted post, think carefully about the direction that you want your career in teaching to take. It is very tempting to take a promotion, especially one that means a salary increase, but how far up the ladder do you envisage yourself going?

4. Consider your priorities and what you really enjoy about the job. Be aware that a move into the higher echelons of management will mean that you spend less time in the classroom, with the kids, and more time dealing with bits of paper.

5. Be aware that your relationship with your colleagues will change once you are promoted. You will be in a position where you must tell people what they should do. It can sometimes be difficult for others to adapt to seeing you in a new light.

6. Remember that the higher up you go, the more time you spend on the job.

A head teacher is always a head teacher, whether inside or outside of school, and will probably play a significant role within the local community.

7. Consider your professional development, and look at the type of training and further education you might need. In some schools, you may be given support to do a further qualification, such as an MA.

8. If you are interested in becoming a senior manager or head teacher, contact the National College for School Leadership (see the Directory for details).

9. Sometimes, a teacher looking for promotion will need to move schools in order to progress. Once you have a few years' experience, look carefully at the opportunities available in your present school, and consider whether you need to move on.

10. Not all promotions or career opportunities take place within the school environment. Consider your career from a wide perspective – you may wish to move into LEA inspection services, freelance writing or consultancy work, or other fields within education.

10 tips for surviving OFSTED

1. Try not to spend the weeks before OFSTED arrive getting worked up about what is going to happen. Don't believe all the scare stories that you will hear. You know already if you're an effective teacher, so focus on gaining something positive from the experience.

2. Don't take the whole process too seriously. An inspection can only ever provide a snapshot of a school, and of you as a teacher. Have confidence in your own abilities within the classroom, and try not to allow a negative judgement of your work to get you down. You know the truth!

3. Think carefully about health and safety in your classroom. Look around with fresh eyes and check carefully for any potential hazards. Consider what your children do with their bags and equipment when they come into the classroom, and any safety implications this may have.

4. Get your lesson planning done well in advance, so you don't have lots of last minute stress. If your school has designed a format that will prove acceptable to OFSTED, use this for your plans. However irritating and contrived it is to have to plan in huge amounts of detail, accept that this is all part of playing the game of inspection.

5. Try to strike a balance in the lessons that you plan. Don't play it too safe, and end up boring your children to tears. On the other hand, this is probably not the time to try out that experimental and whacky new approach to learning.

6. Make sure that you consider the needs of all the children in your class. Show that you are aware of which students have SEN, and what their particular learning needs are. Think carefully about inclusion, equal opportunities and differentiation.

7. Don't expect the inspectors to turn up for a whole lesson, because this will

not necessarily happen. Accept that it is sod's law that they will turn up in the really tricky part of your lesson, or when the children have just decided to riot.

8. Have a copy of your lesson plan to hand, and pass it to the inspector when he or she comes into the room. That way, you can demonstrate the overall structure of the lesson.

9. Make sure the students' exercise books are marked.

10. Make sure that you get the feedback to which you are entitled. Ask the inspector to discuss your lesson with you after the observation, and talk to your line manager if you have any concerns or questions.

Section 4

ICT

17 ICT and the teacher

This chapter deals with ways that the teacher might use ICT to make his or her teaching more effective, both in terms of background work such as planning, preparation and assessment, and also in using computers within the classroom. You'll find information here about the advantages of using computers, both for the teacher and for the student. You'll also get some top tips for working with ICT, and learn about some of the potential hazards or downfalls of computer based learning.

Using ICT

There are a whole range of different ways in which teachers can use ICT in their working lives. Here you'll find a list of some potential uses, both for work done outside the classroom, and also with your students during lessons.

ICT for teachers

- Lesson and scheme planning.
- Undertaking research for lessons.
- Accessing a huge range of educational resources on the internet.
- Creating differentiated worksheets.
- Keeping records of student grades.
- Keeping records of textbooks and other resources.
- Writing reports and other communications with the home.
- Communicating with other teachers and schools via email.

ICT with students

- Creating paper based materials, such as books, newspapers and magazines.
- Presenting class work in a smart and adaptable format.
- Calculating data using spreadsheets.
- Storing and accessing information on a database.
- Researching and downloading information via the internet.
- Communicating globally via the internet and email.

The advantages of ICT

Using ICT is now a natural part of the way that we teach, and it is hard to believe that only 20 or so years ago there was little or no use of computers within the classroom. ICT really does bring many advantages to the world of education: some of these are listed below.

For the teacher

- The ability to create, edit, save and change worksheets, lesson plans and other computerized resources.
- The ease with which a single worksheet can be differentiated for children with different learning needs.
- The motivational qualities of resources that are well presented.
- The generally better behaviour and focus that children have when working on computers.
- The ability to keep, change and work with data and records, for instance of assessments.
- The opportunity to calculate scores and percentages with ease, using spreadsheets.
- The time-saving nature of writing reports on the computer, as well as the more professional looking presentation.
- The huge store of knowledge and information available via the internet.

For the students

- The ability to build a piece of written work, for instance creating an outline of each paragraph, then filling in the text.
- The ease with which changes can be made, without the need for laborious rewrites.
- The ability to make work look good and be professionally finished with pictures and other presentational devices.
- The motivational aspects of creating finished pieces of work.
- The help that ICT offers for children who have SEN, for instance weak spellers, those with poor handwriting, etc.
- The vast store of knowledge and information available on CD-Roms and the internet.
- The ability to communicate quickly and efficiently around the world, via email.
- The importance of being able to use ICT for future career prospects.

Top tips for ICT

Learn to type!

Being able to touch type really will save you a huge amount of time.

Use the 'advanced' functions

If it feels like there should be an easy way of doing a particular task, then there probably is. Use the 'Help' function to find out how!

Ask your students for advice and help

They probably know more than you, and many will welcome the chance to play teacher.

Get to know the ICT teachers

Just as it is well worth developing a good relationship with the head's secretary and the caretaker, so it is well worth having the ICT teachers on side for times when you need help.

Store your work with care

It is all too easy to forget the name you've given a document, or for it to get lost on a network. If possible, store your resources on your own PC or portable, or create your own folder on the network.

Managing ICT use

Using any type of equipment in the classroom will inevitably lead to management issues, and perhaps nowhere is this more so than with electrical and electronic equipment which can so easily be misused or go wrong in the middle of a lesson. If you have only a limited number of computers at your school, you'll find some ideas in the next section about how you can go about maximizing these resources. Other general tips about managing ICT use within the classroom are given below.

- Set out the ground rules for using the computers right from the start, and preferably before your students are actually sitting in front of the machines. Once you get to this point, they will invariably start switching on the PCs and will immediately be distracted from what you are saying.
- Make the boundaries very clear, and the sanctions for misuse of the

machinery equally apparent. If you do need to remove a child from the computers, ensure that you have an alternative task or activity available.

- It can be a good idea to have the children sitting at tables to explain the lesson, before setting them loose on the machines. It is much harder to maintain a group's attention once they are sitting facing a PC. In some schools, you will find that an electronic whiteboard is available, on which you can demonstrate the work to the whole class.
- Encourage an awareness that the computer is a fairly delicate piece of equipment, and that it will respond to being bashed about by freezing, crashing and generally going out of action.
- Spend at least one or two lessons with a class teaching them about the correct use of word processors, spreadsheets, etc. (See the next chapter for some useful tips.) You will find that many children use only the absolute minimum of the full range of functions available.
- Consider ways of introducing more advanced functions, such as section breaks, columns, creating tables, formulating sums, and so on.

Maximizing your resources

There is still a definite disparity between the ICT resources that teachers (and their students) are offered from school to school. In some large secondary schools (especially those with specialist ICT status), there may be numerous suites of computers that teachers can book when they need. In other small primary schools, a large number of children may share a limited number of computers. Here are some tips for maximizing the resources that you do have available at your school.

- If you do not have enough machines for one each, encourage your students to find different ways of sharing the computers.
- One idea for this is to work in pairs, taking it in turns with one student acting as 'reader', the other as 'writer'.
- Use computer time as effectively as possible. Avoid using it for simply typing up work.
- Encourage your students to take very good care of the machines that they do have.
- Book time in a computer room early on in the term – ICT gets very popular when teachers are tired!

ICT hazards

Alongside an awareness of how useful and advantageous ICT can be, the wise teacher also has an understanding of the downsides or hazards of computer use in the school. Many of these hazards are actually to do with the way that you plan for computer use in your classroom or subject, and in the way that you encourage your students to work with ICT. Some of the potential dangers are listed here.

- Viewing word processing as simply a way of presenting work, rather than as a tool for building and editing writing.
- The dangers of time wasting and distraction for your students. These dangers come from a variety of sources, including:
  - the internet (e.g. chat rooms)
  - the excessive editing of written work
  - the overuse of ClipArt.
- An easy sense of achievement, when the presentation looks good, but the content is actually weak.
- The possibility (and indeed likelihood) of plagiarism.
- A lack of decent, reliable and up to date resources.
- Computers which break down, freeze, or crash, causing students to lose their work.
- The abuse of computers by the students, for instance the theft of mouseballs.
- Internet connection problems which can lead to real frustration and in turn to poor behaviour.
- 'Print out mania', whereby the students send endless copies of the same page to the printer.
- Safety issues, for instance relating to use of the internet (for example the dangers of giving out personal information).
- A lack of a really deep knowledge about exactly what computer programs have to offer.

The internet in teaching

At the moment, we're right at the start of internet use in teaching. The full extent of what the net (and all the associated technologies) really offers us still awaits discovery. There's no doubt, though, that whatever age group or subject we teach, there is plenty of potential for teaching and learning via the internet. For a really useful guide to the subject, see *The Internet in Schools* by Duncan Grey (published by Continuum). Some of the possible uses of the internet for the teacher are listed here.

- Publishing our children's writing, for example via a school website or educational site that uses student contributors.
- Researching and finding information on pretty much anything under the sun, both for the teacher and for the student.
- Downloading of programs, documents, etc. Also copying chunks of text from the net onto our computers.
- Educational websites that offer interactive activities with which students can learn.

- Distance teaching and learning, for instance the use of video conferencing.
- Communication locally, nationally and globally, via email.
- Setting up a school or even a class website of your own.

Of course, alongside the many potential benefits that the internet offers, there are also a number of downsides that the wary teacher needs to look out for. Some of these are listed here.

- The ease with which work can be plagiarized. Some sites even offer essays for sale.
- The proliferation of advertising on the internet (both in terms of how irritating it is, and also because of the teacher's responsibility not to expose children to this type of material).
- The huge range of 'adult' sites available, and the need to be fully aware of the content to which our children may be exposed.
- The huge quantity of information available, which may lead to research time being ill spent or wasted.

There are a good number of ways in which many of these problems can be overcome, or at least the difficulties minimized. The tips below focus on ways to avoid squandering research time.

- Find a good search engine to avoid wasted time when research is being done. I recommend 'Google' for the relevancy of its search results and its minimal advertising content.
- Teach your children how to go about using a search engine.
- Encourage focused research and avoid unsuitable sites by doing some background work yourself, giving the children a list of websites to visit.
- Give your students a list of questions to answer, to encourage them to focus on the task in hand, and avoid distraction.

Safety on the internet

Of course, when we use the internet in the classroom, we have a responsibility to be fully aware of the dangers that exist for our children. Before letting them loose on the world wide web, we need to take the time to advise our students about what is and is not acceptable and sensible behaviour. The advice that teachers give their children in school is equally applicable to internet use at home.

- Advise your children that it is essential to keep personal information to themselves, and not to give out their name, address or telephone number over the internet.
- Warn the class that people on the internet can take on false personas, and that the 'child' they meet in a chat room may not be what he or she appears.
- Talk about how easy it is for viruses to find their way onto a PC or network. Tell your students to guard against downloading files, unless they are certain

about the source. The same applies to opening attachments that arrive with emails.

- Discuss the sanctions that the school imposes for those visiting 'adult' sites. It is inevitable, particularly with teenagers, that some at least will try getting away with this!

18 Software

This chapter gives you some general tips about working with software, and specific information about using two common types of computer software: the word processor and the spreadsheet. The tips and instructions given will be helpful to the inexperienced computer user, and also to those with a reasonable level of knowledge which they hope to increase. (Note: I deal with the Microsoft programs here, as these are the most commonly used in schools.)

Some general tips

The following tips should prove useful both for teachers working on their own documents, and also when you are working with children using ICT in the classroom. Some of these tips cover general good practice, others look at some of the common errors that students make (such as hitting the 'Return' button at the end of a line).

- Always save your document a few minutes after you have started working on it. Keep saving it as you go along. There really is nothing quite as frustrating as losing a piece of work because the computer crashes or freezes before you have saved.
- As far as possible, aim to type your work first, then worry about detailed formatting later. This is especially so if you are using a number of different fonts on one page. One of the reasons for this is that if you format as you go along glitches will often appear on the page where the computer defaults to the standard formatting (for instance dropping out of a chosen font and into default Times Roman).
- Use the layout functions of left/right justify and centre, rather than using the space bar or tab button.
- When word processing, only put a return at the end of a paragraph, rather than at the end of each line. Instead, allow the computer's wrap around function to do its work. Many students make this error because they don't know what wrap around does.
- Use 'Ctrl + return' to create a new page instead of adding returns.
- Use the 'Print preview' function to see what a document looks like before sending it to the printer.
- Check at the end of your document for blank pages before sending your work to print.
- Name your documents sensibly, preferably using a separate folder for work in different topic areas.
- Use the shortcut functions, such as 'Ctrl + S' for save and 'Ctrl + B' for

bold. These functions can save a great deal of time and effort, especially once they become second nature.

■ Learn to use more advanced functions, such as section breaks, columns, adapting page layout, creating tables, formulating calculations, and so on. A good way to start working with these functions is by using the 'Help' menus which take you step by step through the processes involved.

Word processing

The word processor really is a wonderful tool for both teacher and student, because of the endless hours of rewriting that it saves us. The word processor also enables us to create professional looking documents relatively easily. You can find information below about putting together a worksheet that will look good and also prove easily accessible for all your students.

Creating a worksheet

The instructions that follow give you guidance in creating a professional looking worksheet to use with your students, using the Microsoft Word program. You can also see a sample of the worksheet that is created. The worksheet is designed for GCSE students studying the novel *Lord of the Flies*. The word processing techniques and layout ideas used can easily be adapted for different ages and subjects.

How do I get started?

■ Use your mouse to point your cursor at the 'Start' button on the bottom left of your screen.
■ Click once with the mouse to open up the menu.
■ Point your cursor to 'Programs', across to 'Word', then click.
■ Alternatively, double click on the 'Word' icon on your desktop.

What happens next?

■ You will see a blank page, basically like a clean sheet of paper.
■ You can view your page in various different layouts, using the 'View' function on the pull down menus.
■ You can also use different sized views of your page, using the '%' box on your toolbar. 100% shows the full sized page, 50% the page at half size, and so on.

How do I create the 'WordArt' title?

- There are a range of pre-formatted 'WordArt' titles available to use, which will make your work look more interesting.
- To add a 'WordArt' title, go to the drop down menu 'Insert', then drag down to 'Picture', and across to 'WordArt'.
- You will see a range of different title styles. Click on your selection, then on 'OK'. A box will appear in which you can type the required text. This box also gives you options about font size and other formatting.
- Click on 'OK' once you are happy with your text. Your title will be inserted onto your blank page, with a 'WordArt' toolbar at the bottom, which you can use to manipulate the title.
- To make any further changes to the title, double click over it and the 'WordArt' editing box will appear.

How do I format text to add bold, underlining, centring, etc?

- To add formatting to a line of text, position your cursor just to the left of the line, then click once. You will find that the whole line is highlighted.
- Alternatively, position your cursor near the line, click down your mouse button and hold, then drag the mouse so that the text is highlighted.
- To add bold, either use the shortcut 'Ctrl + B', or the **B** icon on your toolbar.
- To add italics, use the shortcut 'Ctrl + I', or the *I* icon on your toolbar.
- To align your text (for instance centring), again use the icons on the toolbar. These show a series of lines which offer align left, centre, align right or justify.
- To add bullet points, click on the bullet icon on your toolbar. You can change the type of bullet point used with the drop down menus. To do this, go to 'Format', then 'Bullets and numbering'.

How do I add and manipulate a text box?

- To enclose text in a box, highlight the text that you wish to appear in the box.
- Now use the pull down menus to click on 'Insert', then 'Text box'. A box will appear around the text.
- You can resize the text box to fit your text. Hold your cursor over one of the lines of the box until you see a symbol with four arrows appear.
- Now click once and you will see the box highlighted, and eight small empty boxes appear on the lines. You can now manipulate the size of the box.
- Do this by holding your cursor over one of these boxes until a line with two arrows appears. Now click once, hold down the mouse button and drag the box out or in.
- You can also move the text box around the page. To do this, position your cursor so the four arrows appear. Then click and hold down your mouse button and drag the box to its new position.

- In addition, you can change the formatting of the box. To do this, double click with the four arrows showing, and you will be given a number of options for changing the format.
- In the sample shown, the box fill and line weight have been changed. This allows the teacher to highlight the box in which the outline of activities appears, which will be useful for the weaker student who needs guiding to this part of the sheet.

How do I add and edit a table?

- To add a table to your worksheet, use the drop down menus. Go to 'Table', 'Insert', then drag across to 'Table'.
- A box will appear giving you different options for your table. You can choose the number of columns and rows. You can also use a number of different auto formats.
- To change your table once it has been inserted, again use the 'Table' drop down menu. You can delete or insert rows or columns. There is also a function to sort the text, and various other features.

How do I add AutoShapes to my work?

- To add AutoShapes, view the Drawing toolbar by going to 'View', 'Toolbars', then dragging across to 'Drawing'.
- The toolbar will appear at the bottom of your screen.
- You can use this toolbar to do a number of different things within your document, including changing text colour, adding lines and arrows, 'ordering' your text and pictures (for instance so that a box appears behind or in front of a piece of text), and so on.

How do I add a border to my page?

- To add a border to the page, use the drop down menus. Go to 'Format', then click on 'Borders and Shading'. Now click on 'Page Border'.
- Here you will find a number of different options for adding borders to your page. You can choose an 'Art' border, which features pictures or other frames, or you can use a more straightforward line.
- You can also alter the size of border that will appear.

Lord of the Flies

Themes and Images: Hunting and Ritual

Outline of Activities

Working with a partner.

1. Look again at the six hunts in the novel, reading and making notes.
2. Discuss the morality of hunting, drawing a for/against chart.
3. Make a list of rituals, or ritual behaviours, that are seen in the novel.

Activities

Complete the following tasks, working with your partner.

Kill the pig!

1. There are six hunts in the novel, in chapters 3, 4, 8, 9, 11 and 12.

   ✓ Find the page references for each hunt.
   ✓ Make notes on what happens.
   ✓ Look at who or what is hunted each time.

2. Discuss the morality of hunting. Make a list of points 'For' and 'Against'. Write these down on a table like the one below.

For	Against
Some people see it as a natural form of pest control.	Many people feel it is cruel to the animals involved.

3, Make a list of rituals, or ritual behaviours, that are seen in the novel.

   ✓ Try to find at least five different examples.
   ✓ What purpose do these rituals serve for the boys?

Spreadsheets

The instructions that follow give you all the information you need to create two basic spreadsheets using the Microsoft Excel programme. The spreadsheets that are created will do some basic calculations of student assessments. Examples of what the finished spreadsheets look like are provided at the end of this chapter.

How do I get started?

- Use your mouse to point your cursor at the 'Start' button on the bottom left of your screen.
- Click once with the mouse to open up the menu.
- Point your cursor to 'Programs', across to 'Excel', then click.
- Alternatively, double click on the 'Excel' icon on your desktop.

What happens next?

- A blank workbook (series of spreadsheets) will automatically open, ready for you to use.
- On the top line you will see the workbook's current document name (the default will be book1.xls).
- To change the name of your document, use the pull down menus at the top of your screen. Go to 'File', then 'Save as', and type in the new name of your document.
- The workbook is made up of worksheets (or spreadsheets).

What are worksheets and how do I use them?

- The worksheets are a series of blank spreadsheets, stacked one behind the other like the pages of a book.
- The worksheets are called Sheet 1, Sheet 2, Sheet 3 and so on. The default setting is to open eight worksheets within each workbook.
- You will see the series of worksheets listed at the bottom left of the page on tabs.
- You can move between the worksheets by clicking on these tabs.
- Alternatively, use the shortcut 'Ctrl + Pg Up' (hit both these keys together) to move from sheet 1, to 2, to 3, etc. Use the shortcut 'Ctrl + Pg Dn' to go in reverse order.
- The worksheets allow you to have a range of information within one workbook, and then to formulate sums involving all the worksheets (for instance, finding out average grades over several different classes).
- To rename the worksheets within your workbook:
  - double click on the worksheet tab
  - the original name will be highlighted in black
  - type over the original name with the new name you want.

How do I move around the worksheet?

- On the worksheet you'll see letters going across the top, starting with 'A' and moving alphabetically.
- You'll also see numbers going downwards, in order.
- Each box or 'cell' consequently has an identifying letter/number. The first cell is called A1.
- You can type text or numbers in the cells (or both).
- To move to a cell, click on the box so that it is highlighted. You can then type the text or numbers which you want to appear at that point.

How do I type on the worksheet?

- Click on the cell to highlight the point where you want to type. Now simply type in the text or numbers that you want.
- It doesn't matter if the text you type in is too big for the cell, because you can resize them.
- In the example spreadsheets, the information typed in is:
  - Title of worksheet
  - Student's surname
  - Student's first name
  - Grades and percentages for assignments 1–5
  - Total column (for marks and sum formula)
  - Exclusion of one assignment from the marking (for formula, see below).

How do I resize the columns to fit my text?

- To resize columns individually, move your cursor to the gap between two columns, and hold it there until you see a line with two arrows facing left/right.
- Now hold down your mouse button and pull the column width out until the text fits.
- Alternatively, you can automatically size the columns so that the text fits them exactly. To do this, go to the letter row at the top of the worksheet (A, B, C ...). Click with your mouse in this row and hold down the button.
- Now mark the columns you want to resize by pulling the mouse across until they are highlighted.
- Then simply double click on one of the lines between the columns. The cells will automatically resize to fit your text.
-

How do I use the sum formula?

- To use the 'sum' (or addition) formula, type the marks out of 20 in each of the assignment columns.

- In the 'total' column type ' =sum('. Once you have typed this the computer knows that you are going to add something up to create a formula.
- Now move the cursor to the first point from where you want to add up. In the example this was cell 'C6'.
- Hold the shift button down and mark all the columns you want to add together by moving the cursor along.
- You will see a box with a flashing dotted line around it. Ensure that this box is expanded to cover the area you want to add up. Then hit the 'Enter' or 'Return' button.

Is there another way to add up?

- You can also use the sum icon. This is a Greek 'Epsilon' symbol on the toolbar at the top of your screen (which looks like a funny 'E').
- Click your cursor so that the 'Total' column is highlighted, then double click the 'Epsilon' icon.
- This function will automatically sum up the most logical sequence of numbers from the cell where your cursor is.
- In the example given, the computer works out that you want to add up the five assignment columns to create your total.
- Another method is to use the ' + ' key. Hit the ' + ' while in the 'Total' cell.
- Now move the cursor to the cells you want to add together in turn. The computer will automatically add up these cells.
- Other keys that work in the same way are divide '/' and multiply '*'.

How do I remove one cell from the calculation?

- In the examples, you will see that there is a final column with the marks for Assignment 4 excluded. This might come in useful if, for instance, you suspected a student of cheating in that assignment, or if you felt that the assignment had been too difficult for the class.
- To take out a cell use the '-' key in the same way that you used the ' + ' key above.
- Alternatively, type a formula into the relevant cell. In this case ' + H6' (the name of our total column) '– F6' (the name of the Assignment 4 column).

How do I put in and add up percentages?

- In the second example worksheet, you will see that percentages are used, rather than marks.
- To put in a percentage, type the number in the relevant cell, putting a percentage sign after it. The computer will automatically know that this number is a percentage, and must be treated as such.
- In the total column at the end of the example worksheet, the percentages are added together and then averaged out.

- To do this, type '=sum(' in the 'Total' box. Now use one of the functions described above to add up the columns.
- Click on the 'Total' cell, then in the formula line that appears at the top of your page, showing current formula. Add '/5' after the brackets to tell the computer to divide the sum by 5 (to create an average of the 5 assignments).

How do I format the text on my spreadsheet?

- To format the text, click your cursor in the relevant box, then click on the bold, italic or underline icons (on the toolbar at the top right of your screen).
- Alternatively, you can use the drag down menus as you would in a word processing document.
- To format a group of cells, mark the area you want to format by clicking on the cell, holding down and dragging the mouse across. Then click the formatting icon.
- The large and small 'A' icons can be used to increase and decrease text size.
- To add a box around the spreadsheet, mark the cells to go within the box, then use the icons with borders at the top of the screen.

How do I sort out the layout of my document?

- Use the print preview function (either the icon of a document with a magnifying glass, or the function on the pull down 'File' menu).
- Excel should automatically format your document so that it looks 'correct' on the screen.
- If you are not happy with how it looks, click on the 'Set up' button at the top of the 'Print preview' screen.
- Here you will find options to change the page layout to landscape format, or to fit the text to one page.

ST PATRICKS 2002 – ASSIGNMENT MARKS

SURNAME	FIRST NAME	Assignment 1 mark out of 20	Assignment 2 mark out of 20	Assignment 3 mark out of 20	Assignment 4 mark out of 20	Assignment 5 mark out of 20	Total mark out of 100	excl assign 4 mark out of 80
Baggio	Andrea	1	5	10	5	6	27	22
Bayer	Frans	14	16	11	12	14	67	55
Benson	Sally	9	11	10	10	8	48	38
Davies	Jennifer	18	16	15	17	20	86	69
Du Morier	Nicole	11	9	10	9	12	51	42
Gomez	Maria	14	12	11	12	15	64	52
Jones	Owen	8	9	7	4	9	37	33
Mckay	Angus	17	19	16	17	19	88	71
Singh	Amjan	18	19	18	14	17	86	72
Smith	Bob	13	11	12	11	15	62	51

ST PATRICKS 2002 – ASSIGNMENT MARKS AS PERCENTAGE

SURNAME	FIRST NAME	Assignment 1 as percentage	Assignment 2 as percentage	Assignment 3 as percentage	Assignment 4 as percentage	Assignment 5 as percentage	Total as percentage	excl assign 4 as percentage
Baggio	Andrea	5%	25%	50%	25%	30%	27%	28%
Bayer	Frans	70%	80%	55%	60%	70%	67%	69%
Benson	Sally	45%	55%	50%	50%	40%	48%	48%
Davies	Jennifer	90%	80%	75%	85%	100%	86%	86%
Du Morier	Nicole	55%	45%	50%	45%	60%	51%	53%
Gomez	Maria	70%	60%	55%	60%	75%	64%	65%
Jones	Owen	40%	45%	35%	20%	45%	37%	41%
Mckay	Angus	85%	95%	80%	85%	95%	88%	89%
Singh	Amjan	90%	95%	90%	70%	85%	86%	90%
Smith	Bob	65%	55%	60%	55%	75%	62%	64%

Section 5

The Directory

Art
assessment
Business Studies
careers
Citizenship
curriculum
Design and Technology
Drama
English
examination boards
examinations
further education
general
Geography
government
History
ICT
independent schools
inspection
international education
jobs
languages
library

management
Maths
media
online education
parents
PE
pensions
portals
primary
professional development
PSE
publications
RE
schools information
Science
special educational needs
suppliers (educational products)
supply teaching agencies
support organizations
teacher training
teaching forums and communities
teaching resources
unions

Art

National Society for Education in Art and Design (NSEAD)
The Gatehouse
Corsham Court
Corsham
Wiltshire SN13 OBZ
Website: www.nsead.org
Email: johnsteers@nsead.org
Tel: 01249 714825
Fax: 01249 716138

Assessment

Association of Assessment Inspectors and Advisors (AAIA)
Website: www.aaia.org.uk
Email: vice-president@aaia.org.uk
See also: Examinations

Business Studies

Biz/ed
Website: www.bized.ac.uk
Email: bized-info@bized.ac.uk

The Economics and Business Education Association
1a Keymer Road
Hassocks
West Sussex BN6 8AD
Website: www.ebea.org.uk
Email: ebeah@pavilion.co.uk
Tel: 01273 846033
Fax: 01273 844646

Just Business
Website: www.jusbiz.org
Email: jusbiz@nead.org.uk

Careers

Careers Research Advisory Centre (CRAC)
Sheraton House
Castle Park
Cambridge CB3 0AX
Website: www.crac.org.uk
Email: web.enquiries@crac.org.uk
Tel: 01223 460277
Fax: 01223 311708

Institute of Careers Guidance (ICG)
27a Lower High Street
Stourbridge
West Midlands DY8 1TA
Website: www.icg-uk.org
Email: hq@icg-uk.org
Tel: 01384 376464
Fax: 01384 440830

National Association of Careers and Guidance Teachers
Portland House
4 Bridge Street
Usk NP5 1BG
Tel: 01291 672985
Fax: 01291 672090

Citizenship

The Citizenship Foundation
Ferroners House
Shaftesbury Place
Aldersgate Street
London EC2Y 8AA
Website: www.citfou.org.uk
Email: info@citfou.org.uk
Tel: 020 7367 0500
Fax: 020 7367 0501

Council for Education in World Citizenship (CEWC)
Sir John Lyon House
5 High Timber Street
London EC4V 3PA
Website: www.cewc.org.uk
Email: info@cewc.org.uk
Tel: 020 7329 1500
Fax: 020 7329 8160

Institute for Citizenship
62 Marylebone High Street
London W1U 5HZ
Website: www.citizen.org.uk
Email: info@citizen.org.uk
Tel: 020 7935 4777
Fax: 020 7486 9212

Time for Citizenship
Website:
www.timeforcitizenship.com
Email: via online form

Curriculum

The Basic Skills Agency (BSA)
Commonwealth House
1–19 New Oxford Street
London WC1A 1NU
Website: www.basic-skills.co.uk
Email: enquires@basic-skills.co.uk
Tel: 020 7405 4017
Fax: 020 7440 6626

National Curriculum online
Website: www.nc.uk.net

Design and Technology

Design & Technology Online
Website: www.dtonline.org
Email: dtonline@dialsolutions.co.uk

The Design and Technology Association (DATA)
16 Wellesbourne House
Walton Road
Wellesbourne
Warwickshire CV35 9JB
Website: www.data.org.uk
Email: DATA@data.org.uk
Tel: 01789 470007
Fax: 01789 841955

Design Technology Department
Website: www.design-technology.org
Email: a.davies@design-technology.org

The National Association of Advisers and Inspectors in Design and Technology (NAAIDT)
Gina White, NAAIDT Hon Secretary
6 Birchwood Close
Elton
Cheshire CH2 4RU
Website: www.naaidt.org.uk
Email: gina.white@naaidt.org.uk

Drama

National Drama
Website: www.nationaldrama.co.uk
Email: via website

The Royal National Theatre
Royal National Theatre
South Bank
London SE1 9PX
Website: www.nationaltheatre.org.uk
Email: via online form
Tel: 020 7452 3500
Fax: 020 7452 3535

The Society of Teachers of Speech and Drama (STSD)
Mrs A. Jones
73 Berry Hill Road
Mansfield
Nottinghamshire NG18 4RU
Website: www.stsd.org.uk
Email: stsd@stsd.org.uk
Tel: 01623 627636

English

The English Speaking Union (ESU)
Dartmouth House
37 Charles Street
London W1J 5ED
Website: www.esu.org
Email: esu@esu.org
Tel: 020 7529 1550
Fax: 020 7495 6108

National Association for the Teaching of English (NATE)
50 Broadfield Road
Sheffield S8 OXJ
Website: www.nate.org.uk
Email: natehq@btconnect.com
Tel: 0114 255 5419
Fax: 0114 255 5296

The National Literacy Association (NLA)
Office No. 1
The Magistrates' Court
Bargates
Christchurch
Dorset BH23 1PY
Website: www.nla.org.uk
Email: nla@argonet.co.uk
Tel: 01202 484079
Fax: 01202 484079

The National Literacy Trust
Swire House
59 Buckingham Gate
London SW1E 6AJ
Website: www.literacytrust.org.uk
Email: contact@literacytrust.org.uk
Tel: 020 7828 2435
Fax: 020 7931 9986

Examination boards

Edexcel
Stewart House
32 Russell Square
London WC1B 5DN
Website: www.edexcel.org.uk
Email: enquiries@edexcel.org.uk
Tel: 0870 240 9800
Fax: 020 7758 6960

Joint Examining Board (JEB)
30a Dyer Street
Cirencester
Gloucestershire GL7 2PF
Website: www.jeb.co.uk
Email: jeb@jeb.co.uk
Tel: 01285 641747
Fax: 01285 650449

Northern Examinations and Assessment Board (NEAB)
Website: www.neab.ac.uk

Oxford Cambridge and RSA Examinations (OCR)
1 Regent Street
Cambridge CB2 1GG
Website: www.ocr.org.uk
Email: helpdesk@ocr.org.uk
Tel: 01223 553998
Fax: 01223 552627

Examinations

The Qualifications and Curriculum Authority (QCA)
83 Piccadilly
London W1J 8QA
Website: www.qca.org.uk
Email: info@qca.org.uk
Tel: 020 7509 5555
Fax: 020 7509 6666

QCA Northern Ireland
Website: www.qca.org.uk/ni/
Email: info@qcani.org.uk

Qualifications, Curriculum and Assessment Authority for Wales (ACCAC)
Castle Buildings
Womanby Street
Cardiff CF10 1SX
Website: www.accac.org.uk
Email: info@accac.org.uk
Tel: 029 2037 5400
Fax: 029 2034 3612

Northern Ireland Council for the Curriculum, Examinations and Assessment (CCEA)
Website: www.ccea.org.uk
Email: info@ccea.org.uk
Tel: 028 9026 1200

Scottish Qualifications Authority
Hanover House
24 Douglas Street
Glasgow G2 7NQ
Website: www.sqa.org.uk
Email: helpdesk@sqa.org.uk
Tel: 0141 242 2214
Fax: 0141 242 2244

Further education

Association of Colleges (AOC)
5th Floor, Centre Point
103 New Oxford Street
London WC1A 1RG
Website: www.aoc.co.uk
Email: enquiries@aoc.co.uk
Tel: 020 7827 4600
Fax: 020 7827 4650

The Learning and Skills Council (LSC)
Cheylesmore House
Quinton Road
Coventry CV1 2WT
Website: www.lsc.gov.uk
Email: info@lsc.gov.uk
Tel: 0845 019 4170
Fax: 024 7649 3600

The Learning and Skills Development Agency (LSDA)
Regent Arcade House
19–25 Argyll Street
London W1F 7LS
Website: www.lsda.org.uk
Email: enquiries@lsda.org.uk
Tel: 020 7297 9000
Fax: 020 7297 9001

General

The British Council
10 Spring Gardens
London SW1A 2BN
Website: www.britishcouncil.org
Email:
general.enquiries@britishcouncil.org
Tel: 020 7930 8466
Fax: 020 7839 6347

The Commission for Racial Equality
Elliot House
10–12 Allington Street
London SW1E 5EH
Website: www.cre.gov.uk
Email: info@cre.gov.uk
Tel: 020 7828 7022
Fax: 020 7630 7605

The Duke of Edinburgh's Award
Gulliver House
Madeira Walk
Windsor
Berkshire SL4 1EU
Website: www.theaward.org
Email: info@theaward.org
Tel: 01753 727400
Fax: 01753 810666

National Confederation of Parent Teacher Associations (NCPTA)
18 St Johns Hill
Sevenoaks
Kent TN13 3NP
Website: www.ncpta.org.uk
Email: info@ncpta.org.uk
Tel: 01732 748850
Fax: 01732 748851

National Foundation for Educational Research (NFER)
The Mere
Upton Park
Slough
Berkshire SL1 2DQ
Website: www.nfer.ac.uk
Email: enquiries@nfer.ac.uk
Tel: 01753 574123
Fax: 01753 691632

National Society for the Prevention of Cruelty to Children (NSPCC)
42 Curtain Road
London EC2A 3NH
Website: www.nspcc.org.uk

Email: via the website
Tel: 020 7825 2500
Fax: 020 7825 2525
Child Protection Helpline: 0800 800 5000

Geography

The Council for Environmental Education (CEE)
94 London Street
Reading RG1 4SJ
Website: www.cee.org.uk
Email: njones@cee.org.uk
Tel: 0118 950 2550
Fax: 0118 959 1955

The Geographical Association
160 Solly Street
Sheffield SB1 4BF
Website: www.geography.org.uk
Email: ga@geography.org.uk
Tel: 0114 296 0088
Fax: 0114 296 7176

Ordnance Survey
Customer Contact Centre
Romsey Road
Southampton SO16 4GU
Website: www.ordnancesurvey.co.uk
Email: enquiries@ordsvy.gov.uk
Tel: 0845 605 0505
Fax: 023 8079 2615

Royal Geographical Society
1 Kensington Gore
London SW7 2AR
Website: www.rgs.org
Email: info@rgs.org
Tel: 020 7591 3000
Fax: 020 7591 3001

Government

Department for Education and Skills (DfES)
Sanctuary Buildings
Great Smith Street
London SW1P 3BT
Website: www.dfes.gov.uk
Email: info@dfes.gsi.gov.uk
Tel: 0870 001 2345
Fax: 01928 79 4248
Tel (public enquiries): 0870 000 2288

Also at:
Caxton House, Tothill Street, London SW1H 9FN
Moorfoot, Sheffield S1 4PQ
Mowden Hall, Staindrop Road, Darlington DL3 9BG
Castle View House, East Lane, Runcorn WA7 2DN

Secretary of State for Education and Skills
Rt Hon Estelle Morris MP
Sanctuary Buildings
Great Smith Street
London SW1P 3BT

Department of Education Northern Ireland
An Roinn Oideachais
Mannystrie o Lear
Rathgael House
43 Balloo Road
Bangor Co. Down BT19 7PR
Website: www.deni.gov.uk
Email: mail@deni.gov.uk
Tel: 028 9127 9279
Fax: 028 9127 9100

General Teaching Council for England (GTCE)
3rd Floor
Cannon House

24 The Priory Queensway
Birmingham B4 6BS
Website: www.gtce.org.uk
Email: info@gtce.org.uk
Tel: 0870 001 0308
Fax: 0121 345 0100

Also at:
344–354 Gray's Inn Road, London WC1X 8BP
Fax: 020 7841 2909

General Teaching Council for Scotland (GTCS)
Clerwood House
96 Clermiston Road
Edinburgh EH12 6UT
Website: www.gtcs.org.uk
Email: gtcs@gtcs.org.uk
Tel: 0131 314 6000
Fax: 0131 314 6001

National Grid for Learning (NGfL)
Website: www.ngfl.gov.uk
Email: content@ngfl.gov.uk

Scottish Executive (Education Department)
Victoria Quay
Edinburgh EH6 6QQ
Website: www.scotland.gov.uk/education/teaching/scotexec.html
Email: ceu@scotland.gov.uk
Tel: 0131 556 8400
Fax: 0131 244 8240

Welsh Joint Education Committee (WJEC)
245 Western Avenue
Cardiff CF5 2YX
Website: www.wjec.co.uk
Email: info@wjec.co.uk
Tel: 029 2026 5000

History

The British Museum
Great Russell Street
London WC1B 3DG
Website:
www.thebritishmuseum.ac.uk
Email:
information@thebritishmuseum.ac.uk
Tel: 020 7323 8299

English Heritage
Customer Services Department
PO Box 569
Swindon SN2 2YP
Website: www.english-heritage.org.uk
Email: customers@english-heritage.org.uk
Tel: 0870 333 1181
Fax: 01793 414926

The Historical Association
59a Kennington Park Road
London SE11 4JH
Website: www.history.org.uk
Email: enquiries@history.org.uk
Tel: 020 7735 3901
Fax: 020 7582 4989

ICT

Association for Information Technology in Teacher Education (ITTE)
Website: www.itte.org.uk

British Educational Communications and Technology agency (BECTa)
Milburn Hill Road
Science Park
Coventry CV4 7JJ
Website: www.becta.org.uk
Email: becta@becta.org.uk
Tel: 024 7641 6994

Fax: 024 7641 1418

The IT Network
Website: www.itnetwork.org.uk
Email: itn@itnetwork.org.uk

The National Association of Advisers for Computers in Education (NAACE)
PO Box 6511
Nottingham NG11 8TN
Website: www.naace.org
Email: office@naace.org
Tel: 0870 240 0480
Fax: 0870 241 4115

National Association for Co-ordinators and Teachers of IT (ACITT)
Membership Secretary
138 Inchmery Road
Catford
London SE6 1DF
Website: www.acitt.org.uk
Email: membership@acitt.org.uk

Independent schools

Independent Schools' Association
Boys' British School
East Street
Saffron Walden
Essex CB10 1LS
Website: www.isaschools.org.uk
Email: isa@dial.pipex.com
Tel: 01799 523619
Fax: 01799 524892

Independent Schools Council information service (ISCis)
Grosvenor Gardens House
35–37 Grosvenor Gardens
London SW1W OBS
Website: www.isis.org.uk
Email: isc@iscis.uk.net

Tel: 020 7798 1590
Fax: 020 7798 1591

Scottish Council of Independent Schools (SCIS)
21 Melville Street
Edinburgh EH3 7PE
Website: www.scis.org.uk
Email: information@scis.org.uk
Tel: 0131 220 2106
Fax: 0131 225 8594

Inspection

The Office for Standards in Education (OFSTED)
Alexandra House
33 Kingsway
London WC2B 6SE
Website: www.ofsted.gov.uk
Email: geninfo@ofsted.gov.uk
Tel: 020 7421 6744

International education

European Council of International Schools (ECIS)
21 Lavant Street
Petersfield
Hampshire GU32 3EL
Website: www.ecis.org
Email: ecis@ecis.org
Tel: 01730 268244

Voluntary Service Overseas (VSO)
317 Putney Bridge Road
London SW15 2PN
Website: www.vso.org.uk
Email: enquiry@vso.org.uk
Tel: 020 8780 7200
Fax: 020 8780 7300

Jobs

Education Lecturing Services (ELS – jobs in further education)
Website: els.co.uk

ETeach
Website: www.eteach.com

The Guardian
Education section published weekly on Tuesdays

The Independent
Education section published weekly on Thursdays

The Times Educational Supplement (TES)
Published weekly on Fridays
Website: www.jobs.tes.co.uk

Languages

Association for Language Learning (ALL)
150 Railway Terrace
Rugby CV21 3HN
Website: www.languagelearn.co.uk
Email: info@ALL.languages.org.uk
Tel: 01788 546443
Fax: 01788 544149

Centre for Information on Language Teaching and Research (CiLT)
20 Bedfordbury
London WC2N 4LB
Website: www.cilt.org.uk
Email: library@cilt.org.uk
Tel: 020 7379 5110
Fax: 020 7379 5082

Library

Ask a Librarian
Website: www.ask-a-librarian.org.uk
Email: via online form

Belfast Education and Library Board (BELB)
Education Department
40 Academy Street
Belfast BT1 2NQ
Website: www.belb.org.uk
Email: via the website
Tel: 028 9056 4000
Fax: 028 9033 1714

The British Library
96 Euston Road
London NW1 2DB
Website: www.portico.bl.uk
Email: reader-services-enquiries@bl.uk
Tel: 020 7412 7000

School Library Association (SLA)
Unit 2
Lotmead Business Village
Lotmead Farm
Wanborough
Swindon SN4 OUY
Website: www.sla.org.uk
Email: info@sla.org.uk
Tel: 01793 791787
Fax: 01793 791786

Management

National College for School Leadership
Jubilee Campus
University of Nottingham
Wollaton Road
Nottingham
NG8 1BB
Website: www.ncsl.org.uk
Email: ncsl-office@ncsl.org.uk
Tel: 0870 160 1604
Fax: 0115 846 6952

Maths

Association of Teachers of Mathematics (ATM)
7 Shaftesbury Street
Derby DE23 8YB
Website: www.atm.org.uk
Email: atm@atm.org.uk
Tel: 01332 346599
Fax: 01332 204357

The Institute of Mathematics and its Applications
Catherine Richards House
16 Nelson Street
Southend-on-Sea
Essex SS1 1EF
Website: www.ima.org.uk
Email: post@ima.org.uk
Tel: 01702 354020
Fax: 01702 354111

The Mathematical Association (MA)
259 London Road
Leicester LE2 3BE
Website: www.m-a.org.uk
Email: office@m-a.org.uk
Tel: 0116 221 0013
Fax: 0116 212 2835

Media

BBC
PO Box 1922
Glasgow G2 3WT
Website: www.bbc.co.uk
Tel: 0870 010 0222

The British Film Institute (BFI)
National Film Theatre
Belvedere Road

323

South Bank
London SE1 8XT
Website: www.bfi.org.uk
Email: education.queries@bfi.org.uk
Tel: 020 7957 4787

Education Guardian
Website:
www.guardian.education.co.uk

Online education

Actis Ltd
Website: www.actis.co.uk
Also curriculum websites for various
subjects
Email: welcome@actis.co.uk

BBC
Website: www.bbc.co.uk/education
Email:
homepage.education@bbc.co.uk

Channel 4
Website: www.4learning.co.uk
Email: via online links

Homework High
Website: www.homeworkhigh.com

Learn.co.uk (from The Guardian)
Website: www.learn.co.uk
Email: contact@learn.co.uk

Learning and Teaching Scotland
Website: www.ltscotland.com
Email: enquiries@ltscotland.com

Scottish Virtual Teachers' Centre
Website: www.svtc.org.uk

Parents

**Advisory Centre for Education
(ACE)**
1c Aberdeen Studios
22 Highbury Grove
London N5 2DQ
Website: www.ace-ed.org.uk
Tel (exclusion): 020 7704 9822
Tel (general): 0808 800 5793

PE

**British Association of Advisers and
Lecturers in Physical Education
(BAALPE)**
Peter Whitlam (General Secretary)
Sports Development Centre
Loughborough University
Loughborough
Leicestershire LE11 3TU
Website: www.baalpe.org
Email: baalpe@lboro.ac.uk
Tel/Fax: 01509 228378

**Central Council of Physical
Recreation (CCPR)**
Francis House
Francis Street
London SW1P 1DE
Website: www.ccpr.org.uk
Email: info@ccpr.org.uk
Tel: 020 7854 8500
Fax: 020 7854 8501

**The Physical Education Association
of the United Kingdom (PEA UK)**
Ling House
Building 25
London Road
Reading RG1 5AQ
Website: www.pea.uk.com
Email: enquiries@pea.uk.com
Tel: 0118 931 6240
Fax: 0118 931 6242

Pensions

Teachers' Pensions
England and Wales
Capita Teachers' Pensions
Mowden Hall
Darlington DL3 9EE
Website:
www.teacherspensions.co.uk
Email: via website
Tel: 01325 745746

Teachers' Pensions
Northern Ireland
Department of Education
Teachers' Pensions Branch
Waterside House
75 Duke Street
Londonderry BT47 6FP
Tel: 028 7131 9000

Teachers' Pensions
Scotland
Scottish Public Pensions Agency
Teachers' Benefits Section
St Margaret's House
151 London Road
Edinburgh EH8 7TG

Portals

Online-teachers
Website: www.teachers-online.co.uk

Primary

The British Association for Early Childhood Education
136 Cavell Street
London E1 2JA
Website: www.early-education.org.uk
Email: office@early-education.org.uk
Tel: 020 7539 5400
Fax: 020 7539 5409

The Centre for Language in Primary Education (CLPE)
Webber Street
London SE1 8QW
Website: www.clpe.co.uk
Email: info@clpe.co.uk
Tel: 020 7401 3382
Fax: 020 7928 4624

National Association for Primary Education (NAPE)
University of Leicester
Moulton College
Moulton
Northampton NN3 7RR
Website: www.nape.org.uk
Email: nationaloffice@nape.org.uk
Tel: 01604 647646
Fax: 01604 647660

The Pre-school Learning Alliance
69 Kings Cross Road
London WC1X 9LL
Website: www.pre-school.org.uk
Email: pla@pre-school.org.uk
Tel: 020 7833 0991
Fax: 020 7837 4942

The Times Educational Supplement (Primary)
Website: www.tesprimary.co.uk

Professional development

The College of Teachers
32 John Street
London WC1N 2AT
Website:
www.collegeofteachers.ac.uk
Email: ray@cot3.freeserve.co.uk
Tel: 020 7404 3138

PSE

Kidscape
2 Grosvenor Gardens
London SW1W ODH
Website: www.kidscape.org.uk
Email: webinfo@kidscape.org.uk
Tel: 020 7 730 3300
Fax: 020 7730 7081

Publications

The Times Educational Supplement
Admiral House
66–68 East Smithfield
London E1W 1BX
Website: www.tes.co.uk
Email: via online form
Tel: 020 7782 3000
Fax: 020 7782 3200

The Times Educational Supplement (Scotland)
Website: www.tes.co.uk/scotland

RE

The Inter Faith Network
5–7 Tavistock Place
London WC1H 9SN
Website: www.interfaith.org.uk
Email: ifnet@interfaith.org.uk
Tel: 020 7388 0008
Fax: 020 7387 7968

The Professional Council for Religious Education (PCfRE)
Royal Buildings
Victoria Street
Derby DE1 1GW
Website: www.pcfre.org.uk
Email: cem@cem.org.uk
Tel: 01332 296655
Fax: 01332 343253

The RE Site
Website: theREsite.org.uk

Schools information

DfES School and College Performance Tables
Website: www.dfes.gov.uk/performancetables

Technology Colleges Trust
16th Floor, Millbank Tower
21–24 Millbank
London SW1P 4QP
Website: www.tctrust.org.uk
Email: tctrust@tctrust.org.uk
Tel: 020 7802 2300
Fax: 020 7802 2345

Science

Association for Science Education (ASE)
College Lane
Hatfield
Herts AL10 9AA
Website: www.ase.org.uk
Tel: 01707 283000
Fax: 01707 266532

Institute of Biology (IOB)
20 Queensberry Place
London SW7 2DZ
Website: www.iob.org
Email: info@iob.org
Tel: 020 7581 8333
Fax: 020 7823 9409

Institute of Physics (IOP)
76 Portland Place
London W1B 1NT
Website: www.iop.org
Email: physics@iop.org
Tel: 020 7470 4800
Fax: 020 7470 4848

Special educational needs

The British Association of Teachers of the Deaf (BATOD)
21 The Haystacks
High Wycombe
Buckinghamshire HP13 6PY
Website: www.batod.org.uk
Email: secretary@batod.org.uk
Tel: 01494 464190

The British Dyslexia Association (BDA)
98 London Road
Reading RG1 5AU
Website: www.bda-dyslexia.org.uk
Email: info@dyslexiahelp-bda.demon.co.uk
Tel: 0118 966 2677
Fax: 0118 935 1927
Helpline: 0118 966 8271

The Dyslexia Institute (DI)
133 Gresham Road
Staines
Middlesex TW18 2AJ
Website: www.dyslexia-inst.org.uk
Email: info@dyslexia-inst.org.uk
Tel: 01784 463851
Fax: 01784 460747

The National Association for Gifted Children (NAGC)
Suite 14
Challenge House
Sherwood Drive
Bletchley
Bucks MK3 6DP
Website: www.nagcbritain.org.uk
Email: amazingchildren@nagcbritain.org.uk
Tel: 0870 770 3217
Fax: 0870 770 3219

The National Association for Special Educational Needs (NASEN)
NASEN House
4-5 Amber Business Village
Amber Close
Amington
Tamworth B77 4RP
Website: www.nasen.org.uk
Email: welcome@nasen.org.uk
Tel: 01827 311500
Fax: 01827 313005

The National Autistic Society (NAS)
393 City Road
London EC1V 1NG
Website: www.nas.org.uk
Email: nas@nas.org.uk
Tel: 020 7833 2299
Fax: 020 7833 9666

The National Deaf Children's Society
15 Dufferin Street
London EC1Y 8UR
Website: www.ncds.org.uk
Email: fundraising@ndcs.org.uk
Tel: 020 7490 8656
Fax: 020 7251 5020

Suppliers (educational products)

The Consortium
Hammond Way
Trowbridge
Wiltshire BA14 8RR
Website: www.theconsortium.co.uk
Email: enquiries@theconsortium.co.uk
Tel: 0845 330 7750
Fax: 0845 330 7785

Hope Education
Hyde Buildings
Ashton Road
Hyde

Cheshire SK14 4SH
Website: www.hope-education.co.uk
Email: enquiries@hope-education.co.uk
Tel: 0870 241 2308
Fax: 0800 929139

Supply Teaching Agencies

Note: Some supply agencies only deal with a small geographical area of the UK. Where this is the case, the areas covered are noted below. Some agencies also offer permanent vacancies. Teachers wishing to do supply work in Scotland would normally register for work via their LEA.

ASA Education
Website: www.asagroup.co.uk/eduindex.html
Email: educate@asagroup.co.uk
Tel: 020 7246 4777
Areas – London, surrounding boroughs

Capita Education Resourcing
Website: www.capitaers.co.uk
Email: enquiry.ers@capita.co.uk
Tel: 0800 731 6871 (primary)
0800 731 6872 (secondary)

Castle Recruitment
Website: www.castlerecruitment.com
Email: info@castlerecruitment.com
Tel: 020 8514 3888
Areas – London (secondary teachers)

Concorde Teaching Bank
Website: www.concordeteachingbank.co.uk
Email: concordeteachingbank @cornwall.ac.uk
Tel: 01872 262033

Areas – Cornwall

Cover Teachers
Website: www.coverteachers.co.uk
Email: enquiries@coverteachers.co.uk
Tel: 0117 973 5695
Areas – South West England

Dream Education
Website: www.dream-education.co.uk
Email: teachers@dream-education.co.uk
Tel: 0870 160 5958

Education Recruitment Network
Website: www.ernteachers.com
Email: via online form
Tel: 01633 223747
Areas – Wales, Southern England

Education VIPs
Website: www.educationvips.com
Email: teach@educationvips.com
Tel: 020 8289 6487
Areas – London and Southern England

Hays Education
Website: www.haysworks.com
Email: enquiries@hays-education.com
Tel: 0800 716026

Head Line Teacher Supply Service
Website: www.headline-uk.com
Email: teachers@headline-uk.com
Tel: 01727 840015
Areas – Bedfordshire, Buckinghamshire, Essex, Hertfordshire

International Supply Teachers
Website: www.teachersonthemove.com
Email: info@teachersonthemove.com
Note: This agency charges a registration fee

Key Stage Teacher Supply
Website: www.keystagesupply.co.uk
Email: info@keystagesupply.co.uk
Tel: 01254 298616
Areas – Preston, Burnley, Chorley, Blackburn

Link Education
Website: www.linkteacher.com
Email: enquiries@linkteacher.com
Tel: 01689 878565
Areas – North Kent and surrounding areas

Locum Group Education
Website: www.teachers-uk.co.uk
Email: education@locumgroup.com
Tel: 0800 068 1117

Longterm Teachers
Website: www.longtermteachers.com
Email: info@longtermteachers.com
Tel: 020 7436 4949

Mark Education
Website: www.markltd.com
Email: via online form

Masterlock Education
Website: www.masterlock.co.uk
Email: info@masterlock.co.uk
Tel: 020 7938 1846
Areas – London, Hertfordshire, Bristol

Opus Educational
Website: www.opuseducational.co.uk
Email: info@opuseducational.co.uk
Tel: 01246 224288
Areas – East Midlands

Primetime Education
Website: www.primetime-education.co.uk
Email: northampton.education
@primetime.co.uk
newcastle.education
@primetime.co.uk
watford.education
@primetime.co.uk
Tel: 0800 093 2001
Areas – Northampton, Newcastle, Watford

Protocol Teachers
Website: www.protocol-teachers.com
Email: via online form
Tel: 0845 450 8450

QED Educational Consultants Ltd
Website: www.qed-education.co.uk
Email: info@qed-education.co.uk
Tel: 020 7935 4909

Quality Education
Website: www.qualitylocums.com/QualityEducation.asp
Email: education@qualitylocums.com
Tel: 01992 410088

Quality Teacher Recruitment
Website: qualityteacherrecruitment.co.uk
Email: via online form
Tel: 0800 783 7405
Areas – East Anglia

Recruit Education Services
Website: www.recruiteducation.com
Email: via online form
Tel: 0845 606 0676

Reed Education
Website: www.reed.co.uk/education
Email: education@reed.co.uk
Tel: 0151 708 3813

Scholar UK
Website: www.scholaruk.com
Email: teachers@scholaruk.com
Tel: 0870 0400044

Areas – London, South and South East England, the Midlands

Select Education
Website: www.selecteducation.co.uk
Email: headoffice-ed@select.co.uk
Tel: 0845 600 1234

Standby Teacher Services
Website: www.standbyteachers.com
Email: info@standbyteachers.com
Tel: 0800 146471
Areas – North East England

STEP Teachers
Website: www.stepteachers.co.uk
Email: via online form
Tel: 0800 026 3334

Supply Desk
Website: www.thesupplydesk.co.uk
Email: via online form
Tel: 0845 661 1166

Supply Teachers
Website: www.supplyteachers.com
Email: info@supplyteachers.com
Tel: 01474 328635

Supply Teachers Direct
Website: www.supplyteachersdirect.com
Email: admin@supplyteachersdirect.com
Tel: 01726 66140
Fax: 01726 66166

Supplynet
Website: www.supplynet.org.uk
Email: info@supplynet.org.uk
Tel: 01524 62112/01952 254080
Areas – North West England, West Midlands, Shropshire, Staffordshire

Teachers 'R' Us
Website: www.trus.co.uk
Email: teachers@trus.co.uk
Tel: 020 7328 0000
Areas – London

Teachers Workline
Website: www.teachers-workline.co.uk
Email: enquiries@teachers-workline.co.uk
Tel: 0800 085 2731
Areas – London

Teaching Personnel
Website: www.teachingpersonnel.com
Email: via online form
Tel: 0800 980 8935

The Teaching Supply Agency
Website: www.teaching-agency.co.uk
Email: supply@teaching-agency.co.uk
Tel: 01344 482708
Areas – Berkshire, Surrey, Hampshire

Termwise Teacher Recruitment
Website: www.termwise.co.uk
Email: info@termwise.co.uk
Tel: 01305 268565
Areas – London

TimePlan
Website: www.timeplan.com
Email: via online form
Tel: 0800 358 8040

Support Organizations

Teacher Support Network
Website: www.teacherline.org.uk
Email: customers@teachersupport.info
Tel: 0800 056 2561

Teacher Training

Graduate Teacher Training Registry (GTTR)
Rosehill
New Barn Lane
Cheltenham
Gloucestershire GL52 3LZ
Website: www.gttr.ac.uk
Tel: 01242 544788

National Union of Students (NUS)
Nelson Mandela House
461 Holloway Road
London N7 6LJ
Website: www.nus.org.uk
Email: nusuk@nus.org.uk
Tel: 020 7272 8900
Fax: 020 7263 5713

The Teacher Training Agency (TTA)
Portland House
Stag Place
London SW1E 5TT
Website: www.canteach.gov.uk
Tel (general enquiries): 020 7925 3700
Tel (teaching information line): 0845 6000 991 (English)
0845 6000 992 (Welsh)

Universities and Colleges Admissions Service (UCAS)
Rosehill
New Barn Lane
Cheltenham
Gloucestershire GL52 3LZ
Email: enq@ucas.ac.uk
Website: www.ucas.ac.uk
Tel: 01242 222444

Universities Council for the Education of Teachers (UCET)
58 Gordon Square
London WC1H ONT
Website: www.ucet.ac.uk

Email: ucet@ioe.ac.uk
Tel: 020 7580 8000
Fax: 020 7323 0577

Teaching Forums and Communities

Education.com
Website: www.education.com
Email: via online form

Just for Teachers
Website: www.justforteachers.co.uk
Email: philip@schoolzone.co.uk

Talking Teaching
Website: www.talkingteaching.co.uk
Email: meyrichughes@edcoms.co.uk

Teaching Resources

Clickteaching
Website: www.clickteaching.com
Email: via online form

Quality Teaching Resources
Website: www.qualityteachingresources.co.uk
Email: via online form

Schoolzone
Website: www.schoolzone.co.uk
Email: mail@schoolzone.co.uk

Tagteacher
Website: www.tagteacher.net
Email: feedback@tagteacher.net

Teachit (English teaching online)
Website: www.teachit.co.uk
Email: mail@teachit.co.uk

Topmarks
Website: www.topmarks.co.uk
Email: education@topmarks.co.uk

Unions

Association of Teachers and Lecturers (ATL)
London Headquarters:
7 Northumberland Street
London WC2N 5RD
Website: www.askatl.org.uk
Email: info@atl.org.uk
Tel: 020 7930 6441
Fax: 020 7930 1359

Wales Office:
1st Floor, Empire House
Mount Stuart Square
Cardiff CF10 5FN
Email: cymru@atl.org.uk
Tel: 029 2046 5000
Fax: 029 2046 2000

National Association of Head Teachers (NAHT)
1 Heath Square
Boltro Road
Haywards Heath
West Sussex RH16 1BL
Email: info@naht.org.uk
Website: www.naht.org.uk
Tel: 01444 472472

National Association of Schoolmasters, Union of Women Teachers (NASUWT)
Hillscourt Education Centre
Rose Hill
Rednal
Birmingham B45 8RS
Website: www.teachersunion.org.uk
Email: membership@mail.nasuwt.org.uk
Tel: 0121 457 6211

National Association of Teachers in Further and Higher Education (NATFHE)
27 Britannia Street
London WC1X 9JP
Website: www.natfhe.org.uk
Email: hq@natfhe.org.uk
Tel: 020 7837 3636
Fax: 020 7837 4403
Minicom: 020 7278 0470

National Union of Teachers (NUT)
Hamilton House
Mabledon Place
London WC1H 9BD
Website: www.teachers.org.uk
Email: via website
Tel (new joiners helpline): 0845 300 1669

Professional Association of Teachers (PAT)
2 St James' Court
Friar Gate
Derby DE1 1BT
Website: www.pat.org.uk
Email: hq@pat.org.uk
Tel: 01332 372337
Fax: 01332 290310

PAT Scotland
4/6 Oak Lane
Edinburgh EH12 6XH
Email: scotland@pat.org.uk
Tel: 0131 317 8282
Fax: 0131 317 8111

Scottish Secondary Teachers' Association (SSTA)
15 Dundas Street
Edinburgh EH3 6QG
Website: www.ssta.org.uk
Email: info@ssta.org.uk
Tel: 0131 556 5919
Fax: 0131 556 1419

Secondary Heads Association (SHA)
130 Regent Road
Leicester LE1 7PG
Website: www.sha.org.uk
Email: info@sha.org.uk
Tel: 0116 299 1122
Fax: 0116 299 1123

Index

absences, marking 16
accountability 218, 221
acronyms, list of 279–80
active learning 52–3, 286
    ADHD 144
administration 16, 125, 179–80
advanced skills teachers 118–19
Africa, teaching in 197–8
aims and objectives of lessons 50, 286
appearance 70
application forms 61
    sample 259–61
applying for jobs 61–3
applying for teacher training 23
appraisal 124
art, teaching 33–4, 229
    useful addresses 315
assertive discipline 169–70
assessment 124, 174–5
    downsides of 175–6
    in induction year 85–6
    useful addresses 315, 318
assignments 27
assistant head teachers 109–12

baseline assessments 174
behaviour 13, 17, 44, 96
behaviour management 46, 72–3, 157–9
    books on 55–6
    by form tutors 122–3
    by heads of year 118
    programmes for 169–70
    strategies for 160–9
    by student teachers 30, 48–9, 53–6
    tips for 282–3
body, looking after 78
body language 46
    in interviews 70
boundaries 161, 282
breaks 191
    taking 7, 78, 281, 285
bullying 185
bursars 135

business studies, useful addresses 315

CACHE Specialist Teaching Assistants
        Award 126
calmness 54, 95, 162
Career Entry Profile 83, 88
careers, moving into after teaching
        194–5
    useful addresses 315
caretakers 135
child protection 186–7
Child Protection Officer 187
children's problems, dealing with 184–6
citizenship, useful addresses 315–16
classroom teachers 186
    duties of 124–5
    and special educational needs 144
    student teachers' relationship
        with 47–8, 89
classrooms 153–5
    environment of 44–5, 156
    management of 44, 45–6, 156–7,
        210–11
    organization of 74–5
Code of Professional Values and
        Practice 220, 221–2
colleagues, getting on with 282, 284,
    290
community schools 60
computers 149–50
    see also ICT
confidence 54, 80
cover 124
curriculum 5, 28
    useful addresses 316
    see also National Curriculum
curriculum subjects, plans for 227,
        228–30

'deadly stare' 161, 282
demotivation 175
department development plans 241, 242
deputy headteachers 106–9

Index

design and technology, teaching 229
  useful addresses 316
desks, grouping 153
detentions 165
differentiation 170–1, 230–1, 244
disciplinary procedures 223–4
discipline *see* behaviour management
displays 45
drama 27
  useful addresses 316–17

Early Learning Goals 90
Education Act 1996 165, 167, 168
education welfare officers 130
educational psychologists 129–30
educational shows 195
educational suppliers, addresses 327–8
emotional and behaviour difficulties 144
emotional survival 78–9
English, useful addresses 317
English as a second language 95
equal opportunities monitoring 264
equipment 44, 146–7
European Council of International
  Schools 59
examination boards 317
examinations 125, 174, 183
  helping pupils prepare for 175, 184
  useful addresses 318
expectations 44, 54, 75, 161, 285
extracurricular activities 67, 188–9,
  285–6

faculty system 112
family, combining teaching with 37, 111,
  123–4
financial incentives for teacher
  training 23, 34
form tutors 15–16, 119–24, 186
foundation schools 60
further education, useful addresses 318

General Teaching Councils (GTCs) 217,
  220–3, 320
geography, useful addresses 319
government 221
  useful addresses 320, 326
graduate registered teacher
  programme 127

graduate teacher programme 127
greeting a class 75–6

heads of department 112–14
heads of year 115–18
headteachers 10, 102–6
  skills 104–5
health and safety 124, 167, 169, 244,
  291
history, teaching 218
  primary lesson plan 239–40
  useful addresses 321
home/school divide 79–80
humour 18–19, 161, 284

ICT (Information and Communications
  Technology) 98–9, 149–50, 295
  advantages of 295–6
  hazards of 298–9
  managing 297–8
  software 302–12
  tips for 297, 302
  useful addresses 321
  see also internet
IEPs (individual education plans) 145
inclusion 146
independent schools
  looking for jobs in 59–60
  useful addresses 321–2
individual education plans (IEPs) 145
induction 80–1, 82–6, 88, 97, 99, 281
  in Northern Ireland 81–2
  problems with 86, 87
  in Scotland 81
  of supply teachers 86, 206
  in Wales 81
induction standards 87–8
Initial Teacher Training (ITT)
  students 244–5
INSET (in-service training) 74, 193–4
insults, dealing with 78, 286
International Baccalaureate (IB) 195–6
international education 59, 322
internet 99, 150, 299–300
  job hunting on 58
  safety on 300–1

job hunting 57–60
  on the internet 58

sample forms 259–63
useful addresses 322
job interviews 63–70, 94, 100
pre-interview checklist 64–5
questions 68–9
teaching at 65–6
job offers 71
job satisfaction 108, 110, 219
judging a school 64, 66–7

languages, useful addresses 322
lateral thinking 53, 147
laughter 161, 284
LEAs 58, 82
lesson planning 90–1, 140–2
on teaching practice 33, 41, 49–52,
232
lesson plans 49–52
good/bad 140–1
samples 269–72
lessons
for OFSTED 210
tips for successful 286–7
letters of application 62–3, 262–3
examples 265–8
Literacy Hour 143
literacy planning 230, 234
see also National Literacy Strategy

management 13, 107–8, 110, 112,
113–14
useful addresses 323
mark books 181, 277–8
marking 171–3
close marking 171–2, 275
for specific errors 172, 276
'tick and flick' 171
tips for 283
maths, useful addresses 323
mature entrants 100
media, useful addresses 323–4
media resources 149
medical examinations 71
movement around school 67
moving schools 191–2

National Association of Schoolmasters,
Union of Women Teachers
(NASUWT) 214–16, 332

National Curriculum 142, 146, 243
National Literacy Strategy 91, 143, 243–4
National Numeracy Strategy 91, 143,
243–4
non-contact time, for NQT 97
Northern Ireland 23, 81–2
NQTs (newly qualified teachers) 14, 18,
89–90
responsibility for training 83
in Scotland 35
as supply teachers 206
support for 67, 73, 79, 84, 89, 91, 97
see also induction
numeracy planning 51–2, 230, 235
see also National Numeracy Strategy

observation
during induction period 84–5
on teaching practice 43–7
office staff 134–5, 284
OFSTED (Office for Standards in
Education) 32, 137–8, 208–9, 322
preparing for visit 210–11
tips for surviving 291–2
OFSTED reports 41, 64
online education 324, 325
see also websites
organization
of classrooms 74–5
of resources 147, 231, 243

paperwork 4, 37, 179–80
tips for dealing with 287–8
parents 324
as experts 150
relationships with 118
parents' evenings 10, 187–8
tips for 289–90
pastoral work 117, 119, 123, 184–6
PAT, see Professional Association of
Teachers
Pay, see salaries
pensions 4, 11, 211–12
useful addresses 325
PGCE (Postgraduate Certificate of
Education) courses 15, 23, 105,
116, 127
primary 29–32, 35–8
secondary 32–5

Index

photocopying 148–9, 284
physical attacks 96, 167
physical education, useful addresses
    324
physical intervention 167, 169
physical needs 144
physical survival 77–8
planning 90, 210, 227
    long-term 91, 227, 228, 254–5
    medium-term 91, 227, 228
    for supply teachers 208
    for teaching practice 26–7, 33
    time spent on 229
    see also lesson planning
police checks 71
positivity 18, 54–5, 207
praise 161
primary education 9, 94–7, 139
    useful addresses 325
primary schools
    classrooms 153–5
    planning in 227–40
    typical management structure 101
prioritization 73, 79
private tutoring 195
Professional Association of Teachers
    (PAT) 216–17, 332
professional development 99, 221, 291
    useful addresses 325
professional standards 217, 220
professional time 221
projects 142
promotion 5, 10, 13, 17, 103–4, 191
    qualities for 105
    tips for 290–1
PSHE (personal, social and health
    education) 230
    useful addresses 326
psychological survival 79–80
pupils, getting on with, 67, 118, 284

QCA (Qualifications and Curriculum
    Authority) schemes of work
    228, 232
QTS (Qualified Teacher Status) 24
    skills tests 24, 26, 31
    training for 21, 93–4

reasonable force 167, 168

Reception teaching 90
recording 181
referees 61–2
registered teacher programme 127
religious education (RE), useful
    addresses 326
reports 182–3
    tips for 288–9
    written evidence of
        misbehaviour 165–6
resources, for teachers 18, 31, 91
    see also teaching resources
retention of teachers 221
review 124
rewards 44, 55, 159, 230, 282
risk assessments 244
routes into teaching 12, 14–15, 20–2,
    109
    employment based 21
    postgraduate 21, 22, 23, 29–38
    undergraduate 21, 22, 23, 25–8

safety, see health and safety
salaries 4, 5, 8, 31–2, 69, 190
sanctions 44, 55, 118, 282, 285
    applying 163–4
    types of 164–6
saying 'no' 6, 79
schemes of work 49, 113, 146, 241, 242,
    243
    sample 273–4
school environment 67
school governors 135–6
school inspectors 136–9, 219
school librarians 130–4
school library 132–4
    useful addresses 323
'School Teachers' Pay and Working
    Conditions' 191
science, teaching 229, 243
    Key Stage Two lesson plan 236–8
    Key Stage Three lesson plan 246–8
    Key Stage Four lesson plan 249–53
    practical lessons 243
    useful addresses 326
Scotland 22, 190
    induction 81
    NQTs 35
    pensions 212

Scotland *continued*
    supply teaching   34
    teacher training   23, 34
secondary schools
    planning in   241–56
    teaching in   12–13, 17, 98–9
    typical management structure   101–2
self-evaluation   176–8
SEN, *see* special educational needs
SENCOs (special educational needs
        coordinators)   129, 145
serious incidents   165, 167–9
setting   170
setting standards   75
setting up classrooms   151–5
shouting   46, 54, 55, 77
sickness, during induction period   87, 281
silence, waiting for   160, 282
SIMS report format   181
special educational needs (SEN)   143–5
    coordinators (SENCOs)   129, 145
    inclusion of   146
    statements of   145–6
    useful addresses   327
specialist schools   60
specific learning difficulties   144
spreadsheets   307–12
staff
    treatment of by students   67
    turnover of   67
staff meetings   124
state schools   60
streaming   230–1
strengths   177
stress   4, 78–9
    dealing with   285–6
    for pupils, from assessments   175
student teachers
    books for   38–9
    relationship with classroom
        teachers   47–8, 89
    see also teacher training
subject coordinators   115, 232
supply agencies   58, 203–6, 328–30
supply teachers   34
    General Teaching Council and   222–3
    planning   208
    and school policies   205, 207
    training for   205, 206

supply teaching   90, 202–6
    induction   86
    tips for   206–8
support   13, 17, 79, 212, 283
    for NQTs   67, 73, 79, 84, 89, 91, 97
    organizations   330
    during teacher training   26, 28, 30, 37
survival   6, 8
    of first year   74, 76–80, 281–2
switching off   79–80, 286

target setting   16, 161, 188, 289
Teacher Assistant's Handbook, The   128
teacher training   20–36, 89
    distance learning   36–8
    planning   232
    useful addresses   331
teachers
    good   92, 105, 108, 111, 114, 138,
        219
    see also classroom teachers; NQTs;
        student teachers; supply teachers
teaching   124
    bad moments   12, 17, 90, 96, 114,
        121–2
    good moments   9, 12, 16, 90, 95, 108,
        110–11, 114, 116–17, 121
    in induction year   83
    at interviews   65–6
    leaving   5–6, 10
    as a profession   10–11, 13, 31, 37–8,
        92, 108
    pros and cons   3–4, 12, 16–17
teaching assistants   126–9
    qualifications for   126
teaching degrees   21, 22, 23, 25–8, 89,
    93–4, 103
teaching forums   331
teaching overseas   58–9, 195–201
teaching practice   25–6, 27, 30, 94, 98,
    116, 121
    observing the class   43–5
    observing the teacher   45–7
    planning lessons   33, 41, 49–52, 232
    preparing for   40–2
    problems with   48–9
    relationship with teacher   47–8, 89
    surviving first day   42–3
    teaching   52–3

teaching resources   146–7, 231
  computers as   149–50
  media   149
  organization of   147, 231, 243
  paper-based   147–8
  people as   150–1
  unusual   151
teaching strategies   52–3
teaching styles   231
teaching unions   212, 213–17
  General Teaching Council and   222
  useful addresses   332–3
technicians   149, 243
tests   174
Thailand, teaching in   199–201
theatre groups   150–1
threshold, passing   192
Times Educational Supplement, The   57, 326
timetabling   229, 233
trips   189, 232

unions, see teaching unions

verbal/non-verbal signals   46
videos, use of   149
visiting artists   151
voice
  control of   46, 55, 161, 162, 282, 285
  looking after   77
voluntary aided schools   60
voluntary controlled schools   60

Wales, induction in   81
weaknesses   176
websites   31, 58, 91, 324, 325, 331
whole school behaviour policies   54, 158–9
word processing   303–5
'WordArt' titles   304
working abroad   58–9, 195–201
working conditions   190, 191
working hours   5, 191
worksheets   147–8
written evidence of misbehaviour   165–6